Edward John Long Scott

A Guide to the Manuscripts, Autographs, Charters, Seals, Illuminations and Bindings Exhibited in the Department of Manuscripts and in the Grenville Library

Edward John Long Scott

A Guide to the Manuscripts, Autographs, Charters, Seals, Illuminations and Bindings Exhibited in the Department of Manuscripts and in the Grenville Library

ISBN/EAN: 9783337417390

Printed in Europe, USA, Canada, Australia, Japan

Cover: Foto ©Lupo / pixelio.de

More available books at **www.hansebooks.com**

A GUIDE

TO THE

MANUSCRIPTS,

AUTOGRAPHS, CHARTERS, SEALS,

ILLUMINATIONS AND BINDINGS

EXHIBITED IN

THE DEPARTMENT OF MANUSCRIPTS

AND IN

THE GRENVILLE LIBRARY.

WITH TWENTY PLATES.

PRINTED BY ORDER OF THE TRUSTEES.
1899.

LONDON:
PRINTED BY WILLIAM CLOWES AND SONS, LIMITED,
STAMFORD STREET AND CHARING CROSS.

PREFACE.

Since the last edition of this Guide was published, in 1895, besides minor changes, the Exhibition of Manuscripts has been augmented by a special show-case for Greek Papyri and by the extension of the cases containing Charters.

The present edition also differs from those that have preceded it by including twenty plates of facsimiles. This new feature necessitates an increase in the price, which, it is hoped, will be justified by the additional interest thus given to the text of the descriptions.

EDWARD SCOTT,
Keeper of Manuscripts.

28th February, 1899.

CONTENTS.

	PAGE
ROYAL AUTOGRAPHS	9
HISTORICAL AUTOGRAPHS AND PAPERS	18
CHARTERS	38
LITERARY AND OTHER AUTOGRAPHS (ENGLISH)	52
,, ,, ,, (FOREIGN)	62
AUTOGRAPH LITERARY WORKS, ETC.	67
MANUSCRIPTS :—	
I.—Greek	75
II.—Latin, etc.	82
III.—English	88
IV.—Chronicles of England	90
EARLY BIBLICAL MSS.	109
HISTORICAL DEEDS, ETC.	111
SEALS	113
ILLUMINATED MSS.	119
BINDINGS	129
LIST OF BENEFACTORS	135

DEPARTMENT OF MANUSCRIPTS.

The collections of this Department have been formed partly by the acquisition of private libraries and partly by purchases and donations from year to year. The Manuscripts of Sir Robert Cotton, of Edward Harley, Earl of Oxford, and of Sir Hans Sloane, were among the first collections brought together by the Act of Parliament of 1753, to which the British Museum owes its origin. The Cotton MSS. had been presented to the nation by Sir John Cotton, grandson of Sir Robert, as early as 1700, and the sums paid for the Harley and Sloane MSS. were acknowledged to be much below their real value. The other collections are: The Royal MSS., presented by George II. in 1757; the King's MSS., collected by George III.; the Birch MSS., bequeathed by the Rev. Thomas Birch, D.D., in 1765; the Lansdowne MSS., of William Petty, Marquess of Lansdowne; the Arundel MSS., of Thomas Howard, 14th Earl of Arundel; the Burney MSS., of the Rev. Charles Burney, D.D.; the Hargrave MSS., of Francis Hargrave, K.C.; the Egerton MSS., bequeathed by Francis Egerton, Earl of Bridgewater, in 1829, and since augmented by purchases made from funds provided by him and by Charles Long, Lord Farnborough (1838); the Stowe MSS., collected by George Temple-Nugent-Grenville, Marquess of Buckingham; and the Additional MSS., the largest of all the collections, purchased from the annual parliamentary grant or acquired by donation or bequest. The Department contains upwards of 48,000 volumes; 65,000 charters and rolls; nearly 15,000 detached seals and casts of seals; and over 800 ancient Greek and Latin papyri. A list of the principal benefactors to the Department is given at the end of the Guide.

The selection exhibited to the public* is, roughly speaking, divided into four classes: historical (pp. 9, 90), literary (p. 52), palæographical (p. 75), and artistic (p. 119). The first two classes mainly consist of autographs; the third exemplifies the progress of writing from the third century before Christ to the fifteenth century of our era; and the fourth comprises manuscripts of the tenth to the sixteenth centuries embellished internally by the illuminator and miniaturist, or externally with ornamental bindings. Many of the examples, however, in each class present other elements of interest; and special mention may be made of the "Early Biblical Manuscripts" (p. 109), including the famous "Codex Alexandrinus."

The contents of the first four cases are intended to illustrate the course of English history by a selection of autograph letters and other original documents. They begin (p. 9) with a complete series of autographs of English sovereigns from Richard II. to Victoria, no signature or other handwriting of any earlier sovereign being known to exist. In the last compartment of the same case are also shown autographs of six of the most famous foreign sovereigns from the sixteenth to the nineteenth centuries. Further examples of English royal handwriting will be found in the general series of "Historical Autographs and Papers" in Cases II.–IV. (p. 18). This series begins in the reign of Henry VI., but the earlier periods receive illustration in the Charters exhibited in Cases V. and VI. (p. 38), and in the collection of English Chronicles in the central table-case F (p. 90). The documents are arranged in order of date, and, so far as the limits of space permit, the aim has been, by means of autograph letters, etc., of kings and queens, statesmen, naval and military commanders, ecclesiastics and others, to direct attention to the leading events and most eminent historical characters of each reign.

A few introductory remarks on some of the other classes will be found prefixed to them in their place in the Guide.

* For purposes of study and research the Students' Room is open to all persons provided with reading-tickets, from 10 a.m. to 5 p.m. daily, with the exception of the first four week-days in March and September.

ROYAL AUTOGRAPHS.*

Case I.

[On the left as the visitor enters from the Grenville Library.†]

1. RICHARD II. Particulars of an agreement, in *French*, for the restoration of the castle of Brest to the Duke of Brittany, [A.D. 1397]. Signed by the King, "LE ROY R. S." *i.e.* "Richard Second." [*Cotton MS.* Vesp. F. iii. f. 3.]

2. HENRY IV. Letter, in *French*, to his Council in London, announcing that "la Dame Spenser [Constance, widow of Thomas Despencer, Earl of Gloucester] et lez enfaunz de la Marche [Edmund Mortimer, Earl of March, and Roger his brother, confined at Windsor] sount fuyez par Abyndon" on their way to Glamorgan and Cardiff, and ordering the arrest of a squire named Morgan, whom they had sent to Flanders and France, if he should still be in London. Dated, "a nostre chastiell de Wynd[sor] en hast yeeste dismenge matyn" [? 14 Feb. 1406]. Signed by the king, "H. R., nous prions penser de la mer." [*Cotton MS.* Vesp. F. iii. f. 4.]

3. HENRY V. Portion of a letter relating to the Duke of Orleans and other French prisoners taken at Agincourt in 1415, and to James I. of Scotland, captured on his way to France in 1406, as follows:—"Furthremore I wold that ye convend with my brothre, with the chanceller, with my cosin of Northumbreland, and my cosin of Westmerland; and that ye set a gode ordinance for my north marches, and specialy for the Duc of Orlians and for alle the remanant of my prisoners of France, and also for the K[ing] of Scotelond, for as I am secrely enfourmed by a man of ryght notable estate in this lond that there hath ben a man of the Ducs of Orliance in Scotland and accorded with the Duc of Albany, that this next somer he schal bryng in the manmet of Scotlond to sturre what he may, and also that ther

---

* N.B.—When a letter or document is entirely in one hand it is described as *Holograph*.

† The Manuscripts exhibited in the Grenville Library are described on p. 119.

schold be founden weys to the havyng awey specialy of the Duc of Orlians, and also of the K[ing], as welle as of the remanant of my forsayd prysoners; that God do defende. Wherfore I wolle that the Duc of Orliance be kept stille within the castil of Pontfret with owte goyng to Robertis place or to any othre disport, for it is bettre he lak his disport than we were decoyved. Of alle the remanant dothe as ye thenketh." [A.D. 1419?] *Holograph.* [*Cotton MS.* Vesp. F. iii. f. 5.] *Facsimile* in Ser. ii. no. 1.*

4. HENRY VI. Inspeximus, in *Latin*, confirming a grant by Queen Joanna [of Navarre, widow of Henry IV.] to Edmund Beaufort, Count of Mortain, for the term of her life, of the offices of Constable of Nottingham Castle and Keeper of Sherwood Forest, 20 Jan., 3 Hen. VI. [1425], and an assignment of the same by the said Count to Ralph, Lord Cromwell, 12 June, 12 Hen. VI. [1434], and prolonging the latter's term after the death of the Queen, if he should survive her. Dated, Westminster, 14 Feb, a° 15 [1437]. Signed at the top by the King, "R. H. nous avons grante." [*Cotton MS.* Vesp. F. xiii. f. 41.]

5. EDWARD IV. Letter, in *French*, to his "good cousin" Francis II., Duke of Brittany, praying for assistance in the recovery of his kingdom, from which he had been expelled "by the great treason which was compassed towards me" [the combination of the Earl of Warwick with the Lancastrian party, resulting in Edward's flight from England on 3 Oct. 1470]. Dated, St. Pol, 9 Jan. [1471], two months before his return to England, and three months before his recovery of his kingdom by the battle of Barnet. Written by a secretary, with *autograph* signature, "voster cousyn EDOWARD R." [*Add. MS.* 21,404, f. 5.] *Facsimile* in Ser. iii. no. 1.

6. EDWARD V. A slip of vellum [cut from a volume] containing the three inscriptions, "R. Edwardus quintus"; "Loyaulte me lie. Richard Gloucestre" [Richard, Duke of Gloucester, afterwards RICHARD III.]; and "Souente me souenne. Harre Bokyngham" [Henry Stafford, Duke of Buckingham]. [Apr.—June, 1483.] [*Cotton MS.* Vesp. F. xiii. f. 53.]

7. HENRY VII. Letter, in *Latin*, to King Ferdinand and Queen Isabella of Spain, acknowledging the receipt of their letters in which they announce their agreement to the contract of marriage of the Princess Katherine with Arthur, Prince of Wales, and their intention of sending her to England at the end of the summer, etc. Dated, Canterbury, 20 June, 1500. Signed by the King, "HENRICUS R." [*Egerton MS.* 616, f. 19.]

8. HENRY VIII. Letter to "myne awne good Cardinall" Wolsey, as follows: "I recomando me unto yow with all my hart and thanke yow for the grette payne and labour that yow do dayly take in my bysynes and maters, desyryng yow (that wen yow

* For a full list of facsimiles sold in the department, with prices, see p. 138.

have well establyssyd them) to take summe pastyme and comfort, to the intente yow may the lenger endure to serve us, for allways payne cannott be induryd. Surly yow have so substancyally orderyd oure maters bothe off thys syde the see and byonde that in myne oppynion lityll or no thyng can be addyd . . . Wryttyn with the hand off your lovyng master, HENRY R." [March, 1518.] *Holograph.* [*Cotton MS.* Vesp. F. xiii. f. 71.]

9. KATHERINE OF ARAGON, QUEEN OF HENRY VIII. Letter to the King (then in France), with the news of the battle of Flodden [9 Sept. 1513]: "To my thinking this batell hath bee to your grace and al your Reame the grettest honor that coude bee, and more than ye shuld wyn al the crown of Fraunce: thankend bee God of it, and I am suer your grace forgeteth not to doo this, which shal be cause to sende you many moo suche grete victoryes, as I trust he shal doo. My husband, for hastynesse with Rogecrosse [Rougecroix] I coude not sende your grace the pece of the king of Scottes cote whiche John Glyn now bringeth; in this your grace shal see how I can kepe my promys, sending you for your baners a kings cote. I thought to send hymself unto you, but our Englisshem[en]s hertes wold not suffre it . . . My lord of Surrey, my Henry, wold fayne knowe your pleasur in the burying of the king of Scottes body, . . . and with this I make an ende, praying God to sende you home shortly, for without this noo ioye here can bee accomplisshed." Dated, Woburn, 16 Sept. [1513.] *Holograph.* Signed, "your humble wif and true servant, KATHERINA." [*Cotton MS.* Vesp. F. iii. f. 15.] *Facsimile* in Ser. i. no. 1.

10. ANNE BOLEYN, QUEEN OF HENRY VIII. Letter, written before her marriage, to Cardinal Wolsey, thanking him "for the gret payn and travell that your grace doth take in stewdyeng by your wysdome and gret dylygens howe to bryng to pas honerably the gretyst welth that is possyble to come to any creatour lyvyng, and in especyall remembryng howe wrecchyd and unwrthy I am in comparyng to his hyghnes"; and promising "that after this matter is brought to pas you shall fynd me, as I am bownd in the meane tym, to owe you my servyse, and then looke what thyng in this woreld I can immagen to do you pleasor in, you shall fynd me the gladdyst woman in the woreld to do yt." [A.D. 1528—1529.] *Holograph.* [*Cotton MS.* Vesp. F. xiii. f. 73.] *Facsimile* in Ser. ii. no. 2.

11. EDWARD VI. Letter to the Lord Protector Somerset, on receipt of the news of the victory over the Scots at Pinkie [10 Sept. 1547]: "Derest Uncle, by your lettres and reporte of the messenger, we have at good length understanded to our great comfort the good successe it hathe pleased God to grannt us against the Scottes by your good courage and wise forsight. . . . . So do we give unto you, good Uncle, our most hartie thankes, praying you to thanke also most hartelie in our name

our good cosin therle of Warwike and all the others of the noble men, gentlemen, and others that have served in this journei, of whose service they shall all be well assured we will not (God graunte us lief) shew our selfes unmindfull, but be redy ever to consider the same as anie occasion shall serve." Dated, Oatlands, 18 Sept. [1547]. *Holograph*. Signed, "your good nevew, EDWARD." [*Lansdowne MS.* 1236, f. 16.]

12. LADY JANE GREY, AS QUEEN. Order to Sir John Bridges and Sir Nicholas Poyntz, to levy forces " and with the same to repaire with all possible spend towardes Buckinghamshire, for the repression and subdewing of certain tumultes and rebellions moved there against us and our Crowne by certain seditious men." Dated, Tower of London, 18 July, " in the first yere of our reign" [1553]. Signed at the top, " JANE THE QUEENE." [*Harley MS.* 416, f. 30.]

13. MARY. "Instructions for my lorde previsel [Lord Russell, Lord Privy Seal, sent to receive her husband, Philip of Spain, on his landing at Southampton in July, 1554]. Fyrste, to telle the Kyng the whole state of this Realme with all thynges appartaynyng to the same as myche as ye knowe to be trewe. Seconde, to obey his commandment in all thynges. Thyrdly, in all thynges he shall aske your aduyse to decl[are] your opinion as becommeth a faythfull conceyllour to do. MARYE THE QUENE." *Holograph*. [*Cotton MS.* Vesp. F. iii. f. 12.]

14. ELIZABETH. Draft of a speech from the throne on the occasion of the dissolution of Parliament [2 Jan. 1567], rating the members for their persistence in troubling her on the questions of the succession to the Crown and the liberties of Parliament: " Two visars have blinded the yees of the lokers one in this present session .... and thes be the Succession and liberties. As to the first .... it had bine convenient that so waighty a cause had had his originall from a zelous princes consideration, not from so lippe labored orations out of sucho *iangling* [this word has been cancelled] subiects mouthes, wiche what the[y] be time may teache you knowe and ther demerites wyl make them acknowelege how the[y] have done thor lewde indevour to make all my realme suppose that ther care was muche whan myne was none at all .... I think this be the first time that so waighty a cause passed from so simple mens mouthes as began this cause." After discriminating between various grades of aberration on the part of members, she concludes by advising them to " let this my displing [discipline] stand you in stede of sorar strokes never to tempt too far a princes paciens." A different version of the speech appears in Froude's *History of England*, vii. 484. *Holograph* [with signature from another document]. [*Cotton Charter* iv. 38 (2).]

15. JAMES I. Letter to Charles, Prince of Wales, ordering his return from Spain : " My dearest sonne, I sent you a comandement long agoe not to loose tyme quhaire ye are; but athor to

bring quikelie hoame youre mistresse, quhiche is my earnist
desyre; but if no bettir maye be, rather then to linger any longer
thaire, to come without her, quhiche for manie important reasons
I ame now forcid to renew. And thairfor I charge you upon
my blessing to come quikelie ather with her or without her. I
knowe your love to her person hath enforcid you to delaye the
putting in execution of my former comandement. I confesse it
is my cheifest wordlie ioye that yo love her, but the necessitie
of my effaires enforceith me to tell you that yo musto præferre
the obedience to a father to the love ye carrie to a mistresse.
And so God blesse you. JAMES R." Dated, Cranborne, 10 Aug.
[1623]. *Holograph.* [*Harley MS.* 6987, f. 143.] *Facsimile* in
Ser. ii. no. 7.

16. CHARLES I. Letter to his nephew, Prince Maurice, stating that
he has been obliged to dismiss his brother, Prince Rupert, from
all his commands in the army, in consequence of his surrender
of Bristol [11 Sept. 1645], but adding: " Yet I assoure you that
I am most confident that this great Error of his (which, indeed,
hath given me more Greefe then any Misfortune since this
damnable Rebellion) hath no waise proceeded from his change
of Affection to me or my Cause, but meerly by having his
Iudgement seduced by some rotten-harted Villaines, making
faire pretentions to him; and I am resolved so litle to forgett
his former Services, that, whensoever it shall please God to
enable me to looke upon my Frends lyke a King, he shall thanke
God for the paines he hath spent in my Armys." Dated, New-
toune [co. Montgomery], 20 Sept. 1645. *Holograph.* [*Harley MS.*
6988, f. 190.] *Facsimile* in Ser. iv. no. 9.

17. HENRIETTA MARIA, QUEEN OF CHARLES I. Letter to her son
Charles [afterwards Charles II.], chiding him "because I heere
that you will not take phisike," and threatening that, if he will
not take it to-morrow, "I must come to you and make you take
it." Lord Newcastle, his Governor, is to send word that night
whether the physic has been taken [compare the following
letter, no. 18]. Undated [about 1638]. *Holograph.* [*Harley
MS.* 6988, f. 95.]

18. CHARLES II., AS PRINCE. Letter to the Marquess of Newcastle, advising him not to take too much physic, "for it doth
allwaies make me worse, and I think it will do the like with
you." Undated [about 1638]. *Holograph.* [*Harley MS.* 6988,
f. 101.]

19. OLIVER CROMWELL. Letter to his wife, referring to their
daughter Bettie [Elizabeth Claypole] and other members of
their family: " I praise the Lord I am encreased in strength in
my outward man, but that will not satisfie mee except I gett a
heart to love and serve my heavenly Father better and gett more
of the light of his countenance, which is better then life, and
more power over my corruptions .... Minde poore Bettie of
the Lords late great mercye. Oh, I desire her not only to seeke

the Lord in her necessitye, but indeed and in truth to turne to the Lord and to keepe closse to him," etc. Dated, [Edinburgh], 12 Apr. 1651. *Holograph.* [*Egerton MS.* 2620, f. 9.]

20. CHARLES II. Letter to Sir George Downing, English Ambassador at the Hague, giving instructions for his conduct: "I have thought fitt to send you my last minde upon the hinge of your whole negotiation and in my owne hand, that you may likewise know it is your part to obey punctually my orders, instead of putting yourselfe to the trouble of finding reasons why you do not do so. . . . But upon the whole matter you must allwaies know my minde and resolution is, not only to insist upon the haveing my flag saluted even on there very shoare (as it was alwaies practised) but in haveing my dominion of these seas asserted, and Van Guent exemplarily punished." Dated, Whitehall, 16 Jan. 167½. *Holograph.* [*Stowe MS.* 142, f. 84.]

21. JAMES II. Letter to William Henry, Prince of Orange, referring to the complicity of certain of the magistrates of Amsterdam in the Duke of Monmouth's rebellion, whose names he would transmit: "When I can gett any authentike proffs against them, I shall lett you have it, which I feare will be hard to be gott, tho tis certaine some of them knew of the D[uke] of Mon[mouth's] designe." Dated, Windsor, 25 Aug. 1685. *Holograph.* [*Add. MS.* 28,103, f. 68.]

22. WILLIAM III. Letter, in *French*, to the Prince de Vaudemont, touching on the prospects of the campaign and the progress of the siege of Namur: "L'on va ouvrir la trenchée cette nuit du coste de St Nicola," etc. Dated, "Au Camp devant Namur, ce 11e de Juilliet, 1695, au soir a 9 eures." *Holograph.* [*Add. MS.* 21,493, f. 5.]

23. MARY II. Letter to the Countess of Scarborough, announcing the news of the battle of Steinkirk [24 July, 1692]: "The first I asked after when ye news of ye batle came was your Lord and, finding him not mentioned in any of ye leters, take it for ye best signe, for there is an exact acount come, so much as of ye Lieutenants of ye gards who are eithere wounded or kild, by which, tho you shoud hapen to have no leter, yet you may be sure he is well. I thank God ye King is so, and, tho we have got no victory, yet ye french have had an equal losse, so y^t thay need not brag. We have great reason to thank God for thus much. . . . . Your afectionate kind friend, MARIE R. The batle was fought Sunday last, from 9 till 6." Dated, Kensington, 29 July, 1692, "12 at night." *Holograph.* [*Add. MS.* 20,731, f. 6.] *Facsimile* in Ser. ii. no. 11.

24. ANNE. Letter to the Marquess of Tweeddale [Lord High Commissioner to the Parliament of Scotland], regretting the failure of his negotiations with the Scotch Parliament for the settlement of the succession to the Crown of Scotland, and expressing her intention of not employing those for the future who have opposed and obstructed his endeavours for her service.

Dated, Windsor, 24 July, 1704. *Holograph* [with signature from another letter]. [*Stowe MS.* 142, f. 99.] *Facsimile* in Ser. iv. no. 12.

25. GEORGE I. Letter, in French, to the Emperor Charles VI. on the occasion of sending Abraham Stanian as Ambassador to Constantinople. Dated, Hampton Court, 17 Oct., 1717. *Holograph*. [*Add. MS.* 22,046, f. 48.]

26. GEORGE II. Letter to Thomas Pelham-Holles, Duke of Newcastle, on the formation of the Ministry, which the Duke had undertaken after the dismissal of Pitt from office [6 April, 1757]: "If Pitt will come in with a great number of followers, it is impossible you can direct the Administration, and I know that by inclination he will distress my affairs abroad, which are so enough allready." Dated, 4 June, [1757]. *Holograph*. Eventually Pitt returned to office as Secretary of State under Newcastle, and the victories of the Seven Years War were the result. [*Add. MS.* 32,684, f. 100.] *Presented, in* 1886, *by the Earl of Chichester. Facsimile* in Ser. ii. no. 13.

27. GEORGE III. Paragraph written out by himself for insertion in his first Speech from the Throne:—"Born and educated in this country, I glory in the name of Britain; and the peculiar happiness of my life will ever consist in promoting the welfare of a people whose loyalty and warm affection to me I consider as the greatest and most permanent security of my Throne." [15 Nov. 1760.] *Holograph*. [*Add. MS.* 32,684, f. 121.] *Presented, in* 1886, *by the Earl of Chichester. Facsimile* in Ser. i. no. 16.

28. GEORGE IV. Letter to Louis XVIII., King of France, announcing the death of King George III. and his own accession to the throne. Dated, Carlton House, 31 Jan. 1820. Signed by the King; and countersigned by [Robert Stewart,] Viscount Castlereagh, Secretary of State. [*Add. MS.* 24,023, f. 60.]

29. WILLIAM IV. Codicil to the King's will, bequeathing to the Crown all his additions to the libraries in the several royal palaces; 10 July, 1833. With an *autograph* confirmation, signed and sealed by the King, declaring "that all the Books, Drawings, and Plans collected in all the Palaces shall *for ever* continue Heir-looms to the Crown, and on no pretence whatever to be alienated from the Crown." Dated, Brighton, 30 Nov. 1834. [*Add. MS.* 30,170, f. 8.]

30. VICTORIA. Autograph Signature of Her Majesty, written in pencil, when Princess Victoria, at the age of four years. [1823.] [*Add. MS.* 18,204, f. 12.]

31. VICTORIA. Summons to Dr. Samuel [Butler], Bishop of Lichfield, to attend Her Majesty's Coronation. Dated, St. James's, 9 May, 1838. Signed by the Queen; and countersigned by [Bernard Edward Howard,] Duke of Norfolk, Earl Marshal. [*Add. MS.* 12,093, f. 26.]

(FOREIGN.)

32. CHARLES V., Emperor [1519–1555]. Letter, in *French*, to Queen Mary of England, expressing his desire to see his son Philip, her husband [to whom he was on the point of resigning the crown of Spain]. He refers to delays in the necessary arrangements, but adds that he has now instructed Philip to hasten his journey from England : " Je luy ay escrit pour haster sa venue, laquelle je vous prie tres afectueusement vouloyr auoyr agreable"; and apologises for depriving her of Philip's company, "puis que je voys le contentment que vous aves dicelle, mays jespere que vous vous y acomoderes, puis que ce sera, sil plait a Dieu, pour peu de temps." [1555.] *Holograph*. Signed, "Votre bon pere, frere, cousin et alye, CHARLES." [*Cotton MS*. Titus B. ii. f. 126.] *Facsimile* in Ser. iii. no. 16.

33. HENRY IV., King of Navarre and France [1589–1610]. Letter, in *French*, to Mons. de Turenne, announcing his departure for La Rochelle and the expected attack on Mauléon by the Duc de Nevers. [? October, 1588.] *Holograph*. Signed, "Votre tresafectyoné cousyn et parfayt amy, HENRY." [*Add. MS*. 19,272, f. 53.]

34. LOUIS XIV., King of France [1643–1715]. Letter, in *French*, to Mary of Modena, Queen of James II., congratulating her on the birth of a prince [James Edward, afterwards known as the Pretender]: "J'ai souhaité si ardemment l'heureuse naissance du prince dont vous venes d'accoucher que j'oze dire que personne n'en sauroit avoir plus de joye que moy . . . . . rien n'est plus veritable que la part que prend a tout ce qui vous touche vostre bon frere, LOUIS." Dated, Versailles, 24 June, 1688. *Holograph*. [*Add. MS*. 28,225, f. 279.]

35. PETER THE GREAT, Czar of Russia [1682–1725]. Letter, in *Russian*, to Mr. Noy, ship-builder, in St. Petersburg, instructing him to put a ship in order "so as she came from England," with postscript, " I desire you will pay my compliments to all our fellow ship-builders and the rest." Dated, Colomna, 16 May, 1722. *Holograph*. Signed, "PETER." [*Add. MS*. 5015*, f. 98.]

36. FREDERIC THE GREAT, King of Prussia [1740–1786]. Essay, in *French*, on the military talents of Charles XII., King of Sweden, sent by Frederic, in July, 1757, to Andrew Mitchell, English Ambassador at Berlin in 1756–1763. Among the concluding passages are: " Si lon raproche les diferent traits qui caracterissent ce Monarque singuillier, on le trouvera plus vaillant qu'habile, plus actif que prudant, plus soumi a ses passions qu'ataché a ses interets, ausi audacieux, mais moins russé, qu'Hanibal, tenant plus de Pirhus que d'Allexsandre, ausi brillant que Condé a Rocroy, a Norlingue, a Fribour, en aucun tems ausi admirable que Turene la journée de Gnin, cela de Colmar et durant ses dernieres campagnes. . . . . Pour former un parfait capitaine il faudroit qu'il reunit la valeur, la constance, l'activité de

Charles XII., le coup d'œuil et la politique de Malbouroug, les projets, les resources, et les exspediants du prince Eugene, les ruses de Luxsenbourg, la prudence, la sagesse, la metode de Montecuculi, et l'apropos de monsieur de Turene. Mais je crains quo ce beau fenix ne paraitra jamais." Ends " Finis operi Federicum." *Holograph.* [*Add. MS.* 6845, f. 15.] *Facsimile* in Ser. ii., no. 16.

37. NAPOLEON I., Emperor of the French [1804–1815]. Letter to his brother, Joseph Bonaparte, in Paris, written while in command of the French expedition in Egypt, the victories of which had been sufficiently disputed "to add a leaf to the military glory of this army." He expresses, however, his intention of returning to France in two months, and of retiring to the country in disgust with the world: "Je suis annuié de la nature humaine ! J'ai besoin de solitude et d'isolement ; la grandeur m'annuie, le sentiment est deseché, la gloire est fade ; a 29 ans j'ai tout epuisé ; il ne me reste plus qu'à devenir bien vraiment egoiste." Dated, Cairo, 7 Thermidor [25 July, 1798]. *Holograph*, without signature, but with seal bearing the inscription, " Bonaparte general en chef." A week later the French fleet was destroyed by Nelson in the battle of the Nile ; the letter was intercepted, and is endorsed in Nelson's hand, " Found on the person of the Courier." [*Add. MS.* 23,003, f. 3.] *Facsimile* in Ser. ii., no. 17.

HISTORICAL AUTOGRAPHS AND PAPERS.

Case II.

38. HENRY VI. Articles "For ye goode Reule, demesnyng, and seuretee of ye kynges persone and draught of him to vertue and connyng and eschuying of eny thing that mighte yeve empeschement or let thereto, or cause eny charge, defaulte or blame to be leyd upon ye Erle of Warrewyk [Richard de Beauchamp] at eny tyme withouten his desert": being a series of proposals made by the Earl, as Royal Guardian, to the Privy Council, with their answers to the same; 29 Nov. 11 Henr. VI. [1432]. The king was just completing his eleventh year. The fourth article is to the effect that, as the king's growth in years, in stature and in knowledge of his royal authority "causen him more and more to grucche with chastising and to lothe it," the Earl begs the Council to support him, if necessary, in his chastisement of his pupil, and to bear him scatheless against his anger. At the foot are the signatures of the Council;—H[umphrey Plantagenet, Duke of] Gloucester; J[ohn Kemp, Archbishop of] York; P[hilip Morgan, Bishop of] Ely; W[illiam Grey, Bishop of] Lincoln; J[ohn Stafford, Bishop of] Bath, Chancellor; J[ohn Langdon, Bishop of] Rochester; J[ohn Holland, Earl of] Huntingdon; [William de la Pole, Earl of] Suffolk; and H[umphrey Stafford, Earl of] Stafford. [*Add. Ch.* 17,228.]

39. PERKIN WARBECK, pretended son of Edward IV. Letter to Barnard de la Force, Knt., at Fontarabia, in Spain, desiring him to be his "counseillour and ffrende," as he had been to his father Edward IV. Dated, Edinburgh, 18 Oct. [1496]. Signed, "Your frend RYCHARD OFF ENGLAND." [*Egerton MS.* 616, f. 5.]

40. CARDINAL WOLSEY [b. 1471—d. 1530]. Letter written after his disgrace to Stephen [Gardiner, afterwards Bishop of Winchester], making arrangements respecting appointments in the province of York, and continuing, "that sythyns in thys and all other thynges I have and do moste obedyently submyt and conforme my sylf to hys graces pleasure," he trusts "yt wole now please his maieste to shewe hys pety, compassyon, and bowntuose

goodnes towardes me without sufferyng me any loynger to lye langwyshyng and consumyng awey throwth thys myn extreme sorowe and hevynes." "Wryttyne at Asher [Esher] thys twysday [9 March, 1530] with the rude hand of your dayly bedysman, T[homas] Cardinalis Ebor." *Holograph.* [*Add. MS.* 25,114, f. 28.] *Facsimile* in Ser. ii. no. 3.

41. Sir Thomas More [b. 1480—d. 1535]. Letter to Henry VIII., reminding him that "at such tyme as that great weighty rome and office of your chauncellour . . . . ye were so good and graciouse unto me as, at my pore humble suit, to discharge and disburden me, geving me licence with your gracious favour to bestow the residew of my life, in myn age now to come, abowt the provision for my soule in the service of God," he had the promise of his favour; and now praying "that of your accustumed goodnes no sinistre information move your noble grace to have eny more distruste of my trouth and devotion toward you than I have or shall duryng my life geve the cause"; that in the matter of "the wykked woman of Canterbury" [Elizabeth Barton, the Maid of Kent] he had declared the truth to Cromwell; that, if the King believes him guilty, he is ready to forfeit life and fortune, his compensation being that, "I shold onys mete with your grace agayn in hevyn and there be mery with you," but that, if the King thinks that he has acted according to duty, he will relieve him from the Bill brought against him in Parliament. Dated, "at my pore howse in Chelchith" [Chelsea], 5 March [1534]. *Holograph.* [*Cotton MS.* Cleopatra E. vi. f. 176.] *Facsimile* in Ser. iv. no. 1.

42. Henry VIII. Instructions to the Commissioners for making a survey and valuation of all Church property within the realm. [Jan. 1535]. With *autograph* signature of the King. This survey, known as the 'Valor Ecclesiasticus,' was made in pursuance of the acts of Parliament forbidding the payment of firstfruits and tithes of benefices to the Pope, and granting them to the King. It also served as a basis for the subsequent dissolution of the smaller monasteries in 1536 and the larger in 1538, and the confiscation of their property to the Crown. [*Cotton MS.* Cleopatra E. iv. f. 200.]

43. Thomas Cranmer, Archbishop of Canterbury [b. 1489—d. 1556]. Letter to [Thomas, Lord Cromwell], thanking him "that your Lordeship at my requeste hath not only exhibited the Bible [in English, known as Matthew's Bible] which I sent unto you to the Kinges maiestie, but also hath obteigned of his grace that the same shalbe alowed by his auctoritie to be bowghte and redde within this realme . . . assuryng your Lordeship for the contentacion of my mynde you have shewid me more pleasour herin than yf you hadd given me a thowsande pownde." Dated, Ford, 13 Aug. [1537]. Signed, "Your own bowndman ever, T. Cantuaries." [*Cotton MS.* Cleopatra E. v. f. 348.] *Facsimile* in Ser. i. no. 2.

44. EPISCOPAL DECLARATION, recognising the authority of Christian princes in ecclesiastical matters; [1537]. Signed by T[homas Cranmer], Archbishop of Canterbury; Cuthbert [Tunstall], Bishop of Durham; John [Stokesley], Bishop of London; John [Clerk], Bishop of Bath and Wells; Thomas [Goodrich], Bishop of Ely; Nicholas [Shaxton], Bishop of Salisbury; Hugh [Latimer], Bishop of Worcester; and J[ohn Hilsey], Bishop of Rochester. [*Stowe MS.* 141, f. 36.] *Facsimile* in Ser. ii. no. 4.

45. HUGH LATIMER, Bishop of Worcester [b. 1485?—d. 1555]. Arguments against the doctrine of purgatory, with *autograph* annotations by Henry VIII. in the margin. The greater part of the treatise consists of arguments derived from passages in the Fathers; the concluding paragraph, here exhibited, is an *argumentum ad hominem*: "The fowndyng of monastarys arguyd purgatory to be, so ye pullyng of them down arguyth it nott to be. Whatt uncharitabulnesse and cruellnes semyth it to be to destrowe monasterys yf purgatory be. Now it semyth natt convenyentt the acte of parliament to prech won thyng and tho pulpyd another clean contrary." On which the King comments, "Why then do yow so? turpe enim est doctori cum culpa rederguit cum." [About 1538.] *Holograph*. [*Cotton MS.* Cleopatra E. v. f. 142.] *Facsimile* in Ser. i. no. 3.

46. HENRY VIII. The King's Book, or " Necessary Doctrine for a Christian Man "; published in 1543, being a revision by Henry of the Bishops' Book, or "Institution of a Christian Man," published in 1537. The draft is in a secretary's hand, with *autograph* corrections by Henry. The passage exhibited relates to the claims of the Papacy (the words printed in italics being those inserted by Henry himself): " Herby it may appere that the busshop of Rome contrary to Goddes lawes doth chalenge superioritie and| preeminence *over all, and to make an appearance that itt shuld be so hath and dothe wrest Scripture for that porpose contrary bothe to the trw menyng off the same and the auncyent doctors interpretations of the chyrche, so that by that chalenge he wolde nott do wrong wonly to this chyrche off England but also to all other chyrchys in claymeyng superioryte w^t ought any auctoryte by God so to hym gyffen*." [*Cotton MS.* Cleopatra E. v. f. 34.]

47. EDWARD VI. Letter of the King and his Council to the Bishops, in confirmation of the use of the Book of Common Prayer, and ordering them to collect and "deface and abholish" all the old service-books. Dated, Westminster, 25 Dec. a^o 3 [1549]. Signed at the top, "EDWARD." [*Stowe MS.* 142, f. 16.]

48. EDWARD VI. Diary of his reign, written with his own hand, the page exhibited including: "18 [March, 1551]. The L[ady] Mary my sister came to me to Whestmnster, wheare after salutacious she was called with my counsel into a chambre, where was declared how long i had suffered her masse *against my will* [erased] in hope of her reconciliation, and how now being no hope, wich i perceived by her lettres, except i saw some short

amendement, i could not beare it. She answerid that her soul was God['s] and her faith she wold not chaung, nor dissemble hir opinion with contrary doinges. It was said i constrained not her faith, but willed her not as a king to rule but as a subject to obey. And that her exaumple might breed to much inconvenience. 19. Th' emperours embassadour came with short messag frome his master of warre, if i wold not suffre his cosin the princesse to use hir masse. To this was no aundswer given at this time." *Holograph.* [*Cotton MS. Nero C. x. f. 30 b.*] *Facsimile* in Ser i. no. 4.

49. LADY JANE GREY. Letter from her, as Queen, to [William Parr] Marquess of Northampton, Lord Lieutenant of Surrey, etc., announcing her entry into possession of the kingdom of England, and requiring his allegiance against the " fayned and untrowe clayme of the Lady Marye, bastard daughter to our greate uncle Henry th' eight." Dated, from the Tower, 10 July, " the first yere of our reign " [1553]. Signed, "JANE THE QUENE." [*Lansdowne MS.* 1236, f. 24]. *Facsimile* in Ser. iii. no. 4.

50. QUEEN MARY. Order of her adherents to Sir N. Pelham and to "all other the gentilmen of the Shere of Sussexx," requiring them to proclaim her Queen in that county, and denouncing " the ladie Jane, a quene of a new and pretie invencion." Dated, 19 July [1553]. Signed by Henry [Neville], Lord Abergavenny, [Sir] T[homas] Wyat, and others. [*Add. MS.* 33,230, f. 21.] *Presented, in* 1887, *by the Earl of Chichester.* *Facsimile* in Ser. iii. no. 5.

51. SIR PHILIP SIDNEY [b. 1554—d. 1586]. Letter to [Lord Burghley?] on the condition of his garrison of Flushing : " The garrison is weak, the people by thes cross fortunes crossly disposed ; and this is ye conclusion : if these 2 places be kept, her Ma{tt} hath worth her monei in all extremities; if thei shoold be lost, none of the rest wold hold a dai." Dated, Flushing, 14 Aug. 1586 [about five weeks before his mortal wound in the battle of Zutphen, on 22 Sept.]. *Holograph.* [*Stowe MS.* 150, f. 50.]

52. MARY, QUEEN OF SCOTS. Letter, in *French*, to Queen Elizabeth, complaining of the rigour of her imprisonment: " Bien que je ne veuille vous importuner de ce qui concerne mon estat, laquele conoissant vous ettre si peu chere je remets a la misercorde de Dieu . . . . je vous priray aussi (a ce forcee par le zelle de ma consience) de me permettre avvoir ung prestre de lesglise catolique, de la quelle je suis membre, pour me consoller et sollisiter de mon devvoyr; lesquelles resquestes acordees, je priray Dieu et en prison et en mourant de rendre vottre cueur tel qui luy puisse estre agreable et a vous salutayre, et si j'en suis refeusee je vous laysse la charge den respondre devvant Dieu. . . . Il me reste encores vous fayre une autre resquesto de peu d'importence pour vous et dextresme consolation pour moy, cest quil vous playse, ayant pitiay dune desolee mere d'entro les bras de qui on a arasché son seul enfant et esperance de

future joye en ce monde, me permetre decriro a tout le moingns lettres ouvertes pour m'enquerir a la veritay de ces nouvelles et luy ramentevoir sa triste mere." Dated, "de mon estroite prison de Chefild" [Sheffield], 29 Oct. [1571]. *Holograph.* Signed, "Votre bien bonne sœur et [cousine] MARIE R." [*Cotton MS.* Caligula C. iii. f. 239 b.] *Facsimile* in Ser. i. no. 5.

53. WILLIAM CECIL, LORD BURGHLEY [b. 1520—d. 1598]. Letter to Sir Christopher Hatton concerning the trial of Anthony Babington for conspiring to assassinate Queen Elizabeth and release Mary, Queen of Scots, delivering Elizabeth's pleasure with regard to the evidence to be given as to the complicity of Mary, namely "that ther be no enlargment of hir cryme, butt brefly declared for mayntenance of the endyttment that she allowed of Babyngtons wrytyng or lettre; nether wold she that ether by my L. Cobham, your self, or by any other, any sharp speches be used in condemnation or reprooff of the Scotts Quene cryme." Dated, 12 Sept. [1586], the day before the trial. *Holograph.* [*Egerton MS.* 2124, f. 30.] *Facsimile* in Ser. ii. no. 5.

54. MARY, QUEEN OF SCOTS. Rough sketch by Lord Burghley of the arrangement of the hall of Fotheringhay Castle for the Queen's trial, on 12 Oct. 1586, the "chayre for ye Q. of Scotts" being placed in the centre just above a dividing rail across the hall. [*Cotton MS.* Calig. C. ix. f. 587.]

55. JAMES VI. of Scotland. Letter to Robert Dudley, Earl of Leicester, congratulating him on his absence from England at the time of "the pretendit condemnation" of his mother, Mary, Queen of Scots, and desiring him to exert his influence that "the rest of this tragedie may be unperfytid." Dated, Holyrood House, 4 Dec. 1586. *Holograph.* [*Add. MS.* 32,092, f. 56.]

56. MARY, QUEEN OF SCOTS. An account of her execution at Fotheringhay, 8 Feb. 158⅚, sent to Lord Burghley and endorsed by him "The manner of ye Q. of Scotts deth at Fodryngbay, wr[itten] by Ro[bert] Wy[ngfield]." The final scene is thus described: "Then lying upon the blocke most quietly and stretching out her armes [she] cryed, ' *In manus tuas Domine,*' etc., three or fowre tymes, then she lying very still on the blocke, one of the executioners holding of her slitely with one of his handes, she endured two strokes of the other executioner with an axe, she making very smale noyse or none at all, and not stirring any parte of her from the place where she lay .... Then one of the executioners espied her litle dogg which was crept under her clothes, which could not be gotten forth but by force, yet afterward wold not departe from the dead corpes but came and lay betweene her head and her shoulders." [*Lansdowne MS.* 51, ff. 99–102.]

57. THE SPANISH ARMADA. Resolution of a Council of War of the English commanders, after the defeat of the Armada off Gravelines: "1 Augusti, 1588. We whose names are herunder written have determyned and agreede in counsailo to folowe and

pursue the Spanishe Fleete untill we have cleared oure owne coaste and broughte the Fritho weste of us, and then to returne backe againe, as well to revictuall oure ships (which stand in extreme scarsitie) as alsoo to guard and defend oure owne coaste at home; with further protestatione that, if oure wantes of victualles and munitione were supplied, we wold pursue them to the furthest that they durste have gone." Signed by C[harles] Howard, Lord] Howard [of Effingham, Lord High Admiral], George [Clifford, Earl of] Cumberland, [Lord] T[homas] Howard, Edmund [Sheffield, Lord] Sheffield, [Sir] Francis Drake, [Sir] Edward Hoby, [Sir] John Hawkins, and [Capt.] Thomas Fenner. [Add. MS. 33,740, f. 6.] Facsimile in Ser. i, no. 6.

58. SIR WALTER RALEGH [b. 1552?—d. 1618]. Letter to Robert Dudley, Earl of Leicester, Governor of the Low Countries for Queen Elizabeth, protesting his zeal in the performance of his commissions: "But I have byn of late very pestilent reported in this place, to be rather a drawer bake then a fartherer of the action whor yow govern. Your Lordshipe doth well understand my affection towards Spayn and how I have consumed the best part of my fortune hating the tirranus sprosperety of that estate, and it were now strang and mounsterous that I should becum an enemy to my countrey and conscience . . . In the mean tyme I humble beseich yow lett no poeticall scrib worke your Lordshipe by any device to doubt that I am a hollo or could sarvant to the action, or a mean wellwiller and follower of your own." Dated, "from the Court," 29 March, 1586. In a postscript Ralegh adds, "The Queen is in very good tearms with yow, and, thank be to God, well pacified, and yow ar agayne her sweet Robyn." *Holograph*. [Harley MS. 6994, f. 2.] *Facsimile* in Ser. iii. no. 6.

59. SIR FRANCIS DRAKE [b. 1540—d. 1596] and SIR JOHN HAWKINS [b. 1520—d. 1595]. Letter to Lord Burghley on the eve of their departure on their last voyage, the expedition against Porto Rico: "We humbly thanke your lordship for your manyfold favours, which we have allwayes fownd never varyable, but with all favour, love, and constancye, for which we can never be suffyeyently thankfull, but with our prayers to God long to blesse your good lordship with honour and hellthe. . . . And so lokyng daylyo for a good wynd, we humbly take our leve." Dated, Plymouth, 18 Aug. 1595. Neither returned from this voyage, Hawkins dying off Porto Rico on 11 Nov. 1595, and Drake off Porto Bello on 28 Jan. 1596. *Autograph* signatures. [Harley MS. 4762, f. 84.]

Case III.

[Immediately opposite Case II.]

60. SIR FRANCIS BACON [b. 1561—d. 1626]. Letter to Lord Keeper Puckering, with reference to the office of Solicitor-General, which he was anxious to obtain: "Thear hath nothing happened to

me in the course of my busines more contrary to my expectacion then your L[ordship] failing me and crossing me now in the conclusion when frendes are best tryed.... And I for my part thowgh I have much to alledg, yet neverthelesse, if I see her Ma[jesty] settle her choise upon an able man, such a one as Mr. Sergeaunt Flemyng, I will make no means to alter it. On the other side, if I perceyve any insufficient obscure idole man offred to her Ma[jesty], then I thinke my self dowble bownd to use the best meanes I can for my self, which I humbly pray your L[ordship] I may do with your favour." Dated, Gray's Inn, 28 July, 1595. *Holograph.* Fleming was appointed, and Bacon did not become Solicitor-General until 1607. [*Harley MS.* 6997, f. 72.] *Facsimile* in Ser. ii. no. 6.

61. QUEEN ELIZABETH. Letter to James VI. of Scotland [afterwards James I. of England], vehemently repelling some charges brought against her policy by the King of Spain, and warning him against believing them. She begins, "Hit pleaseth me not a litel that my true intentz without glosis or giles ar by you so gratefully taken, for I am nothinge of the vile disposition of suche as while ther neghbors house is or likly to be afire wyl not only not helpe but not afourd them water to quenche the same"; and ends, "Thus you se how, to fulfil your trust reposed in me, wiche to infring I never mynde, I have sincerely made patente my sinceritie, and thogh not fraught with much wisedome yet stuffed with great good wyl. I hope you wyl beare with my molesting you to long with my skrating hand, as proceding from a hart that shall ever be filled with the sure affection of your loving and frendely sistar, ELIZABETH." [5 Jan. 1603, two months before her death.] *Holograph.* [*Add. MS.* 18,738, f. 39.] *Facsimile* in Ser. i. no. 7.

62. ROBERT CECIL, EARL OF SALISBURY, Secretary of State [b. 1550—d. 1612]. Letter to Sir T. Edmondes, ambassador at Brussels, giving a detailed account of the discovery of the Gunpowder Plot. "the most cruell and detestable practize against the person of his Majestie and the whole Estate of this Realme that ever was conceaved by the harte of man, at any time, or in any place whatsoever.... The person that was the principall undertaker of it is one Johnson" [the assumed name of Guy Fawkes] "a Yorkshire man and servant to one Thomas Percye.... I must needs do the Lord Chamberlain" [the Earl of Suffolk] "his right, that hee would take noe satisfaction untill hee might search to the bottome, wherein I must confesse I was lesse forward, not but that I had sufficient advertisement that most of those that now are fled had some practize in hande for some sturre this parliament, but I never dreamed it should have bin of such a nature, because I never red nor heard the like in any state to be attempted in grosse, without some distinction of persons." Dated, Whitehall, 9 Nov. 1605. *Autograph* signature. [*Stowe MS.* 168, f. 213.]

63. ARABELLA STUART. Letter to her cousin James I., after her arrest for marrying William Seymour, thanking him for a relaxation of her imprisonment and begging for his favour : . . . . "And since it hath pleased your Majesty to give this testimony of willingnesse to have me live a while, in all humility I begge the restitution of those comforts without which every houre of my life is discomfortable to me, the principall whearof is your Majestys favour, which none that breathes can more highely esteeme then I." [1610.] *Holograph.* [*Harley MS.* 7003, f. 89.]

64. THOMAS WENTWORTH, VISCOUNT WENTWORTH, afterwards EARL OF STRAFFORD [b. 1593—d. 1641]. Letter, as Lord Deputy of Ireland, to the Earl of Carlisle, explaining his difficulties, arising from the attempts of his subordinates to keep all knowledge from him : " I am purposed on the other side to open my eyes as wide as I can, and dispaire not in time to be able to sounde the depthe they covett soo much to reserve from me. . . . . I shall be sure to doe the uttermost that lies in me, for I have a hartte can willingly sacrifise all that ever I have for his Majesty (if I doe not deceave myself) with a chearfullnesse and faithe extraordinary, only I am fearefull that, whilst impossibilities are exspected at my hands, the best I can doe should not be accepted, nay imputed unto me as a crime." Dated, Dublin, 27 Aug. 1633. *Holograph.* [*Egerton MS.* 2597, f. 150.] *Facsimile* in Ser. ii. no. 8.

65. WILLIAM LAUD, Archbishop of Canterbury [b. 1573—d. 1645]. Letter to Lord Conway, with reference to the Scotch invasion : " If the Scotts come into England and that Newccastle be taken, I will not dare to wright what I thinke of ye busynes. But if they gett such footinge in ye North, the South beinge affected, or rather infected, as they ar, it may prove that which I beleeve ye Enimye yett expects not. . . . . God send us well out of these darke tymes." Dated, Croydon, 14 Aug. 1640. *Holograph.* [*Add. MS.* 21,406, f. 13.] *Facsimile* in Ser. iii. no. 7.

66. CHARLES I. Instructions to Sir Edward Herbert, Attorney-General, relative to the impeachment of Lord Kimbolton [Viscount Mandeville] and the Five Members [3 Jan. 1641½]. *Holograph.* It is evident that Mandeville's impeachment was an afterthought, the King having at first, as appears from the erasures, included his name among the peers whom he intended to call as witnesses. [*Egerton MS.* 2546, f. 20.] *Facsimile* in Ser. i. no. 8.

67. EDWARD HYDE, afterwards EARL OF CLARENDON [b. 1608—d. 1674]. Letter to the Countess of Carnarvon, on the eve of the Civil War, urging her to secure the adhesion of an unnamed person (probably her father, the Earl of Pembroke) to the royal cause : " 'Tis not possible for me to say more in the argument to him then I have, nor can I imagyne what ill spiritt can engage him thus to venture his fortune and his fame, his honour and the honour of his house, in a vessell where none but desperate

persons have the goverment. . . . . I know not what argument they have at London for ther confidence, but truly they seeme to have very few frendes in these partes, and I doe not thinke ther condicion is much better in other places. . . . . I am not yet out of hope of kissinge your Ladyshyps handes before the summer endes." Dated, Nottingham, 22 July, 1642. *Holograph*. [*Stowe MS.* 142, f. 47.]

68. JOHN HAMPDEN [b. 1594—d. 1643]. Letter to Colonel Bulstrode and others commanding parliamentary troops, written a few days after the battle of Edgehill [23 Oct.], which was followed by the retreat of the Parliamentarian army: "The army is now at North Hampton, moving every day nearer to you. If you disband not, wee may be a mutuall succour, each to other; but, if you disperse, you make yourselves and your country a pray." Dated, Northampton, 31 Oct. [1642]. [*Stowe MS.* 142, f. 49.] *Facsimile* in Ser. iv. no. 8.

69. JOHN PYM [b. 1584—d. 1643]. Letter to Sir Thomas Barrington, on the fall of Bristol and the efforts being made to save Gloucester: "It is true that Bristow is a great loss, and may endanger all the west if not quickly prevented, and therefor wee use all the meanes we can to raise a considerable army to send into those partes. . . . . In the North, God be thanckd, matters goe reasonable prosperously. Col. Cromwell in the taking of Burlye House [Burghley House, in Lincolnshire] took 5 troups of Horse, 3 of Dragoones, 3 companyes of foot. Since that they have beaten Generall Kings forces before Gainsboroughe, and if my L[ord] of Newcastles whole army had not come upon them in the very instant, they had had a more compleat victory. Wee are studiying all the ways we can to save Gloucester, Exeter and the other western townes now in danger upon the loss of Bristowe." Dated, Westminster, 2 Aug. 1643 [four months before his death]. *Holograph*. [*Egerton MS.* 2643, f. 13, b.] *Facsimile* in Ser. ii. no. 9.

70. JAMES GRAHAM, MARQUESS OF MONTROSE [b. 1612—d. 1650]. Letter to Lord Fairfax, with reference to an exchange of prisoners: "Mr. Darly being ane parlament man and on that hitherto hes beane much imployed and wery usefull to your party, and the other only in the degree of a cornell, bot admitt of the odes [*i.e.* odds], iff your l[ordship] will dispent it, the difference shall be maide up. Iff otherwayes you will be rather gallantly pleased to make it a curtesye, ane wery thankfull and acceptable returne shall, I hope, (er long) be randered your l[ordship]." Dated, 22 July, 1644. *Holograph*. [*Sloane MS.* 1519, f. 78.]

71. OLIVER CROMWELL. Letter to William Lenthall, Speaker of the House of Commons, reporting the victory of Naseby: "Wee after 3 howers fight, very doubtful, att last routed his [the King's] Armie, killed and tooke about 5000, very many officers, but of what quallitye wee yett know not, wee tooke alsoe about

OLIVER CROMWELL.

200 carrag[es], all hee had, and all his gunns. . . . Sir, this is non[e] other but tho hand of God, and to him aloane belongs the Glorie." After high commendations of tho General, Sir T. Fairfax, Cromwell proceeds: " Honest men served you faythfully in this action. Sir, they are trustye, I beseech you in the name of God not to discorage them. I wish this action may begett thankfullnesse and humilitye in all that are concerned in itt. Hee that venters his life for the libertyo of his euntrie, I wish hee trust God for the libertye of his conscience, and you for the libertye hee fights for." Dated, Haverbrowe [Market Harborough], 14 June, 1645, the day of the battle. *Holograph.* [*Add. MS.* 5015,* f. 13.] *Presented, in* 1758, *by Mr. Wright.*

72. PRINCE RUPERT [b. 1619—d. 1682]. Letter to Sir Edward Nicholas, Secretary of State, referring to aspersions upon him as being unfavourable to open counsels; and on military movements: " As for military disignes ye king will faile as [he] ded last if ho [trust] not to his officers opinions." Dated, Bristol, 5 July, [1645]. *Holograph*; partly in cipher, with decipherings by Sir E. Nicholas. [*Add. MS.* 18,738, f. 80.]

73. SIR THOMAS FAIRFAX, afterwards LORD FAIRFAX [b. 1612—d. 1671]. Letter, written while Generalissimo of the Parliamentary army, to his father, reporting his defeat of Goring's army at Langport [10 July, 1645, about a month after Naseby]: " I have taken this occasion to let your Lordship know God's great goodnes to us in defeating Gen. Goring's army: 2000 prisoners are taken, 2 peeces of ordinance, many armes and coulers [colours] both of horse and foot, but not many slaine. . . . The King had given Gooring strickt commands not to ingage befor himselfe with the Welch forces were joynd with him and Greenwel with those out of the west, which altogether would have maid [a] very great army . . . . so as we cannot esteme this marcy less, al things considerd, then that of Neasby fight." Dated, Chedsey, 11 July, 1645. *Holograph.* [*Add. MS.* 18,979, f. 204.]

74. CHARLES I. Letter, when prisoner at Carisbrooke, to Henry Firebrace, relative to plans for his escape, etc. Dated, 24 July, 1648. Written, partly in cipher, in a feigned hand, speaking of himself in the third person. *Holograph.* [*Egerton MS.* 1788, f. 34.]

75. OLIVER CROMWELL. Letter during his Irish campaign to Lord Fairfax, congratulating him on " the prosperityo of your affaires, wherin the good of all honest men is soe much concerned," and announcing the capture of Wexford : " The Lord shewes us great mercyo heere, indeed Hee, Hee only gave this stronge towne of Wexford into our handes." Dated, Wexford, 15 Oct. 1649. *Holograph.* [*Egerton MS.* 2620, f. 7.] *Facsimile* in Ser. i. no. 9.

76. OLIVER CROMWELL. Order of the Council of State requiring the presence and assistance of the Lord Mayor and the Aldermen of the City of London on the 19th December [1653] at the procla-

mation of "his Highness Oliver Cromwell" as "Lord Protector of the Common Wealth of England, Scotland, and Ireland and the Dominions therunto belonging." Dated, Whitehall, 17 Dec. 1653. With the *autograph* signatures of the members of the Council of State, John Disbrowe [or Desborough], J[ohn] Lambert, P[hilip], Viscount] Lisle [afterwards Earl of Leicester], E[dward] Mountagu [afterwards Earl of Sandwich], [Sir] Gil[bert] Pickering, Wal[ter] Strickland, Phi[lip] Jones, Ric[hard] Maijor, F[rancis] Rous, W[illiam] Sydenham, [Sir] Ch[arles] Wolseley, [Sir] An[thony] Ashley Cooper [afterwards Earl of Shaftesbury], and He[nry] Lawrence. [*Add. MS.* 18,739, f. 1.] *Facsimile* in Ser. iii. no. 8.

77. OLIVER CROMWELL and JOHN MILTON. Warrant to Gualter Frost, Treasurer to the Council of State, to pay a quarter's salary to various persons. Dated, Whitehall, 1 Jan. 165$\frac{3}{4}$. With *autograph* signature of Cromwell as Lord Protector, "OLIVER P." Appended are the receipts, with the *autograph* signatures of the persons concerned, among them being John Thurloe, principal Secretary to the Council of State (quarter's salary £200), and John Milton, Secretary for Foreign Tongues (quarter's salary £72 4s. 7$\frac{1}{2}$d). [*Stowe MS.* 142, ff. 60, 61.]

78. ROBERT BLAKE [b. 1599—d. 1657]. Letter, as General in command of the fleet, to the Commissioners for the Admiralty and Navy, on the eve of his departure for the Mediterranean, asking for the payment of his salary "unto the day of the date hereof, it being uncertain whether I may live to see you againe another. Howere my comfort is and I doubt not but wee shall meet together at the last day in the joyfull fruition of that One Faith and Hope of the common salvacion in the Lord, upon whome alone I do waite and to whose free grace and everlasting goodnes I do heartily recommend you." Dated, Plymouth, 25 Aug. 1654. *Holograph.* [*Add. MS.* 9304, f. 89.] *Facsimile* in Ser. iii. no. 9.

79. GENERAL CHARLES FLEETWOOD. Letter to General George Monck, in "behalfe of that distressed familie of his late Highnes [Richard Cromwell], whose condicion I thincke is as sad as any poore familie in England, the debts contracted during y^e goverment falling upon my Lord Richard Cromwell." Dated, Wallingford House, 14 Jan. 16$\frac{59}{60}$. *Autograph* signature. [*Egerton MS.* 2618, f. 58.]

80. RICHARD CROMWELL, late Lord Protector of England. Letter to General George Monck, asking his interest with the Parliament "that I bee not left liable to debts which I am confident neither God nor Conscience can ever reckon mine." Dated, 18 Apr. 1660. Signed, "R. CROMWELL." [*Egerton MS.* 2618, f. 67.] *Facsimile* in Ser. iv. no. 10.

81. CHARLES II. Letter, in *French*, to his sister Henrietta, afterwards Duchess of Orleans, written the day after the Restoration: "J'estois si tourmenté des affaires a la haye [Hague] que je ne

pouvois pas vous escriro devant mon depart, mais j'ay laissé ordre avec ma sœur de vous envoyer un petit present de ma part, que j'espere vous receverés bien tost. J'arrivay hire a douer [Dover], ou j'ay trouvay Monke avec grande quantité de noblesse, qui m'ont pensé acablé d'amitié et de ioye pour mon retour. J'ay la test si furieusement étourdy par l'acclamation du peuple et le quantité d'affaires que je ne scay si j'escrive du sen ou non; s'est pour quoy vous me pardonneres si je ne vous dy pas davantage, seulement que je suis tout a vous. C." Dated, Canterbury, 26 May, [1660]. *Holograph.* [*Add. MS.* 18,738, f. 102.] *Facsimile* in Ser. i. no. 10.

82. CHARLES II. Speech to the Members of the House of Commons, in the Banqueting Hall at Whitehall, 1 March, 166½, thanking them for their zeal and affection, urging them to settle a liberal revenue on the Crown, and warning them against precipitation and impatience in the matter of religion: " I thank you for it, since I presume it proceedes from a good roote of piety and devotion, but I must tell you I have the worst lucke in the world, if, after all the reproches of being a papist whilst I was abroade, I am suspected of being a presbiterian now I am come home." *Holograph.* [*Egerton MS.* 2546, f. 30.]

83. JOHN GRAHAM, OF CLAVERHOUSE, afterwards VISCOUNT OF DUNDEE [b. 1650—d. 1689]. Letter to [George Livingston] Earl of Linlithgow, Commander-in-Chief in Scotland, giving an account of the skirmish with the Covenanters at Drumclog: " We keeped our fyr till they wer within ten pace of us; they recaived our fyr and advanced to the shok. The first they gave us brought down the coronet, Mr. Crafford, and Captain Bleith . . . . which so disincoroged our men that they sustined not the shok but fell unto disorder. There horse took the occasion of this and perseud us so hotly that we got no tym to ragly. I saved the standarts, but lost on the place about aight ord ten men, beseids wounded; but the dragoons lost many mor." Dated, Glasgow, 1 June, 1679. *Holograph.* [*Stowe MS.* 142, f. 95.] *Facsimile* in Ser. ii. no. 10.

84. JAMES, DUKE OF MONMOUTH [b. 1649—d. 1685]. Letter to the Queen Dowager, after the failure of his insurrection, begging her to intercede for his life: " Being in this unfortunate condision and having non left but your Majesty that I think may have some compasion of me, and that for the last Kings sake, makes me take this boldnes to beg of you to intersed for me. I would not desire your Majesty to doe it, if I wear not from the botom of my hart convinced how I have bene disceaved into it, and how angry God Almighty is with me for it, but I hope, Madam, your intersesion will give me life to repent of it, and to shew the King how realy and truly I will serve him hear after." Dated, Ringwood, 9 July, 1685 [the day after his capture]. *Holograph.* [*Lansdowne MS.* 1236, f. 229.] *Facsimile* in Ser. i. no. 11.

85. WILLIAM, PRINCE OF ORANGE [afterwards William III. of England]. Letter, in *French*, to Admiral Arthur Herbert [afterwards Earl of Torrington], announcing the landing of his troops at Torbay and his intention of marching on Exeter, and making arrangements for sending on the baggage to Exmouth Dated, "Au camp de Torbay," $\frac{6}{16}$ Nov. 1688. *Holograph.* [*Egerton MS.* 2621, f. 39.]

86. GILBERT BURNET, afterwards Bishop of Salisbury [b. 1643—d. 1715]. Letter to Admiral Arthur Herbert [afterwards Earl of Torrington], written while accompanying the Prince of Orange on his march from Torbay to London during the Revolution, and giving details of public events, of the desertion of the King by the Princess of Denmark and others, of the arrival of Commissioners to treat with the Prince, etc. Dated, Hungerford, 9 Dec. 1688. *Holograph.* [*Egerton MS.* 2621, f. 69.]

87. WILLIAM III. Instructions to Admiral Arthur Herbert for the disposal of the person of the late King James II., in case of his capture at sea. Dated, Whitehall, 16 March, 168$\frac{8}{9}$. With signatures and seal of William III. and countersignature of [Daniel Finch,] Earl of Nottingham, Secretary of State. [*Egerton MS.* 2621, f. 87.] *Facsimile* in Ser. i. no. 12.

Case IV.

88. MARY II. Order, in the absence of William III., to Admiral Arthur [Herbert], Earl of Torrington, to engage the French fleet: "We apprehend ye consequences of your retiring to ye Gunfleet to be so fatall, y^t we choose rather y^t you should upon any advantage of ye Wind give battle to ye Enemy then retreat farther then is necessary to gett an advantage upon ye Enemy." Dated, Whitehall, 29 June, 1690. Signed at the top, "MARIE R."; and countersigned by [Daniel Finch,] Earl of Nottingham, Secretary of State. The result of this order was the battle of Beachy Head [30 June], in which the English and Dutch force was defeated by a superior French fleet, Torrington, who did not wish to fight, refusing to engage his squadron closely. [*Egerton MS.* 2621, f. 91.]

89. JAMES EDWARD STUART, THE PRETENDER [b. 1688—d. 1766]. Letter to Simon Fraser, Lord Lovat, promising, in consideration of his ancestors' services, "and now your own so freely hasarding your life in comeing hither upon so important an occasion," to create him an Earl, "and that in preference to all I shall create in the Kingdome of Scotland, ... so as that you shall become an argument to encourage others to serve me zealously." Dated, St. Germains, 3 May, 1703. Signed, "JAMES R."; with the royal signet. *Holograph.* [*Add. MS.* 31,249, f. 17.] *Facsimile* in Ser. i. no. 13.

90. JOHN CHURCHILL, DUKE OF MARLBOROUGH [b. 1650—d. 1722]. Letter, in *French*, to George Louis, Elector of Hanover [after-

wards George I. of England], giving an account of his victory at Ramillies [23 May] : "Le combat se shauffa et dura assez long tems avec une tres grand fureur, mais enfin les ennemis furent obliges de plier. . . . Ansi le bon Dieu nous a donné un victoire complet." Dated, Louvain, 25 May, 1706. *Holograph.* [*Stowe MS.* 222, f. 412.] *Facsimile* in Ser. i. no. 14.

91. SARAH CHURCHILL, DUCHESS OF MARLBOROUGH [b. 1660—d. 1744]. Letter to James Craggs [afterwards Secretary of State] on her dismissal from Court : "The message the Queen sent me, that I might take a lodging for ten shillings a week to put my Lord Marlboroughs goods in, sufficiently shews what a good education and understanding the wolf has, who was certainly the person that gave that advise." [April, 1710.] *Holograph.* [*Stowe MS.* 751, f. 1.]

92. ROBERT HARLEY, afterwards EARL OF OXFORD [b. 1661—d. 1724]. Letter to George Louis, Elector of Hanover [afterwards George I. of England], announcing the removal of the Duchess of Marlborough from the Queen's service, " as a further instance of her Majesties desire on all occasions to improve that good correspondence which is so necessary. . . . The causes of this ladys disgrace have been so public and of so many years continuance that it wil be needless to troble your Electoral Highness on that head." Dated, $\frac{19}{30}$ Jan. 171$\frac{0}{1}$. *Holograph.* [*Stowe MS.* 224, f. 16.] *Facsimile* in Ser. iii. no. 11.

93. HENRY ST. JOHN, VISCOUNT BOLINGBROKE [b. 1678—d. 1751]. Letter to George Clarke, formerly Secretary-at-War, giving his reason for removing from Paris, relying on the good opinion of his friends and " a conscience void of guilt," with which supports " I hope to wade thro' that sea of troubles into which I have been the first plung'd ; tho' I confess I do not see the shore on which one may hope to land." Dated, Belle Vue near Lyons, 27 June, 1715. *Holograph.* [*Egerton MS.* 2618, f. 217.] *Facsimile* in Ser. iii. no. 12.

94. SIR ROBERT WALPOLE [b. 1676—d. 1745]. Letter, written as First Lord of the Treasury, to the Duke of Newcastle, Secretary of State, respecting action to be taken in regard to the prosecution by the House of Commons of John Huggins, late Warden of the Fleet Prison, for cruelty to prisoners. [1730.] *Holograph.* [*Add. MS.* 32,687, f. 397.] *Presented, in* 1886, *by the Earl of Chichester. Facsimile* in Ser. iv. no. 13.

95. JAMES EDWARD STUART, THE PRETENDER [b. 1688—d. 1766]. Declaration, under the title of "James the Third," to all his "loving subjects," previous to the Rebellion of 1745. Dated, "at our Court at Rome," 23 Dec. 1743, "in the 43^d year of our reign." Signed, "JAMES R."; with privy seal. [*Add. MS.* 33,380.]

96. WILLIAM, DUKE OF CUMBERLAND [b. 1721—d. 1765]. Letter to Sir John Ligonier, with reference to the battle of Culloden, etc.: "Yesterday I received your kind congratulations on our Victory.

Would to God the enemy had been worthy enough for our troops.
Sure never were Soldiers in such a temper. Silence and Obedience
the whole time and all our Manœuvres were perform'd without
the least confusion. I must own that [you] have hit my weak
side when you say that the Honour of our troops is restored.
That pleases beyond all the Honours done me." Dated, Inverness, May, 1746. *Holograph.* [*Stowe MS.* 142, f. 113.]

97. HENRY BENEDICT STUART, afterwards CARDINAL OF YORK [b. 1725
—d. 1807], the last of the Stuarts. Letter, in *French*, commending the Duke of Perth to the protection of the French
King, as one of those "qui ont servi le Prince mon frere en
Ecosse," and who have consequently to take refuge in France.
Dated, Navarre, 26 June, 1746. *Holograph.* [*Add. MS.* 21,404,
f. 25.]

98. CHARLES EDWARD STUART, THE YOUNG PRETENDER [b. 1720—
d. 1788]. Letter to his brother Henry, Cardinal of York, with
reference to the transfer of some books to his wife, from whom
he was separated, and with whom he declined to hold direct
communication; " for it is not possible for me to have to say
with my wife in anny shepe, untill shee reppents. I am so fatigued
in writing this, you cannot immagin, my head being so much
bothered." [Florence, July, 1781.] Signed, " CHARLES R."
Holograph. [*Add. MS.* 34,634, f. 9.]

99. ROBERT CLIVE, afterwards LORD CLIVE [b. 1725—d. 1774].
Letter to the Duke of Newcastle, as First Lord of the Treasury,
reporting his recovery of Calcutta [after the tragedy of the Black
Hole, 21 June, 1756] and defeat of the Nawáb's army (50,000
strong) with a force of 600 Europeans and 800 natives: " A
little before day break wee entred the camp and received a very
brisk fire. This did not stop the progress of our Troops, which
march'd thro' the enemy's camp upwards of 4 miles in length.
Wee were more then 2 hours in passing, and what escaped the
Van was destroyd by the Rear . . ." Dated, " Camp near
Calcutta," 23 Feb. 1757. *Holograph.* [*Add. MS.* 32,870, f. 216.]
Presented, in 1886, by the Earl of Chichester. Facsimile in Ser. ii.
no. 12.

100. WILLIAM PITT, afterwards EARL OF CHATHAM [b. 1708—
d. 1778]. Letter to the Duke of Newcastle, complaining of the
concealment from him of a correspondence between Major Gen.
Joseph Yorke, Minister at the Hague, and an unknown lady at
Paris, concerning proposals of peace, made in the course of the
Seven Years War. The letter ends: " I acknowledge my unfitness for the high station where His Majesty has been pleased to
place me, but while the King deigns to continue me there, I trust
it is not presumption to lay myself at His Majesty's feet and
most humbly request his gracious permission to retire, whenever
His Majesty thinks it for his service to treat of a Peace in the
vehicle of letters of amusement and to order his servants to
conceal, under so thin a covering, the first dawnings of informa-

perity of this young & rising country, cannot but be gratefully received by all its citizens, and every lover of it. — One means to the contribution of which, and its happiness; is very judiciously portrayed in the following words of your letter " to be little heard of in the great world of Politics" These words I can assure your Lordship are expressive of my sentiments on this head; and I believe it is the sincere wish of United America to have nothing to do with the Political intrigues, or the squabbles of European Nations; but on the contrary, to exchange Commodities & live in peace & amity with all the inhabitants of the earth; and this I am persuaded they will do, if rightfully it can be done. — To administer justice to, and receive it from every Power with whom they are connected will, I hope, be always found the most prominent feature in the administration of this Country; and I flatter myself that nothing short of imperious necessity can occasion a breach with any of them. — Under such a system if we are

Your Lordship's most
Ob'd't & ble Servant
G. Washington

GEORGE WASHINGTON.

tion relative to so high and delicate an object." Dated, Hayes, 23 Oct. 1759. *Holograph.* [*Add. MS.* 32,897, f. 314.] *Presented, in* 1886, *by the Earl of Chichester. Facsimile* in Ser. i. no. 15.

101. "JUNIUS." The "Dedication to the English Nation," in the hand of Junius, of Woodfall's first edition of the Collected Letters of Junius, 1772. *Holograph.* [*Add. MS.* 27,775, f. 15.] *Facsimile* in Ser. iii. no. 13.

102. WARREN HASTINGS, Governor-General of India [b. 1732—d. 1818]. Letter to his wife, referring to his duel with Mr. (afterwards Sir) Philip Francis, Member of the Council: "I have desired Sir John Day to inform you that I have had a meeting this morning with Mr. Francis, who has received a wound in his side, but I hope not dangerous. . . . . I am *well* and *unhurt*. But you must be content to *hear* this good from me. You cannot see me. I cannot leave Calcutta while Mr. Francis is in any danger." Dated, Calcutta [17 Aug. 1780]. *Holograph* [with signature from another letter]. [*Add. MS.* 29,197, f. 13.]. *Facsimile* in Ser. iii. no. 14.

103. GEORGE WASHINGTON [b. 1732—d. 1799]. Letter to the Earl of Buchan, partly on the principle which should guide the United States, viz.: "to be little heard of in the great world of Politics." . . . . "I believe it is the sincere wish of United America to have nothing to do with the Political intrigues or the squabbles of European nations; but, on the contrary, to exchange commodities and live in peace and amity with all the inhabitants of the earth; and this I am persuaded they will do, if rightfully it can be done. . . . . To evince that our views are expanded, I take the liberty of sending you the Plan of a New City [*i.e.* Washington] situated about the centre of the Union of these States, which is designed for the permanent seat of the Government, and we are at this moment deeply engaged and far advanced in extending the inland navigation of the River (Potomac) on which it stands, and the branches thereof, through a tract of as rich country—for hundreds of miles—as any in the world." Dated, Philadelphia, 22 April, 1793. *Holograph.* [*Add. MS.* 12,099, f. 28.] *Facsimile* in Ser. i. no. 17.

104. WILLIAM PITT, the younger [b. 1759—d. 1806]. Letter to a member of his Cabinet [probably the Duke of Leeds], on the negotiations with the leaders of the French National Assembly, then being privately conducted by Mr. [afterwards Sir] Hugh Elliot: "I am in hopes you will think that it [a despatch to Elliot] steers quite clear of any thing like *Cringing* to France, which I agree with you ought to be avoided *even* in the present moment of their weakness, and certainly in all others." [October, 1790.] *Holograph.* [*Add. MS.* 33,964, f. 21.] *Facsimile* in Ser. ii. no. 14.

105. EDMUND BURKE [b. 1730—d. 1797]. Letter to Bishop Douglas, asking advice as to the propriety of presenting a copy of a new work [the *Appeal from the New to the Old Whigs*] to the King,

and commenting on affairs in France, with especial reference to the Queen, Marie Antoinette: "A worthy friend of mine at Paris writes me an account of the condition of the Queen of France, which makes it probable that the life of that persecuted Woman will not be long . . . What a lesson to the great and the little! How soon they pass from the state we admire and envy to that the most cruel must pity! I find I am preaching to a Bishop—but they are things and events that now preach, and not either Clergy or Laity." Dated, Margate, 31 July, 1791. *Holograph.* [*Egerton MS.* 2182, f. 72.] *Facsimile* in Ser. ii. no. 15.

106. CHARLES JAMES FOX [b. 1749 — d. 1806.] Letter to the Duchess of Leinster, relative to the petition against the bill of attainder of her son Lord Edward Fitzgerald, concluding with the words, "nor can anything make me have, I will not say a friendly, but even a patient feeling towards the Government of this country till his poor children are reinstated in their rights." Dated, Holkham, 21 Oct. [1798]. *Holograph.* [*Add. MS.* 30,990, f. 45.] *Facsimile* in Ser. iii. no. 15.

107. RICHARD BRINSLEY SHERIDAN [b. 1751—d. 1816]. Notes for a speech in the House of Commons, on 30 April, 1805, charging Pitt with misapplication of the public money, in connection with the charge against Lord Melville. *Holograph.* [*Add. MS.* 29,964, f. 58.] *Facsimile* in Ser. iv. no. 14.

108. SIR JOHN MOORE [b. 1761—d. 1809]. Letter, when Lieut.-Colonel Moore, to General Paoli, on his summary recall from Corsica: "I shall present myself to the King and to his Ministers with confidence, conscious of no conduct that deserves reproach—indeed I feel that I am incapable of an improper or unbecoming action. I hope the person who is the cause of my leaving Corsica [*i.e.* the viceroy, Gilbert Elliot, afterwards Earl of Minto] may upon his return be able to say as much." Dated, Corté, 6 Oct. 1795. *Holograph.* [*Add. MS.* 22,688, f. 114.]

109. CAROLINE, QUEEN OF GEORGE IV. Letter to the King, written on the day of his coronation, to which she had been refused admittance, claiming "that, after the publick insult her Majesty has received this morning, the King will grant her just Rights, to be crowned as next Monday." Dated, 19 July, 1821. *Holograph.* Signed "CAROLINE R." [*Add. MS.* 34,486, f. 93.]

110. HORATIO, VISCOUNT NELSON [b. 1758—d. 1805]. Sketch-plan of the Battle of Aboukir, generally called the Battle of the Nile, 1 Aug. 1798. In the corner is the following attestation:—"This was drawn by Lord Viscount Nelson's left hand, the only remaining one, in my presence, this Friday, Feb. 18th, 1803, at No. 23, Piccadilly, the house of Sir William Hamilton, late Ambassador at Naples, who was present. ALEXANDER STEPHENS." [*Add. MS.* 18,676.]

111. HORATIO, VISCOUNT NELSON. Letter written two days before the battle of Trafalgar to Lady Hamilton, telling her

Battle, may heaven bless you prays your Nelson Bronte. Oct'. 20th in the morning we were close to the mouth of the Straights but the Wind had not come far enough to the Westward to allow the Combined fleets to weather the Shoals of Trafalgar but they were counted as far as forty Sail of Ships of War which I suppose to be 34 of the Line and Six frigates, a Group of them was seen off the Lighthouse of Cadiz this Morn'g but it blows so very fresh I think I rather believe they will go into the Harbour before night. May God almighty give us success over these fellows

LORD NELSON.

that the enemy's combined fleets are coming out of port, and that he hopes to live to finish his letter. Dated, on board the Victory, 19 Oct. 1805. A postscript, written on the 20th Oct., the eve of the battle, is added, as follows: "Oct 20th. In the morning, we were close to the mouth of the streights, but the wind had not come far enough to the westward to allow the combined fleets to weather the shoals off Traflagar [sic]; but they were counted as far as forty sail of ships of war, which I suppose to be 34 of the Line and six frigates. A group of them was seen off the Lighthouse of Cadiz this morning, but it blows so very fresh and thick weather that I rather believe they will go into the Harbour before night. May God Almighty give us success over these fellows and enable us to get a Peace." *Holograph.* Below is written in the hand of Lady Hamilton: "This letter was found open on *his* Desk and brought to Lady Hamilton by Captain Hardy. Oh, miserable wretched Emma! Oh, glorious and happy Nelson!" [*Egerton MS.* 1614, f. 125.]*
Facsimile in Ser. i. no. 18.

112. ARTHUR WELLESLEY, DUKE OF WELLINGTON [b. 1769—d. 1852]. Enumeration of the cavalry under his command at the battle of Waterloo, 18 June, 1815. *Holograph.* Given by the Duke to Sir John Elley, Deputy Adjutant General, previous to the battle. [*Add. MS.* 7140.] *Presented, in* 1828, *by the Rt. Rev. John Jebb, D.D., Bishop of Limerick. Facsimile* in Ser. i. no. 19.

113. ARTHUR WELLESLEY, DUKE OF WELLINGTON. Letter to Lord Hill (his former second in command in the Peninsula), offering him the succession to himself in the chief command of the army: "You will have heard that in consequence of my being employed in the Government [as First Lord of the Treasury] I have been under the painful necessity of resigning my office of Commander in Chief . . . . In consequence of my resignation I have been under the necessity of considering of an arrangement to fill the office which I have held; and I have naturally turned towards you. There is no doubt that your appointment will be highly satisfactory to the country as well as the army; but it has occurred to some of the Government that, considering the place in which you stand on the list, it is better in relation to the senior officers of the army, some of whom have high pretensions, that you should be Senior General upon the Staff performing the duties of Commander in Chief than Commander in Chief." Dated, London, 1 Feb. 1828. *Holograph* [with signature from another letter]. Lord Hill held the post of General Commanding in Chief from 1828 to 1842. [*Add. MS.* 35,060, f. 512.] *Facsimile* in Ser. iv. no. 15.

114. HENRY JOHN TEMPLE, VISCOUNT PALMERSTON [b. 1784—d. 1865]. Letter, as Secretary of State for Foreign Affairs, to R. B.

---

* Beside this letter of Lord Nelson is a small box made from a splinter of the *Victory*, knocked off by a shot in the Battle of Trafalgar, and containing a portion of Nelson's hair. *Presented, in* 1865, *by Capt. Wm. Gunton.*

Hoppner, British representative at Lisbon, on the course to be followed in the case of an outbreak of hostilities at Lisbon on the landing of Dom Pedro. Dated, 18 June, 1832. *Holograph.* [*Egerton MS.* 2343, f. 6.]

115. SIR ROBERT PEEL [b. 1788—d. 1850]. Letter to Sir Robert Inglis, on the impossibility of increasing a Civil List pension. Dated, Whitehall, 27 Feb. 1843. *Holograph.* [*Add. MS.* 32,441, f. 379.] *Presented, in* 1884, *by Mrs. A. Bennett.*

116. LORD JOHN RUSSELL, afterwards EARL RUSSELL [b. 1792—d. 1878]. Letter, written while Prime Minister, to Bishop Maltby of Durham, with reference to the Papal Bull creating Roman Catholic bishops in England, commonly known as "the Durham Letter": "I agree with you in considering 'the late aggression of the Pope upon our Protestantism' as 'insolent and insidious,' and I therefore feel as indignant as you can do upon the subject .... There is a danger, however, which alarms me much more than any aggression of a foreign Sovereign. Clergymen of our own Church, who have subscribed the thirty-nine Articles and acknowledged in explicit terms the Queen's Supremacy, have been the most forward in leading their flocks 'step by step to the very verge of the precipice.' The honour paid to Saints, the claim of infallibility for the Church, the superstitious use of the sign of the Cross, the muttering of the liturgy so as to disguise the language in which it is written— the recommendation of auricular confession, and the administration of penance and absolution—all these things are pointed out by clergymen of the Church of England as worthy of adoption .... But I rely with confidence on the people of England, and I will not bate a jot of heart or hope so long as the glorious principles and the immortal Martyrs of the Reformation shall be held in reverence by the great mass of a nation which looks with contempt on the mummeries of superstition, and with scorn at the laborious endeavours which are now making to confine the intellect and enslave the soul." Dated, Downing Street, 4 Nov. 1850. *Holograph.* [*Add. MS.* 35,068, ff. 3–5.] *Presented, in* 1896, *by Lieut. G. R. Maltby.*

117. BENJAMIN DISRAELI, afterwards EARL OF BEACONSFIELD [b. 1805 —d. 1881]. Letter to Macvey Napier, editor of the *Edinburgh Review*, offering to write an article on *Zohrab the Hostage*, an Oriental romance by J. P. Morier: "With a great reluctance to hurt the feelings of so gentlemanlike a fellow as Morier, I must say that I have a great desire to show the public the consequence of having a tenth-rate novelist [Lockhart] at the head of a great critical journal [the *Quarterly Review*, which had praised the book], for really a production in every respect more contemptible than *Zohrab* I have seldom met with. My acquaintance with Oriental life would not disqualify me from performing the operation." Dated, St. James, 23 Feb. 1833. *Holograph* [with signature from another letter, in which the

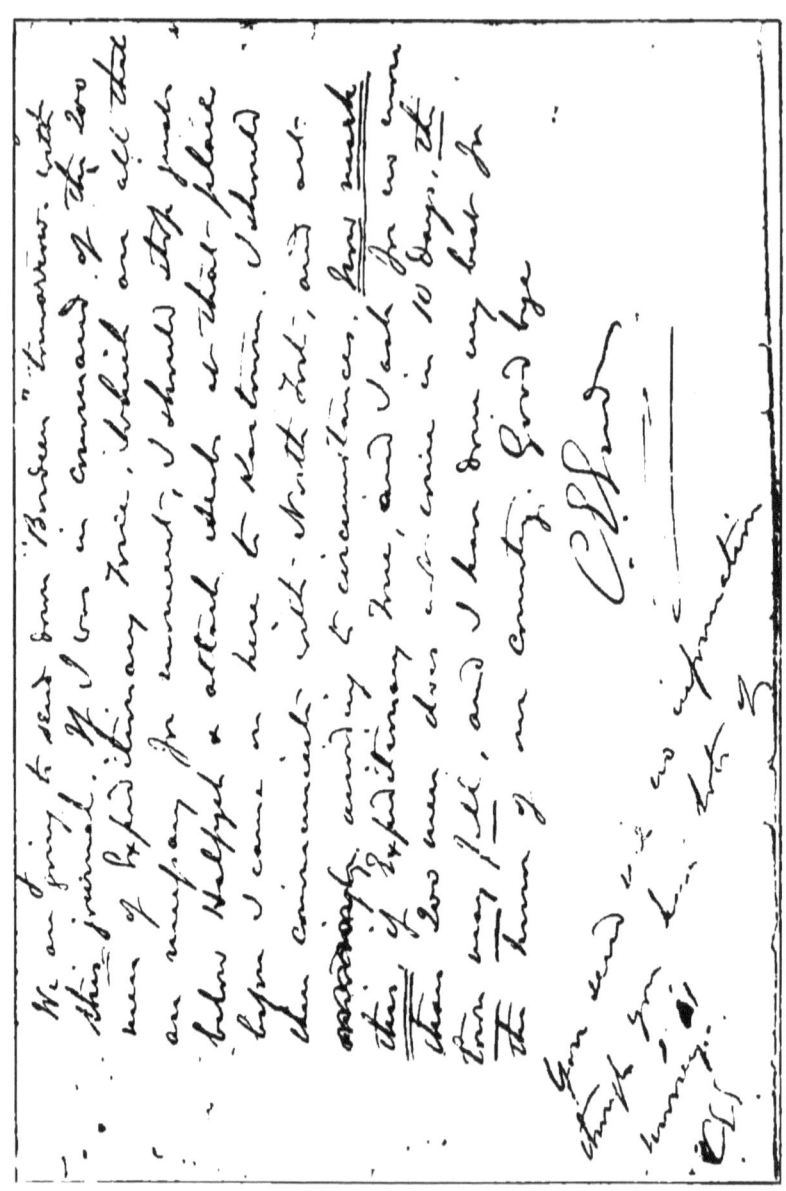

CHARLES GEORGE GORDON.

proposed article is abandoned, on account of political engagements]. [*Add. MS.* 34,616, f. 45.]
118. WILLIAM EWART GLADSTONE [b. 1809—d. 1898]. Letter to A. Panizzi, Principal Librarian of the British Museum, with reference to literary work and foreign politics: "I am no Achilles, and have had no provocation, great or small; nor am I, nor can I well be, asked to render any help, when the help i should render would be in the wrong direction. My ideas of foreign policy are, I fear, nearly the contradictories of those now in vogue [under the Palmerston government]. I am for trusting mainly to the moral influence of England, for uttering no threats except such as I mean to execute, for declining to revile to-day the men whom I lauded yesterday .... in short, for a long list of heresies which the *Times* daily anathematizes *ex cathedra,* and for which I am most thankful not to be burned by a slow fire." Dated, Hawarden, 29 Nov. 1856. *Holograph.*
119. CHARLES GEORGE GORDON, Governor-General of the Soudan [b. 1833—d. 1885]. The last page of his Diary at Khartoum, 14 Dec. 1884, written on the backs of telegraph forms: "We are going to send down 'Bordeen' to-morrow with this journal. If I was in command of the 200 men of Expeditionary Force, which are all that are necessary for moment, I should stop just below Halfyeh and attack Arabs at that place before I came on here to Kartoum. I should then communicate with North Fort and act according to circumstances. *Now mark this,* if Expeditionary Force, and I ask for no more than 200 men, does not come in 10 days, *the town may fall,* and I have done my best for the honor of our country. Good bye. C. G. GORDON." *Holograph.* [*Add MS.* 34,479, f. 108.] *Bequeathed, in* 1893, *by Miss M. A. Gordon. Facsimile* in Ser. i. no. 20.
120. QUEEN VICTORIA. Letter to Miss M. A. Gordon, thanking her for the gift of a Bible which had formerly belonged to her brother, General C. G. Gordon: "It is most kind and good of you to give me this precious Bible, and I only hope that you are not depriving yourself and family of such a treasure if you have no other. May I ask you during how many years your dear heroic brother had it with him?" Dated, Windsor Castle, 16 March, 1885. *Holograph.* Signed, "VICTORIA R.I." [*Add. MS.* 34,483, ff. 7 b, 8.] *Bequeathed, in* 1893, *by Miss M. A. Gordon. Facsimile* in Ser. i. no. 21.

CHARTERS.

The term Charter (Lat. *Charta*, papyrus, paper) includes not only royal grants of privileges and recognitions of rights, such as the "Magna Charta" of King John and the Charters of municipal and other corporations, but any formal document of the nature of a covenant or record, whether public or private. Examples of various kinds, chiefly English, are here shown, including two papal Bulls (so called from the "bulla" or leaden seal used by the Popes) and a Golden Bull of the Emperor Baldwin II. They have been selected not only for the interest of their contents, but in order to illustrate the progress and changes of the chancery and charter hands, as distinguished from the book hand (see p. 75), between the eighth and the sixteenth centuries.

The usual mode of attestation after the Norman Conquest was by means of a seal without a signature: "Magna Charta," for example, was not actually *signed* in writing by the King, but had his great seal appended. The seal was in fact the *signum* or legal signature; and written signatures only became common, and eventually necessary, when ability to write was more general. In Saxon times, before Edward the Confessor, seals were very rarely employed; the names (usually of the King and his Witan or Council) were written by the same hand as the body of the document, and a cross prefixed or added. Some of the Charters here have the seal still attached; and a special selection of royal and other seals, many of which are of great artistic beauty, is exhibited in Cases L. M. (p. 113.)

Case V.

[At right angles to Case III., the numbers beginning on the left.]

1. Grant by OFFA, King of the Mercians, to Ealdbeorht, his "minister" or thegn, and his sister Seleðryð [Abbess of Lyminge] of land of 14 ploughs in the province of the Cantuarii at Iocc ham and Perham stede [Ickham, and Parmested in Kingston, co. Kent], with swine-pasturage in the Andred wood, etc. Witnesses: King Offa, Iaenbeorht, Archbishop of Canterbury, Cyneðryð, the Queen, and others. Dated at the Synod of Celchyð [Chelsea], A.D. 785. *Latin.* [*Stowe Ch.* 5.]

2. Grant by EADRED, King of the English, to Ælfwyn, a nun, of six "mansae," or in the Kentish tongue "syx sulunga," of land at Wic ham [Wickham Breaux, co. Kent], for two pounds of the purest gold. Witnesses: King Eadred, Eadgifu his mother, Oda, Archbishop of Canterbury, Wulfstan, Archbishop of York, and others. Dated A.D. 948. *Latin*, with the boundaries of the land in *English.* [*Stowe Ch.* 26.]

Charters. 39

3. Grant by CNUT, King of the English, to Ælfstan, Archbishop [of Canterbury], at the petition of Queen Ælfgyfu, of a grove in the forest of Andredesweald, known as Haesclerse [co. Kent]. Witnesses: King Cnut, Wulfstan, Archbishop [of York], Ælfgyfu, the Queen, and others. Dated A.D. 1018. *Latin*, with the boundaries in *English*. [*Stowe Ch.* 38.]

4. Notification by EDWARD THE CONFESSOR to Archbishop Eadsige (d. 1050) and others, of his confirmation of all grants made by Earl Leofric and Godgyva his wife [Godgyfu, or Godiva] to St. Mary's Abbey, Coventry. [1043-1050.] *English*. [*Add. Ch.* 28,657.]

5. Notification by WILLIAM I., the Conqueror, King of the English, to Peter, Bishop of Chester [Lichfield and Coventry], Will. FitzOsbern, Earl [of Hereford], Hugh, Earl of Chester, and others, "Francis et Anglis," of his confirmation to Abbot Leofwin and St. Mary's Abbey, Coventry, of the grants of Earl Leofric as confirmed by King Edward (*cf.* no. 4). Witnesses: Odo, Bishop of Bayeux, Gosfrid, Bishop of Coutances, Robert, Count of Mortain, and others. [About 1070.] *Latin*. With seal. [*Add. Ch.* 11,205.]

6. Notification by WILLIAM II. to Osmund [de Séez], Bishop of Salisbury, and all his barons and lieges, French and English, in Wiltshire, of his grant to the Church of St. Martin de Bello [Battle Abbey, co. Sussex], by order of his father, of the manor of Bromham [co. Wilts]. Witnesses: Eudo the Dapifer, Roger Bigot, and others. Dated at Winchester, [1087-1099]. *Latin*. [*Cotton MS.* Aug. ii. 53.]

7. Charter of Anselm, Archbishop of Canterbury ("Dorobernensis ecclesie"), restoring to the monks of the same [*sc.* of Christ Church, Canterbury] the moiety of the altar of Christ, which he had after the death of Lanfranc his predecessor, who had restored the other moiety; and at the same time restoring the manor of Stistedo [Stisted, co. Essex], which was known to belong to them. Witnesses: William, Archdeacon of Christ Church, Haimo the Sheriff, and others. [About 1095.] *Latin*. With seal. [*Campb. Ch.* vii. 5.] This charter and no. 9 are apparently not originals, though genuine seals are attached.

8. Notification by HENRY I. to Robert, Bishop of Lincoln, Simon, Earl [of Northampton], and Gilbert the Sheriff, and to the men "francigeni et angligeni" of co. Huntingdon, of an agreement between Aldwin, Abbot of Ramsey, and William the King's "Dispensator," whereby the latter is to hold the land of Elintuna [Ellington, co. Hunts] of the abbey till his death, the whole lordship then to revert to the abbey, to provide food for the monks. Witnesses: Randulf the Chancellor, Will. de Curci, Roger de Oli, and others. Dated, "apud nemus Wardbergam" [co. Hunts, about 1106-1114.] *Latin*. [*Add. Ch.* 33,250.]

9. Confirmation by HENRY I. to Archbishop William and the monks of Christ Church, Canterbury, of all the lands and

D 2

privileges which they had in the time of King Edward and of William his father. [1123?] *Latin.* Followed by an *English* version, beg. " H. þurh godesgeuu ænglelandes kyning grete ealle mine bisscopes and ealle mine eorles and calle mine scirgereuan and calle mine ðegenas frencisce and ænglisce," etc. With seal, sewed up in a cover of green damask. [*Campb. Ch.* XXXI. 6.]

10. Grant by MATILDA, Empress [of the Romans], daughter of King Henry 1. and Queen of the English, to St. Mary's Abbey, Reading, co. Berks, for her soul's health, and for the soul of King Henry her father and for the preservation of Geoffrey, Count of Anjou, and the lord Henry her son [Henry II.], etc., of the land of Windesor [Windsor, co. Berks.], and Cateshell [Catshill in Godalming, co. Surrey], which belonged to Geoffrey Purcell, and which he gave to the Monastery when he became a monk there. Witnesses: Henry [of Blois], Bishop of Winchester [brother of King Stephen], Alexander, Bp. of Lincoln, Nigel, Bp. of Ely, Bernard, Bp. of St. David's, Rodbert [de Bethune], Bp. of Hereford, Robert, Earl of Gloucester [natural son of Henry I.], Reginald [de Dunstanvill], Earl [of Cornwall, natural son of Henry I.], Rodbert his brother, Brien Fitz-Count, Milo [de Gloucester] the Constable, John the Marshal. Dated at Reading, [May, 1141?] *Latin.* [*Add. Ch.* 19,576.]

11. Notification by King STEPHEN of his grant, for the health of his soul and those of Matilda his queen, of Eustace his son, and of his other children, and for the soul of King Henry I., his uncle, to St. Mary's Abbey, Reading, of his manor of Bleberia [Blewbury, co. Berks.], with free customs, etc. Witnesses: M[atilda] the Queen, "my wife," H[enry of Blois], Bishop of Winchester, "my brother," Count E[ustace], "my son," and others. Dated at London, [about 1144]. *Latin.* With seal. [*Add. Ch.* 19,581.]

12. Confirmation by Gilbert [de Clare], Earl [of Pembroke], to St. Mary's Priory, Southwark, of the land of Perenduna [Parndon, co. Essex], which John the Steward and Nich. de Epinges granted to it, with William fil. Eadmundi, whose land it was, free of all service except *sentage;* and when one Knight [*sc.* one Knight's fee] gives 20 sh., that land shall give 2 sh., and when one Knight gives one mark, it shall give 16d., etc. Witnesses: Richard his son, Isabel the Countess, Hervieus his brother, and others. [1138–48.] *Latin.* [*Cotton MS.* Nero C. iii. f. 228.]

13. Charter whereby William, Earl of Warenne, confirms to the monks of St. Pancras [*sc.* Lewes Priory] all the lands, etc., which they hold of his fee, undertaking to acquit them of Danegeld and all other services due to the King, and moreover grants to them tithe of corn, hay, lambs, fleeces and cheeses, and the tenth penny of all his rents in England. This charter, he goes on to say, he granted and confirmed at the dedication of the church of St. Pancras; and he gave the church seisin of the

tenth penny of his rents by hair cut with a knife from his own head and his brother's by Henry, Bishop of Winchester, before the altar ("quos abscidit cum cultello de capitibus nostris ante altare Hen. ep. Winton."). Witnesses: Theobald, Archb. of Canterbury, Henry, Bp. of Winchester, Robert, Bp. of Bath, and Ascelin, Bp. of Rochester, who dedicated the church, William [de Albini], Earl of Chichester, and others. [1142–1147.] *Latin.* [*Cotton Ch.* xi. 56.]

14. Grant by William fil. Audoeni to St. Denis Priory, near Hamton [Southampton], by the hand of Henry, Bishop of Winchester, of his land of Norham [Northam], with confirmation by the oblation of a knife ("per hunc cultellum.") Witnesses: Antelm the Prior, Walter his canon. Henry, Chancellor of the Bp. of Winchester, Osbert, Constable of Hamton, and others. Dated 1151. *Latin.* [*Harley Ch.* 50 A. 8.]

15. Treaty of peace between Rannlph [de Gernons], Earl of Chester, and Robert [de Beaumont], Earl of Leicester, providing for the surrender of the castle of Mount Sorrel, co. Leic., to the Earl of Leicester, the demolition of the castle of Ravenstone, co. Leic., etc.; made in presence of "the second" Robert [de Chesney], Bishop of Lincoln, and adherents of the two parties. [1147–1151.] *Latin.* [*Cotton MS.* Nero C. iii. f. 178.]

16. Grant by HENRY II. to the cathedral church of Winchester of the manors of Meonis [East Meon, co. Southt.] and Weregrana [Wargrave, co. Berks], with their churches, chapels, etc.; together with an addition of eight days to Winchester Fair, so that it may now last 16 days instead of eight as in the time of King Henry his grandfather. Witnesses: Theobald, Archb. of Canterbury, Hugh, Archb. of Rouen, and others. Dated at London, [Dec. 1154?] *Latin.* [*Add. Ch.* 28,658.]

17. Grant by HENRY II. to William and Nicholas, sons of Roger, son-in-law of Albert, of the charge of his galley ("ministerium meum de esnecca mea"), with the livery ("liberatio") belonging thereto, and all the lands of their father. Witnesses: Theobald, Archb. of Canterbury, Henry, Bp. of Winchester, T[homas Becket], Chancellor, and others. Dated at Oxford, [Jan. 1155?]. The word "esnecca" preserves the memory of the "Snekkar," or Serpents, as the Northmen called their long war-galleys. *Latin.* [*Campb. Ch.* xxix. 9.]

18. Confirmation by William, Count of Boulogne and Warenne, for the health of his soul and that of Isabella his wife [daughter and heir of William, 3rd Earl of Surrey and Warenne], and for the souls of King Stephen his father, Queen Matilda his mother, and Count Eustace his brother, of a grant from King Stephen to the Church of Saltereia [Sawtrey Abbey, co. Hunts.] of lands in Gamalingeia [Gamlingay, co. Cambs.]. Witnesses: Reinald de Warenne, Seher de Quinci, and others. Dated at Acre [Castle Acre, co. Norf., about 1155]. *Latin.* [*Harley Ch.* 83 A. 25.]

19. Confirmation by HENRY II. to Bromfield Priory, co. Salop, of the church of Bromfield, with the lands and vills of Haverford [Halford], Dodinghopa [Dinchope], Esseford [Ashford], Felton, etc.; granted on the reconstitution of the Priory under the Benedictine Order in 1155. *Latin.* [*Cotton Ch.* xvii. 4.]

20. Grant from Hugh Talebot, with the assent of Ermentrude his wife and Gerard, Geoffrey, Hugh and Richard his sons, to the Abbey of St. Mary and St. Laurence of Beaubec, in Normandy, of his land of Fautewella [Foltwell, co. Norf.], from which Aeliza de Cokefelt and Adam her son paid him yearly 100 shillings. Dated 1165. *Latin.* With seal. [*Harley Ch.* 112 D. 57.]

21. Grant by Richard, Bishop of St. Andrews, to the church of the Holy Cross [Holyrood Abbey] of the church of Egglesbrec, "que varia capella dicitur" [now Falkirk, co. Stirling], and all the land he had there, paying yearly one "petra" of wax to his chapel. Witnesses: Geoffrey, Abbot of Dunfermline, John, Abbot of Kelso, Osbert, Abbot of Jedworth, and others. Dated in full chapter at Berwick, 1166. *Latin.* [*Harley Ch.* 111 B. 14.]

22. Grant from Robert [Trianel], Prior, and the Priory of St. Andrew at Northampton to Christian, Abbot, and the Abbey of Aunay in the diocese of Bayeux in Normandy, of two parts of the tithage of Aissebi [Ashby-Mears, co. Northampton], the Abbey in return to pay yearly six measures of winnowed corn into the Priory grange at Ashby. Witnessed by six priests, three from either House. Dated 1176. *Latin.* [*Harley Ch.* 44 A. 1.]

23. Fine at Oxford "in Curia Regis" before Rich. Giffard, Roger fil. Reinfrid and John de Caerdif, the King's Justices, on the feast of SS. Peter and Paul [*sc.* 29 June, 1176] next after the King took the allegiance of the barons of Scotland at York, whereby Ingrea and her three daughters quit to the canons of Oseney their claim to certain land in Oxford for 20 sh. *Latin.* This is the earliest known original record of the legal process known as a Fine or Final Concord. [*Cotton Ch.* xi. 73.]

24. Agreement whereby the Knights Hospitallers of St. John of Jerusalem surrender to Richard [Toclive], Bishop of Winchester, the charge and administration of the Hospital of St. Cross without the walls of Winchester, the Bishop raising the number of poor there entertained from 113 to 213 (of whom 200 were to be fed and 13 fed and clothed), assigning to the Knights Hospitallers the churches of Morduna [Mordon, co. Surrey] and Haninctona [Hannington, co. Southampton], and releasing them from the yearly payment to the monks of St. Swithin of 10 marks and two candles of 10 lbs. of wax. Dated at Dover, 10 Apr. 1185, in presence of Henry II., Eraclius, Patriarch of Jerusalem, and others. *Latin.* With autograph signatures of Bishop Toclive and Roger de Molins, Master of the Hospital of St. John of Jerusalem. Appended are the leaden "bulla" of R.

de Molins and the seals of the Bishop and of Garnerius de Neapoli, Prior of the Hospitallers in England. [*Harley Ch.* 43 I. 38.]

25. License by RICHARD I. to Reginald [Fitz-Jocelin], Bishop of Bath, and his successors for their hounds to hunt through the whole of Somerset, to take all beasts except hart and hind, buck and doe, and to pursue all that shall escape from their parks, with a penalty of 10 pounds against any who shall disturb them in so doing. Witnesses: Baldwin, Archb. of Canterbury, and others. Dated by the hand of W[illiam de Longchamp], Bishop-elect of Ely, Chancellor, at Canterbury, 26 Nov. 1st year [1189]. Latin. [*Harley Ch.* 83 C. 10.]

26. Confirmation by RICHARD I. to Alured de St. Martin, his steward, of a grant made to him for life by Henry, Count of Eu, on the death of Alice his [Henry's] mother [who married A. de St. Martin as her 2nd husband], of the dower-lands of the said Alice in Eleham and Bensinton [Elham and Bilsington, co. Kent]. Witnesses: H[ugh de Puisac], Bp. of Durham, and others. Dated, "per manum Will. de Longo Campo, Cancellarii nostri, Elyensis electi," at Canterbury, 30 Nov. 1st year [1189]. Latin. With seal. [*Egerton Ch.* 372.]

27. Grant by Waleran [de Newburgh], Earl of Warwick, to Peter Blund of lands in Scenegefeld and Tromkewull [Shinfield and Trunkwell, near Mortimer Stratfield, co. Berks], at a rent of two bezants or four shillings. Witnesses: William [de Longchamp], Bp. of Ely, Godfrey [de Lucy], Bp. of Winchester, and many others. [1190–1.] Latin. [*Harley Ch.* 83 A. 4.]

28. Grant by John, Count of Mortain, Lord of Ireland [King JOHN], to Hamo de Valoniis of the town of Waterford, in Ireland, to support him in the Count's service until the latter can restore to him the lands he had lost for his sake or give him an equivalent. Witnesses: Will. de Wenn[evall], Reginald de Wassunville, and others. Dated at Dorchester, 7 July, 4 Rich. I. [1193]. Latin. [*Lansd. Ch.* 33.]

29. Confirmation by RICHARD I. to Alan Basset, his knight, of the manor of Winterburn [Winterborne-Basset, co. Wilts] granted to him by Walter de Dunstanvill. Witnesses: Otho, son of the Duke of Saxony, "our nephew," Baldwin de Bethune, and others. Dated at Chinon, by the hand of W[ill. de Longchamp], Bishop of Ely, Chancellor, 12 Dec. 6th year [1194]. With re-confirmation as follows, "Is erat tenor carte nostre in primo sigillo nostro, quod, quia aliquando perditum fuit et, dum capti essemus in Alemannia, in aliena potestate constitutum, mutatum est," i.e. "Such was the tenor of our charter under our first seal, but as this seal was at one time lost, and, while we were in captivity in Germany, was in the power of others, it has been changed." Witnesses: Baldwin [de Bethune], Earl of Albemarle, William Marshal, and others. Dated, by the hand of E[ustace], Bishop of Ely, Chancellor, "apud Rupem auree

vallis" [Orival-sur-Seine, in Normandy], 22 Aug. 9th year [1198]. *Latin.* With *second* Great Seal. [*Cotton Ch.* xvi. 1.]

30. Confirmation by Earl David, brother of the King of Scots, [as Earl of Huntingdon], to the Priory of St. James of Huntingdon [*al.* Hinchingbrooke Priory] of a yearly rent of 30d. from the mill of Little Hameldon [Hambleton, co. Rutland]. Witnesses: Hugh de Lisors, Simon de Seinliz, and others. [About 1200.] *Latin.* [*Add. Ch.* 34,255.]

31. Grant by Hasculf de Pinchencia to Helias de Englefeld of the meadow of Middelham [in Englefield, co. Berks?], to be held for the service of a sor-hawk yearly at the time of the taking of hawks (" per unum nisum sor quem reddet annuatim mihi in tempore de espreueitesun "), the grantee moreover giving to the said Hasculf 4 marks of silver, to Gillo his son and heir a shod hunting-horse (" unum chazeur ferratum ") and to Matildis his wife half a mark. [Late 12th cent.] *Latin.* With seal. [*Add. Ch.* 7201.]

32. Grant by Ranulph, Earl of Chester, to Roger, his Constable, of a free boat on the river Dee at Chester, for the yearly service of a pair of gilt spurs, with rights of fishing above and below Chester bridge and at Etton [Eaton], by day and by night, "cum flonettis et draghenettis et stalnettis," and all kinds of nets, and of doing what he will with the fish they shall take. Witnesses: Rob. de Monte alto, Seneschal of Chester, and others. [Late 12th cent.] *Latin.* With fragment of seal. [*Harley Ch.* 52 A. 17.]

33. Confirmation by King JOHN to the Order of Bonshommes de Grammont (" Bonis hominibus Grandi Montis ") of the foundation made by his father Henry II. of their house [Notre Dame du Parc] near Rouen, and of his grant to them for their victuals of 200 livres of Anjou from the Vicomté of Rouen. Witnesses: R[oger], Bp. of St. Andrews, Will. Lunge Espee, Earl of Salisbury, and others. Dated, by the hands of Symon, Archdeacon of Wells, and John de Gray, at Chinon, 26 Sept. 1st year [1199]. *Latin.* [*Add. Ch.* 11,314.]

34. Deed of sale by Alan de Witcherche to Will. de Englefeld, for one mark of silver, of his three " nativi," sons of Bernard the miller of Scofeld [Sheffield, near Englefield, co. Berks]. [About 1200.] *Latin.* With seal. [*Add. Ch.* 20,592.]

35. Grant by King JOHN to William de Belver [Belvoir], son of William de Albeni, of a weekly market and a three-day fair at Brigtford [Bridgford, co. Notts]. Witnesses: R[obert], Earl of Leicester, William, Earl of Salisbury, and others. Dated, by the hand of Hugh of Wells, at " Sagium " [Séez, in Normandy], 28 Jan., 4th year [1203]. *Latin.* With seal. [*Harley Ch.* 43 C. 34.]

36. Grant by Brother Robert the Treasurer, Prior of the Knights Hospitallers in England, to Robert, son of Ivo de Wicham, of land in Wicham [Wykeham, near Nettleton, co. Linc.] at a

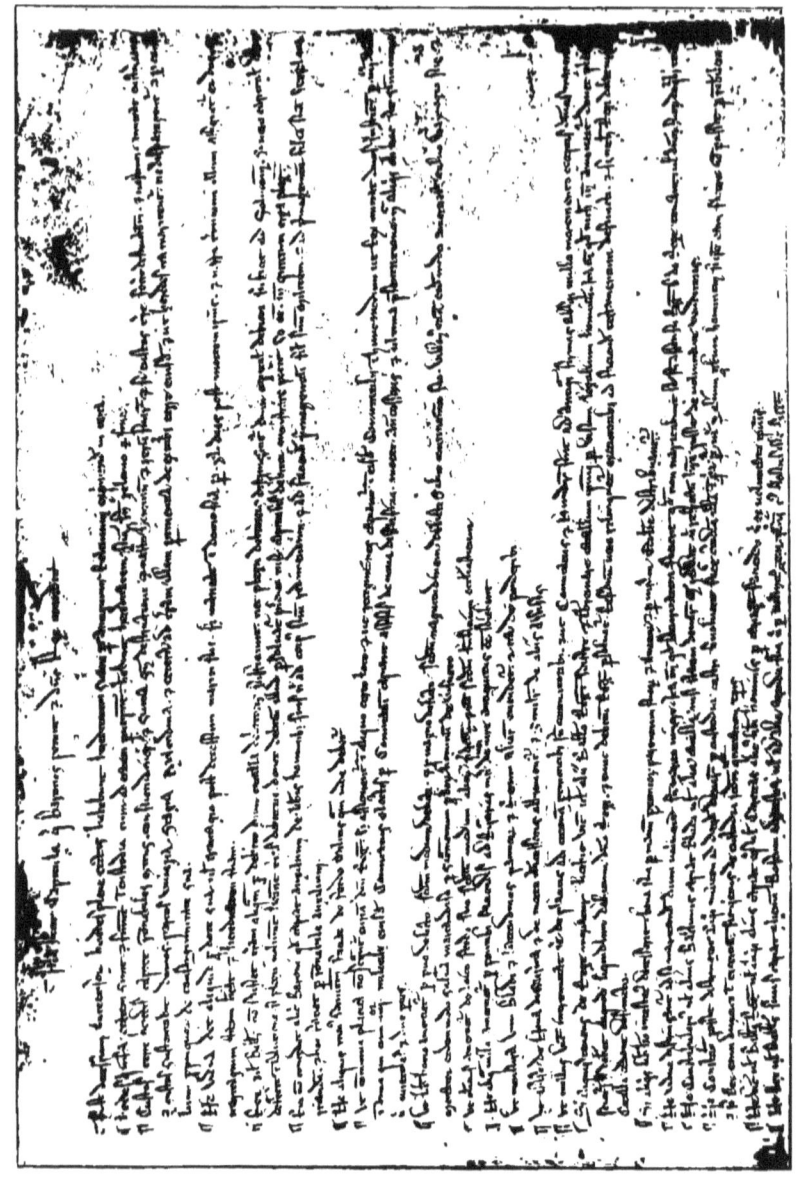

ARTICLES OF MAGNA CHARTA.

yearly rent of 12d., a third part of the chattels of the grantee and his heirs to pass on death to the Hospital. Witnesses: Brother Reimbald, and others. Dated, at the Chapter of St. Hilary, at Oscinton [Ossington, co. Notts], 1205[6]. *Latin.* [*Harley Ch.* 44 E. 21.]

37. Surrender by William "Walensis" and Isabel his wife and by Robert [de Hagley], son and heir of the said Isabel, to Sir Roger de Mortimer [d. 1214] of land in the vale of Wigemor [Wigmore, co. Hereford] held of him by the service of being his huntsmen, the said service being long in arrear and Sir Roger having paid to them 40 marks of silver. Witnesses: Sir Ralph, Abbot of Wigmore, and others. [Before 1214.] *Latin.* With seals. [*Cotton Ch.* xxx. 8.]

38. Bull of Pope Innocent III. ratifying the offering and grant made by King John, by counsel of his barons, of his kingdoms of England and Ireland to the Holy Roman Church; in return for which he takes the King and his heirs and the two kingdoms under the protection of St. Peter and himself, and grants the kingdoms to John in fee on condition of public recognition and oath of fealty by each successive King at his coronation. Attested by the "sentence" of the Pope, viz. "Fac mecum, domine, signum in bonum" [Ps. lxxxv. 17], his name, autograph S [for "signum" or "signavi"] and monogram "Bene Valete," followed by the autograph signatures of 12 cardinals and 3 bishops. Dated at the Lateran, 2 Non. Nov. [4 Nov.], 1213. With leaden "bulla" appended. The Bull recites the letters of John, dated Dover, 15 May, 1213, in which he notifies his surrender of his kingdoms and his receiving of them back as feodatory in presence of Pandulph, subdeacon and familiar of the Pope, promising for himself and his successors fealty and homage and a yearly payment of 1000 marks. *Latin.* [*Cotton MS.* Cleop. E. i. f. 149.]

39. Grant by Louis, eldest son of [Philip II.] King of France, to William de Huntingfeld, of the town of Grimeby [Grimsby, co. Linc.] until he shall assign to him 100 librates of land elsewhere to be held for a service of two Knights' fees. Witnesses: [Seiher de Quincy], Earl of Winchester, Robert Fitz-Walter [commanding the forces of the English Barons], Ursio the Chamberlain, Vicomte of Melun, Master Simon de Langton [brother of Archb. Stephen Langton, and Chancellor to Louis], and others. Dated at the siege of Hertford, 21 Nov. 1216. *Latin.* With fine seal. [*Harley Ch.* 43 B. 37.]

40. Articles of Liberties, demanded by the Barons of King John in 1215, and embodied in MAGNA CHARTA. *Latin.* A collotype copy of the original preserved in the Department and presented, in 1769, by Philip, Earl Stanhope.* A portion of the Great Seal remains. [*Add. MS.* 4838.]

---

* The collotype copy and the printed text can be purchased in the Museum.

Case VI.

[In a line with Case V., at right angles to Case II.]

41. Genealogical and historical roll, 16 feet long, of the Kings of England from Egbert [d. 839] to Henry III. [d. 1272]; preceded by an account, within an illuminated border, of the Seven Saxon Kingdoms, commonly called the Heptarchy. Written during the reign of Hen. III., the date of his death being added by another hand. *Latin.* [*Add. MS.* 30,079.]

42. Confirmation by Baldwin, "Imperator Romanie et semper Augustus" [*i.e.* Baldwin II., de Courtenay, Emperor of Constantinople 1228, dethroned 1261], of a grant by his uncle Philip [I], Marquis of Namur [1196–1212], to the church of St. Bavon at Ghent, of the patronage of Biervliet [in Zeeland]. Dated at Biervliet, May, 1269. *Latin.* With the emperor's golden "bulla" or seal. [*Add. Ch.* 14,365.]

43. Bequest by Richard Morin to Reading Abbey of his body to be therein buried, with lands, etc., at or near Grimesdich [Grim's Ditch], Niweham [Newnham], Waldich, Munge-welle [Mongewell], and Wallingford [co. Berks], and a recognition of a fishing right in the Thames, between Mongewell and Wallingford Bridge. Witnesses: Richard [Poore], Bishop of Salisbury, Richard [afterwards Earl of Cornwall], son of King John, and others. [About 1220-1.] *Latin.* [*Add. Ch.* 19,615.]

44. Lease from Juliana, widow of John Frusselov, to Robert, Abbot of Abingdon, and the convent of the same, of all her dower-lands in Dumbelton [Dumbleton, co. Glouc.] for 10 years from "Hocke dai" [2nd Tuesday after Easter], 14 Hen. III. [1230]. Witnesses: Henry de Tracy, Richard, Dean of Dumbleton, etc. [1230.] *Latin.* [*Harley Ch.* 75 F. 36.]

45. Assignment by R., Prior of Sempringham, to the nuns of Bullington, co. Lincoln, with the assent of Prior William and the convent of the same, of a yearly rent of five marks from land in Friskney, etc., co. Linc., for buying their smocks ("ad camisias illarum inperpetuum emendas"). Dated 1235. *Latin.* [*Harley Ch.* 44 I. 14.]

46. Notification by the Priors of Reading, Sherborne and Poughley, as papal delegates, of a composition between Sir Will. de Englefeld and Missenden Abbey in a dispute concerning the services of a chantry in the chapel of Sipplake [Shiplake, co. Oxon], whereby the said Sir William agrees to augment the endowment and the Abbey to provide a chaplain and do all that is required except repair of the fabric, with stipulations as to services, etc. Witnesses: John de S. Egidio, Archdeacon of Oxford, and others. Dated, the Eve of St. Andrew [29 Nov.], 1242. *Latin.* With seals of the three Priors, of the Abbey and of the Abbot. [*Add. Ch.* 20,372.]

47. Agreement between William, Lord of Melebery Osmund [Melbury Osmond, co. Dorset], and John Picot, whereby they mutually renounce the right of pasture on each other's lands in Melebery, etc. Witnesses: Sir William, son of Henry, Sir William Maubanc, Sir Benedict de Bere, Knts., Sir Richard, vicar of Gateministre [Yeatminster], etc. Dated, St. Margaret's day, 27 Hen. III. [20 July, 1243]. *Latin.* [*Harley Ch.* 53 D. 36.]

48. Confirmation by ALFONSO the Wise, King of Castile, of royal grants to the hospital near the monastery of Santa Maria Real in Burgos. Dated at Burgos, 30 Dec., era 1292 [A.D. 1254], in which year, it is added, Edward [afterwards Edward I.], eldest son of Henry [III.], King of England, received knighthood from Alfonso in Burgos. *Spanish.* With a cross for the royal signature, surrounded by the inscription, "Signo del Rey Don Alfonso," and by the confirmation of Don Juan Garcia, in concentric circles, and attested by the Moorish kings of Granada, Murcia, and Niebla, and by seventy-seven prelates and noblemen. The witnesses were assembled, no doubt, to celebrate Edward's marriage with Eleanor, the King of Castile's sister. The royal seal, impressed on lead, is appended. [*Add. Ch.* 24,804.]

49. Notification by S[imon] de Monte Forti, Earl of Leicester P[eter] de Sabaudia [Savoy], Geoffrey and Guy de Lezeniaco [Lusignan], and Hugh Bigod, of their acceptance, as English plenipotentiaries, of a treaty of peace with France. Dated at Paris, 1 June, 1258. With four seals. *Latin.* [*Add. Ch.* 11,297.]

50. Letter of HENRY III. appointing Humphrey de Bonn, Earl of Hereford and Essex, Constable of England, and William de Fortibus, Earl of Albemarle, his procurators to swear upon his soul in his own presence ("ad iurandum in animam nostram in presencia nostra") that he will keep the peace with France lately made at Paris. Dated at Westminster, 9 Feb. 43rd year [1259]. *Latin.* With seal. [*Add. Ch.* 11,299.]

51. Covenant by Eleanor, Queen of Henry III., and Edward her son [EDWARD I.] to Spinellus Symonetti, Janucius Beaumondi and Renucius Ardingi and their fellows, Florentine merchants, to indemnify them in the matter of a bond in 1700 marks, in which the name of Walter de Merton, Chancellor, was inserted without his seal being attached. Dated at Westminster, 7 June, 1262. *Latin.* With fragments of seals. [*Harley Ch.* 43 C. 42.]

52. Bequest by Margaret, widow of Walter de Clifford, to Aconbury Priory near Hereford of her heart to be therein buried, with 15 marks in alms and the expenses of burial. Witnesses: Brother Hen. de Marisco, Sir Bernard, sub-prior of Kingswood, and others. Dated at Ross, [16 Dec.] 1263. *Latin.* With seals of Marg. de Clifford, Samson, Abbot of Kingswood, and Henry, Abbot of Dore. [*Harley Ch.* 48 C. 31.]

53. Covenant by Pain de Chaworth and Robert Tybetot to serve Edward, eldest son of King [Henry III.], in the Holy Land with

12 knights for one year from the next passage in September, for 1200 marks and their passage, i.e. hire of ship, water and horses. Dated at Westminster, 20 July, 54 Hen. III. [1270]. *French.* With seals. [*Add. Ch.* 19,829.]

54. Commission from Edward, eldest son of King [Henry III.], W[alter Giffard], Archbishop of York, Sir Philip Basset and others, to raise funds for the repayment within October next of 5000 marks lent to him by divers merchants on the guarantee of the Knights Hospitallers at Acre, in order that his good fame may not perish and access to credit with others be closed to him ("ut fama nostra non depereat, nec aditus credencie penes alios precludatur"). Dated at Acre, 6 Apr. 56 Hen. III. [1272]. *Latin.* With seal. [*Harley Ch.* 43 C. 48.]

55. Confirmation by Henry de Lascy, Earl of "Nichole" [i.e. Lincoln], Constable of Chester, etc., to the Priory of Bernecestre [Bicester, co. Oxon.] of grants by Sir Gilbert Basset and Sir William Lunge-espe, of pasturage for three teams of oxen, fuelwood out of Bernewode in the manor of Bernecestre, and a mill with suit of the tenants, saving free grinding thereat to the grantor. Witnesses: Mons. Robord fitz Roger, and others. Dated at Bernecestre, 2 Jan. 14 Edw. I. [1286]. *French.* [*Add. Ch.* 10,624.]

56. Grant by EDWARD I., as "superior dominus regni Scocie," to Gilbert [de Clare], Earl of Gloucester and Hertford, of the marriage of Duncan, son and heir of Duncan, late Earl of Fife [murdered in 1288], provided he be not disparaged. Dated at Berwick, 25 June, 20th year [1292]. *Latin.* With Edward's Great Seal for Scotland. [*Harley Ch.* 63 D. 1.]

57. Appointment by Prince Edward [EDWARD II.] of John [de Pontissera], Bishop of Winchester, Amedeo, Count of Savoy, Henry de Lacy, Earl of Lincoln, and Otho de Grandison, Knt., as proctors to carry out the treaty of marriage between him and Isabella, daughter of Philip [IV.] of France. Dated at Rokesbourgh [Roxburgh], Ascension Day [16 May], 1303. *Latin.* [*Add. Ch.* 11,303.]

58. Counterpart of a grant in tail by Anthony [de Bek], Bishop of Durham, to Edward, Prince of Wales [EDWARD II.], of Eltham manor, with lands, etc., in Crayo and Cateford, etc., co. Kent. Witnesses: Robert [de Winchelsea], Archbishop of Canterbury, John [de Aldreby], Bp. of Lincoln, Walter [de Langton], Bp. of Coventry and Lichfield, Henry [de Lacy], Earl of Lincoln, Thomas, Earl of Lancaster, Humfry [de Bohun], Earl of Hereford, and others. Dated at Doncaster, 20 April, 33 Edw. I. [1305]. *Latin.* With seal of Prince Edward. [*Harley Ch.* 43 D. 12.]

59. Grant by Robert de Meysi to Sir Will. de Englefeud of Ivo his "nativus" and all his issue, "and for this grant he gave to me a hawk" ("et pro hac donacione dedit mihi ancipitem," sc. accipitrem). Witnesses: Sir Peter Achard and others. [*Temp.* Edw. I.]. *Latin.* With seal. [*Add. Ch.* 20,251.]

60. Letters of Queen Philippa [wife of EDWARD III.] to the Dean and Chapter of St. Paul's, London, desiring them to confirm for life to Master Robert de Chikewell, her Chancellor, a lease to him from Master Henry de Idesworth, Canon of St. Paul's, of houses in Ivy-lane [in London], upon which he is otherwise unwilling to carry out costly improvements. Dated at Antwerp, 16 July, 13 [Edw. III., 1339]. *French.* [*Harl. Ch.* 43 E. 10.]

61. Letters of Edward, Prince of Wales, etc. [the Black Prince], reciting letters of his father Edward III., dated at Calais, 28 Oct. 1360, whereby the term for the fulfilment by the King of France of the articles of the Peace of Bretigny is extended from Michaelmas to All Saints day [1 Nov.]; and swearing upon the consecrated body of Christ to observe the same. Dated at Boulogne, 31 Oct. [1360]. *French.* With seal. [*Add. Ch.* 11,308.]

62. Charter of Abbot Peter and the convent of Bitlesden [co. Bucks], admitting to the privileges of confraternity Sir Robert Corbet and Sir Robert Corbet his son, knights, Beatrice wife of Robert the elder, Sibilla his late wife, Alice late wife of Robert the younger, and their children, living or dead; the two knights undertaking in return to warrant to the Abbey an acre of land and the advowson of the church in Eberton [Ebrington, co.Glouc.]. Dated, Feast of the Conversion of St. Paul [25 Jan.], 1379[80]. *Latin.* With seal of arms of Robert Corbet. [*Harl. Ch.* 84 F. 5.]

63. Covenant by William de Wyndesore with Richard II. to serve in war for one year under Thomas of Wodestok, Earl of Buckingham, Constable of England, in his expedition to Brittany and France, with a retinue of 200 men-at-arms and 200 archers; the said William to find 100 men-at-arms for the first half-year at his own cost (save an allowance of 200 livres) by reason of the King's grant to him of lands taken from Alice his wife [Alice Perrers, mistress of Edward III.] in the King's first Parliament, and the other 100 men-at-arms to consist of himself, one other banneret, 20 knights, and the rest esquires. Dated at Westminster, 10 May, 3rd year [1380]. *French.* With fragment of the King's Privy Seal. [*Add. Ch.* 7378.]

64. Notarial certificate of the process by which possession was taken of Tilbury church, co. Essex, by William Tannere, Master of Cobham College, co. Kent, to which it had lately been appropriated, describing how he laid hold of the door-handle ("annulum hostii"), entered the church, proceeded to the High Altar and touched the chalice, vestments, books, etc., how he then rang the bells, celebrated Mass, and received oblations, how he next went to the rectory ("mansum rectorie"), laid hold of the door-handle, and ate food and drank wine and beer in the hall with divers of the parishioners, and how he finally appointed Rich. Burle, of Tilbury, as his proctor to continue possession. Witnesses: Sir Walter Chridham, rector of Staplehurst, Sir Roger Wyle, vicar of Tilbury, and others. Dated, 18 Dec. 1390. *Latin.* [*Harley Ch.* 44 C. 35.]

65. Letters Patent of HENRY IV. taking into his protection Sir John Holt and Sir William de Burgh, Knts., [late Justices of Common Pleas], who, with Sir Robert Bealknape [late Chief Justice of Common Pleas], had been banished to Ireland, 11 Rich. II. [1388], but had been recalled by statute, 22 Jan. 20 Rich. II. [1397]. Dated at Westminster, 20 Feb. 1 Hen. IV. [1400]. Latin, the recited statute in French. [Add. Ch. 19,853.]

66. Grant of indulgence from Brothers John Seyvill and William Hullis, of the Order of St. John of Jerusalem, as Proctors of Pope Alexander V., to Sir William Fitz-Hugh, Knt., and Margery his wife, as contributors to the refortifying of the castle of St. Peter at Budrum, lately captured from the infidels. Dated at Clerkenwell Priory, 1414. Latin. [Cotton Ch. iv. 31.]

67. Indenture whereby Richard Courtenay, Bishop of Norwich, Treasurer of the King's Chamber and Keeper of his Jewels, delivers to Robert Asshefeld, esq., retained to serve the King with three archers beyond sea, certain gold and silver plate as security for £13 11s. 11d., a quarter's wages. Dated at Westminster, 22 June, 3 Hen. V. [1415]. French. [Harley Ch. 42 I. 25.]

68. Quitclaim by Robert de Bridelyngton, of Beverley, "sherman" [clothworker], and Alan Thomson, of Riston, to Robert Dowthorp, of Beverley, "barker" [tanner], of the moiety of two tenements in Beverley, co. York, one near the cucking-stool pond ("iuxta le cokestulepitt") and the other in Spineslane. Dated at Beverley, 10 Apr. 8 Hen. V. 1420. Latin. [Add. Ch. 5761.]

69. Petition by Sir Ralph Cromwell to Henry VI. for a writ to the Exchequer to stay proceedings against him for certain homages, reliefs, etc., during his absence beyond sea in the King's service; supported by the signatures of Humphrey, Duke of Gloucester, Henry Beaufort, Cardinal, Henry Chicheley, Archb. of Canterbury, John Kemp, Archb. of York, Chancellor, and other members of the Council. Endorsed with a note of the grant of a writ, 16 Mar. 9 Hen. VI. [1431]. French. [Cotton MS. Vesp. F. iii. f. 9.]

70. Bull of Pope Eugenius IV., granting permission to the Provost and officials of the New College of Eton to lease out their lands, and to receive the rents and apply them to the uses of the College. Dated at Florence, [1 Feb.], 1445. Latin. [Add. Ch. 15,570.]

71. Bond of the Mayor of Plymouth as surety for the King for the observance of the treaty of friendship and commerce made between Henry VII. and Philip, Archduke of Austria and Duke of Burgundy, on 24 Feb. last past. Dated, 24 Mar. 1495[6]. Latin. With seal. [Add. Ch. 37,639.]

72. Deed of Fr. Ralph Bekwith, "minister domus de Houndeslowe" [Hounslow, co. Midd.], and the convent of the same, of the Order of the Holy Trinity and of the Redemption of Captives, admit-

ting Henry, Prince of Wales [HENRY VIII.], to the confraternity of the Order. Dated 1508. At the foot is the form of absolution. *Latin.* With an illuminated initial enclosing Henry's arms, and an ornamental border of red Tudor roses, with the arms of the Trinitarians and the duchy of Cornwall and an arbitrary coat for Prince Henry bearing the three ostrich feathers. [*Stowe Ch.* 617.]

LITERARY AND OTHER AUTOGRAPHS.

The letters and other documents here shown are divided into two series, English and Foreign, and include not only autographs of eminent poets and prose-writers, but those of actors, artists, musicians, philosophers, and theologians.

(*ENGLISH.*)

[The first three attached to the pilaster on the right of the large upright case C; the rest in Case VII. on the left of the entrance to the Students' Room.]

1. WILLIAM SHAKESPEARE [b. 1564—d. 1616]. Collotype facsimile of a Mortgage by "William Shakespeare, of Stratford upon Avon, Gentleman," and others, to Henry Walker, citizen of London, of a dwelling-house within the precincts of "the late Black Fryers." Dated, 11 March, 10 Jas. I. 1612 [1613]. Four labels with seals are attached, on the first of which is the signature "Wm SHAKSPE[,]."

[signature facsimile]

The first two labels bear seals with the initials H.L., probably belonging to Henry Lawrence, servant to the scrivener who prepared the deed. The original is in the Department.*
[*Egerton MS.* 1787.]

2. EDMUND SPENSER [b. 1552—d. 1599]. Grant from Edmund Spenser, styled "of Kilcolman, Esq.," to — McHenry (a member of the Roche family) of the custody of the woods of Balliganin, etc., in the county of Cork, Ireland. Not dated [1588-1598]. *Holograph.* [*Add.MS.* 19,869.]

3. JOHN MILTON [b. 1608—d. 1674]. Original Articles of Agreement, dated 27 April, 1667, between John Milton, gentleman, and Samuel Symmons, printer, for the sale of the copyright of "a Poem intituled *Paradise Lost*," the sum paid to the poet being £5 down, with three further payments of £5 each on the sale of three editions, each of 1,300 copies. Signed "JOHN MILTON," with his seal of arms affixed. [*Add. MS.* 18,861.] *Presented, in* 1852, *by Samuel Rogers, Esq.*

---

* Copies of this collotype are sold in the Museum, price two shillings.

Case VII.

4. JEREMY TAYLOR, Bishop of Down and Connor [b. 1613—d. 1667]. Letter to Christopher Hatton, Lord Hatton: will send over in the spring the tracts D[uctor] D[ubitantium], etc.; the king has forgiven the Irish clergy their first fruits and twentieths, and sends over a lieutenant who will excel the Earl of Strafford in his kindness to the church. Dated, Dublin, 23 Nov. 1661. *Holograph*. [*Add. MS.* 29,584, f. 6.]

5. SIR CHRISTOPHER WREN [b. 1632—d. 1723]. Report on the design for the Monument of the Fire of London, recommending a brass statue, 15 feet high, for the top of the pillar, as "the noblest finishing that can be found answerable to soe goodly a worke in all mens judgments," though he considers "a ball of copper, 9 foot diameter, cast in severall peeces, with the flames and gilt .... will be most acceptable of anything inferior to a Statue, by reason of the good appearance at distance, and because one may goe up into it, and upon occasion use it for fireworkes." Dated, 28 July, 1675. *Holograph*. [*Add. MS.* 18,898, f. 2.] *Facsimile* in Ser. ii. no. 19.

6. JOHN DRYDEN [b. 1631—d. 1700]. Letter to [Laurence Hyde, Earl of Rochester, First Lord of the Treasury]: "I know not whether my Lord Sunderland has interceded with your Lordship for half a yeare of my salary. But I have two other advocates, my extreame wants, even almost to arresting, and my ill health. .... If I durst, I wou'd plead a little merit and some hazards of my life .... but I onely thinke I merite not to sterve. .... Be pleasd to looke on me with an eye of compassion; some small employment wou'd render my condition easy. The king is not unsatisfyed of me, the Duke has often promisd me his assistance; and your Lordship is the conduit through which their favours passe. Either in the Customes or the Appeales of the Excise, or some other way; meanes cannot be wanting, if you please to have the will. 'Tis enough for one age to have neglected Mr Cowley and sterv'd Mr Buttler." [1682.] *Holograph*. [*Add. MS.* 17,017, f. 49.] *Facsimile* in Ser. i. no. 22.

7. JOHN LOCKE [b. 1632—d. 1704]. Letter to Dr. [afterwards Sir Hans] Sloane, with a proposal for the reformation of the Calendar, and referring to the performances of a strong man in London and to a new edition of his *Essay on the Human Understanding*: "The storys I have heard of the performances of the strong man now in London would be beyond beleif were there not soe many witnesses of it. I think they deserve to be communicated to the present age and recorded to posterity. And therefor I think you cannot omit to give him a place in your transactions, his country, age, stature, bignesse, make, weight, and then the several proofs he has given of his strength, which may be a subject of speculation and enquiry to the philosophical world. I took the liberty to send you just before I left the

town the last edition of my Essay. I doe not intend you shall have it gratis. There are two new Chapters in it, one of the *association of Ideas*, and another of *Enthusiasme*; these two I expect you should read and give me your opinion frankly upon." Dated, Oates, 2 Dec. 1699. *Holograph.* [*Sloane MS.* 4052, f. 5 b.] *Facsimile* in Ser. iv. no. 21.

8. SIR ISAAC NEWTON [b. 1642—d. 1727]. Letter to William Briggs, M.D., commending his "New Theory of Vision," but dissenting from certain positions in it: "I have perused your very ingenious Theory of Vision, in which (to be free with you, as a friend should be) there seems to be some things more solid and satisfactory, others more disputable, but yet plausibly suggested and well deserving the consideration of the ingenious," etc. Dated, Trinity College, Cambridge, 20 June, 1682. *Holograph.* [*Add. MS.* 4237, f. 32.] *Facsimile* in Ser. iii. no. 19.

9. JONATHAN SWIFT, Dean of St. Patrick's, Dublin [b. 1667—d. 1745]. Letter to Mrs. Howard [afterwards Countess of Suffolk], complaining of the Queen [Caroline, queen of George II.] having neglected her promise to give him a medal: "I must now tell you, Madam, that I will receive no medal from Her Majesty, nor any thing less than her picture at half length, drawn by Jervas, and if he takes it from another original, the Queen shall sit at least twice, for him to touch it up. I desire you will let Her Majesty know this in plain words, although I have heard that I am under her displeasure. But this is a usual thing with Princes as well as Ministers, upon every false representation, and so I took occasion to tell the Queen upon the quarrel Mr. Walpole had with our friend Gay. . . . . Mr. Gay deserved better treatment amongst you, upon all accounts, and particularly for his excellent unregarded fables dedicated to Prince William, which I hope His Royal Highness will often read for his instruction. I wish Her Majesty would a little remember what I largely sayd to her about Ireland, when before a witness she gave me leave and commanded to tell here what she spoke to me upon that subject, and ordered me that if I lived to see her in her present station to send her our grievcances, promising to read my letter and do all good offices in her power for this miserable and most loyall Kingdom, now at the brink of ruin, and never so near as now." Dated, Dublin, 21 Nov. 1730. *Holograph* [with signature from another letter]. [*Add. MS.* 22,625, f. 20.] *Presented, in* 1858, *by the executors of the Right Hon. J. W. Croker.*

10. ALEXANDER POPE [b. 1688—d. 1744]. Letter to Lord Halifax, First Lord of the Treasury, submitting to him a portion of his translation of Homer, [prior to its publication in June, 1715], and thanking him for past and promised favours: "While you are doing justice to all the world, I beg you will not forget Homer, if you can spare an hour to attend his cause. I leave him with you in that hope, and return home full of acknowledg-

ments for the Favors your Lordship has done me, and for those you are pleasd to intend me. . . . . Your Lordship may either cause me to live agreably in the Towne, or contentedly in the Country; which is really all the Difference I sett between an Easy Fortune and a small one." Dated, 3 Dec. 1714. *Holograph.* In subsequently publishing this letter Pope omitted some of the expressions of gratitude, his expectations from Halifax not having been fulfilled. [*Add. MS.* 7121, f. 43.] *Bequeathed, in* 1829, *by N. Hart. Facsimile* in Ser. iii. no. 20.

11. SIR RICHARD STEELE [b. 1671—d. 1729]. Letter to Henry Pelham, asking whether the Duke of Newcastle will recall the order of silence imposed upon Drury Lane Theatre; "but if My Lord insists to keep me out of my right, I must plainly tell you, that is, His Grace by you, that the right of petitioning the King in Council, the Parliament sitting, or the Judges in Westminster Hall, shall be utterly taken from me before I will suffer my very good Lord to send my children a starving." Dated, 27 May, 1720. *Holograph.* [*Add. MS.* 32,685, f. 31.] *Presented, in* 1886, *by the Earl of Chichester. Facsimile* in Ser. ii. no. 20.

12. JOSEPH ADDISON [b. 1672—d. 1719]. Letter to J. Robethon, Secretary to George I., on the King's accession: "You will find a whole nation in the Highest Joy and throughly sensible of the great Blessings which they promise themselves from His Majestys accession to the Throne. I take the liberty to send you enclosed a poeme written on this occasion by one of our most Eminent hands [? Ambrose Philips], which is indeed a Masterpiece in its kind and tho very short has touched upon all the topics which are most popular among us. I have likewise transmitted to you a Copy of the preamble to the prince of Wales's Patent, which was a very gratefull task imposed on me by the Lords Justices." Dated, St. James's, 4 Sept. 1714. *Holograph.* [*Stowe MS.* 227, f. 419.] *Facsimile* in Ser. i. no. 23.

13. SAMUEL RICHARDSON, the Novelist [b. 1689—d. 1761]. Letter to [Cox Macro, D.D.], in defence of "the compromise between Sir Charles Grandison and Clementina in the article of religion." Dated, Salisbury Court, Fleet Street, 22 March, 1754. *Holograph.* [*Add. MS.* 32,557, f. 176.]

14. PHILIP DORMER STANHOPE, EARL OF CHESTERFIELD [b. 1694—d. 1773]. Letter, in *French*, to his son, on the duty of politeness to inferiors: "On ne fait pas des complimens a des gens audessous de soy, et on ne leur parle pas de l'honneur qu'ils vous font; mais en même tems il faut les traitter avec bonté et avec douceur. . . . . Il faut donc agir avec douceur et bonté envers tous ceux qui sont audessous de vous et ne pas leur parler d'un ton brusque ni leur dire des duretéz, comme si ils etoient d'une differente espece." Dated, Isleworth. *Holograph;* without signature. [*Add. MS.* 21,508, f. 41.]

15. WILLIAM HOGARTH [b. 1697—d. 1764]. Notes on his intentions in desiguing the pictures "Beer Street," "Gin Lane," and "The

Four Stages of Cruelty" [executed in 1751]: "Beer St. and Gin Lane were done when the dredfull consequences of gin drinking was at its height. In Gin Lane every circumstance of its horrid effects are brought to view. . . . . Beer Street its companion was given as a contrast, were (sic) that invigorating liquor is recommend[ed] in orders (sic) [to] drive the other out of vogue. . . . . The Four Stages of Cruelty were done in hopes of preventing in some degree that cruel treatment of poor Animals which makes the streets of London more disagreable to the human mind than any thing whatever." *Holograph.* [*Add. MS.* 27,991, f. 49 b.] *Facsimile* in Ser. ii. no. 21.

16. JOHN WESLEY [b. 1703—d. 1791]. Letter to Samuel [Bradburn], concerning the progress of evangelical work, and expressing his strong opinion that the Methodists ought not to leave the Church of England: " Bro. Jackson should advise bro. Ridel, not to please the Devil by preaching himself to death. I still think, when the Methodists leave the Church of England, God will leave them. Every year more and more of the Clergy are convinced of the truth, and grow well affected toward us. It wou'd be contrary to all common Sense, as well as to good conscience, to make a separation now." Dated, Birmingham, 25 March, 1783. *Holograph.* [*Add. MS.* 27,457, f. 6.] *Presented, in* 1866, *by Prof. George Stephens. Facsimile* in Ser. iv. no. 26.

17. OLIVER GOLDSMITH [b. 1728—d. 1774]. Agreement (never carried out) to write for James Dodsley, the publisher, a "Chronological History of the Lives of eminent persons of Great Britain and Ireland," at the rate of 3 guineas a sheet. Dated, 31 March, 1763. In Goldsmith's handwriting, and signed by both parties. [*Add. MS.* 19,022, f. 8.] *Presented, in* 1852, *by Samuel Rogers, Esq. Facsimile* in Ser. iii. no. 23.

18. SIR JOSHUA REYNOLDS, P.R.A. [b. 1723—d. 1792]. Letter to the Duke of Newcastle, making an appointment to come and see some pictures put in their frames. Dated, Leicester Fields, 26 Aug. 1765. *Holograph.* [*Add. MS.* 32,969, f. 195.] *Presented, in* 1886, *by the Earl of Chichester.*

19. SAMUEL JOHNSON [b. 1709—d. 1784]. Letter to Warren Hastings, Governor of Bengal, soliciting his support for a translation of Ariosto by John Hoole: "Amidst the importance and multiplicity of affairs in which your great Office engages you I take the liberty of recalling your attention for a moment to literature, and will not prolong the interruption by an apology which your character makes needless. . . . . It is a new thing for a Clerk of the India House to translate Poets. It is new for a Governor of Bengal to patronise Learning. That he may find his ingenuity rewarded, and that Learning may flourish under your protection is the wish of, Sir, your most humble Servant, SAM: JOHNSON." Dated, 29 Jan. 1781. *Holograph.* [*Add. MS.* 29,196, f. 4.] *Facsimile* in Ser. iii. no. 24.

20. JAMES BOSWELL [b. 1740—d. 1795] and SAMUEL JOHNSON. Note to John Wilkes and his daughter, enclosing a card from Dr. Johnson in refusal of an invitation, and regretting that "so agreable a meeting must be deferred till next year." Dated, South Audley Street, 25 May, [1783]. *Holograph.* [*Add. MS.* 30,877, f. 97.]

21. THOMAS CHATTERTON [b. 1752—d. 1770]. Letter to William Barrott, in reply to remonstrances against his expressed intention of committing suicide: "In regard to my Motives for the supposed rashness, I shall observe that I keep no worse Company than *myself*. . . It is my Pride, my damn'd, native, unconquerable Pride, that plunges me into Distraction. . . I must either live a Slave, a Servant; to have no Will of my own, no Sentiments of my own which I may freely declare as such;— or Die. Perplexing Alternative! but it distracts me to think of it." Signed "T. C." [1769.] *Holograph.* [*Add. MS.* 5766 B. f. 91.] *Bequeathed, in* 1800, *by R. G. Clobery, M.D. Facsimile* in Ser. iv. no. 25.

22. DAVID HUME [b. 1711—d. 1776]. Letter to Richard Davenport, with reference to a proposal to obtain a pension from the government for Jean Jacques Rousseau: "I see that this whole Affair is a Complication of Wickedness and Madness; and you may believe I repent heartily that I ever had any Connexions with so pernicious and dangerous a Man. He has evidently been all along courting, from Ostentation, an Opportunity of refusing a Pension from the King, and at the same time of picking a Quarrel with me, in order to cancel at once all his past Obligations to me." Dated, 8 July, 1766. *Holograph.* [*Add. MS.* 29,626, f. 19.] *Facsimile* in Ser. iii. no. 25.

23. EDWARD GIBBON [b. 1737—d. 1794]. Letter to his aunt Hester, on his departure for Lausanne: "Your good wishes and advice will not, I trust, be thrown away on a barren soil; and whatever you may have been told of my opinions, I can assure you with truth, that I consider Religion as the best guide of youth and the best support of old age: that I firmly believe there is less real happiness in the business and pleasures of the World, than in the life, which you have chosen, of devotion and retirement." Dated, Sheffield Place, 30 June, 1788. *Holograph.* [*Add. MS.* 34,486, f. 31 b.] *Presented, in* 1893, *by Miss Sarah Law. Facsimile* in Ser. ii. no. 23.

24. DAVID GARRICK [b. 1716—d. 1779]. Letter to Edward Gibbon, repeating laudatory remarks of Lord Camden on the first volume of his *History of the Decline and Fall of the Roman Empire,* which had just appeared: "Lord Camden call'd upon me this morning and before Cumberland declar'd that he had never read a more admirable performance than Mr. Gibbon's History . . . . *such depth, such perspicuity, such language, force, variety, and what not?*" Dated, Adelphi, 8 March, 1776. *Holograph.* [*Add. MS.* 34,886, f. 59 b.] *Facsimile* in Ser. iii. no. 26.

25. JOHN PHILIP KEMBLE [b. 1757—d. 1823]. Letter to Samuel Ireland, desiring him to send the manuscript of the play of "Vortigern" [alleged to be by Shakespeare, but in fact forged by W. H. Ireland]. Dated, 27 Dec. 1795. *Holograph.* [*Add. MS.* 30,348, f. 62.]

26. SARAH SIDDONS [b. 1755—d. 1831]. Letter to Samuel Ireland, regretting her inability through illness to act in "Vortigern." [29 March, 1796.] *Holograph.* [*Add. MS.* 30,348, f. 93.]

27. EDMUND KEAN [b. 1787—d. 1833]. Letter to R. Philips, apologising for an insult offered to him under his roof. Dated, 5 June, [1829]. *Holograph.* [*Egerton MS.* 2159, f. 89.]

28. JOHN FLAXMAN, R.A. [b. 1754—d. 1826]. Letter to William Hayley on a design for a monument for Capt. Quantock in Chichester Cathedral, and on differences between W. Hayley and his wife. Dated, 14 Feb. 1813. *Holograph.* [*Add. MS.* 30,805, f. 42.]

29. SIR DAVID WILKIE, R.A. [b. 1785—d. 1841]. Letter to Perry Nursey, reporting the progress of some of his pictures, mentioning the election of Constable as A.R.A., and stating that the copies for the English market of the new novel "Ivan-Hoe," by the "great unknown," which "is said to be a very fine thing," are reported to have been lost at sea. Dated, Kensington, 28 Dec. 1819. *Holograph.* [*Add. MS.* 29,991, f. 22.]

30. JOSEPH MALLORD WILLIAM TURNER, R.A. [b. 1775—d. 1851]. Letter to Dawson Turner, of Yarmouth, thanking him for a present of bloaters; Mr. Phillips is recovering; is sorry to see by the paper that Sir A. W. Callcott, R.A., is dead, and that a robbery has been committed on the bank of Samuel Rogers. Dated, 26 Nov. 1844. *Holograph.* [*Add. MS.* 29,960 B.]

31. WILLIAM COWPER [b. 1731—d. 1800]. Letter to the Rev. William Unwin, commenting on Dr. Johnson's *Lives of the Poets*: "With one exception, and that a swingeing one, I think he has acquitted himself with his usual good sense and sufficiency. His treatment of Milton is unmercifull to the last Degree. A Pensioner is not likely to spare a Republican, and the Doctor, in order, I suppose, to convince his Royal Patron of the sincerity of his Monarchical Principles, has belabor'd that great Poet's Character with the most Industrious Cruelty. . . . . I am convinced by the way that he has no ear for Poetical Numbers, or that it was stopp'd by Prejudice against the Harmony of Milton's. . . . . Oh! I could thresh his old Jacket till I made his Pension jingle in his Pocket." Dated, 31 Oct. 1779. *Holograph.* [*Add. MS.* 24,154, f. 18.] *Facsimile* in Ser. ii. no. 22.

32. ROBERT BURNS [b. 1759—d. 1796]. Song, "Here's a health to them that's awa'," written in support of the Whigs, about the end of 1792; with references to "Charlie, the chief of the clan" [*i.e.*, Charles James Fox], and "Tammie, the Norland laddie, who lives at the lug o' the law" [*i.e.*, Thomas Erskine,

afterwards Lord Erskine]. *Holograph.* [*Egerton MS.* 1656, f. 27.] *Facsimile* in Ser. ii., no. 24.

33. SAMUEL TAYLOR COLERIDGE [b. 1772—d. 1834]. Letter to Basil Montagu, concerning the doctrines of Edward Irving, etc. [1 Feb. 1826.] *Holograph.* [*Add. MS.* 21,508, f. 55.]

34. WILLIAM WORDSWORTH [b. 1770—d. 1850]. Letter on receiving the news of the death of Coleridge, addressed to H. N. Coleridge, the poet's nephew and son-in-law : " I cannot give way to the expression of my feelings upon this mournful occasion ; I have not strength of mind to do so. The last year has thinned off so many of my friends, young and old, . . . that it would be no kindness to you were I to yield to the solemn and sad thoughts and remembrances which press upon me. It is nearly 40 years since I first became acquainted with him whom we have just lost; and though . . . I have seen little of him for the last 20 years, his mind has been habitually present with me." Dated, 29 July, [1834]. *Holograph.* [*Add. MS.* 34,225, f. 193.] *Facsimile* in Ser. i. no. 25.

35. CHARLES LAMB [b. 1775—d. 1834]. Letter to John Clare, thanking him for a present of his poems and criticising his use of provincial phrases ; with a recipe for cooking frogs, " the nicest little rabbity things you ever tasted." Dated, India House, 31 Aug. 1822. *Holograph.* [*Egerton MS.* 2246, f. 99.] *Facsimile* in Ser. ii. no. 27.

36. GEORGE GORDON, LORD BYRON [b. 1788—d. 1824]. Letter to J. Hanson, his solicitor, with reference to his pecuniary difficulties : " It is in the power of God, the Devil, and Man, to make me poor and miserable, but neither the *second* nor *third* shall make me sell Newstead, and by the aid of the *first* I will persevere in this resolution." Dated, Athens, 11 Nov. 1810. *Holograph.* [*Egerton MS.* 2611, f. 214.] *Facsimile* in Ser. ii. no. 25.

37. PERCY BYSSHE SHELLEY [b. 1792—d. 1822]. Letter to Miss Curran, at Rome, concerning designs for a monument [to his infant son William, who died on 7 June preceding], and mentioning that he has nearly finished his " Cenci " and wishes " to get a good engraving made of the picture in the Colonna Palace." Dated, Livorno. 5 Aug. 1819. *Holograph.* [*Add. MS.* 22,130, f. 94.] *Facsimile* in Ser. ii. no 26.

38. JOHN KEATS [b. 1795—d. 1821]. Letter to his sister Fanny [afterwards Señora Llanos], at the beginning of his last illness : " 'Tis not yet Consumption, I believe, but it would be were I to remain in this climate all the winter ; so I am thinking of either voyageing or travelling to Italy. Yesterday I received an invitation from Mr. Shelley, a Gentleman residing at Pisa, to spend the winter with him. . . . I am glad you like the Poems" [*Hyperion, Lamia,* etc., then just published]. [14 Aug. 1820.] *Holograph.* [*Add. MS.* 34,019, f. 81.] *Presented,* in 1891, *by Señorita Rosa Llanos-Keats. Facsimile* in Ser. i. no. 26.

39. ALFRED, LORD TENNYSON [b. 1809—d. 1892]. Letter to Mr. W. C. Bennett, with a sketch of the pile of letters which awaited him, "penny-post maddened," on his return from abroad, including "MS. poems," "printed proof-sheets of poems," requests for subscriptions, etc., topped with "letters for autographs," "anonymous insolent letters," and "letters asking explanation of particular passages." [22 Oct. 1864.] *Holograph.* [*Egerton MS.* 2805, f. 1.] *Facsimile* in Ser. ii. no. 28.

40. ELIZABETH BARRETT BROWNING [b. 1806—d. 1861]. Letter to H. F. Chorley, with reference to a poem by her ["A Tale of Villa Franca," published in *Poems before Congress*, 1860], recently printed in the *Athenæum* sending him an additional stanza which had been omitted in the preliminary publication, "because it seemed to me likely to annul any small chance of Athenæum-tolerance," and discussing the state of Italian politics since the battle of Solferino, and other matters: "Is it really true that 'Adam Bede' is the work of Miss Evans? The woman (as I have heard of her) and the author (as I read her) do not hold together." Dated, Siena, [Sept.–Oct. 1859]. *Holograph.* [*Add. MS.* 35,155 H.] *Presented, in* 1897, *by R. Barrett Browning, Esq.*

41. ROBERT BROWNING [b. 1812—d. 1889]. Letter to William G. Kingsland, thanking him for his sympathy with his writings: "I can have little doubt but that my writing has been, in the main, too hard for many I should have been pleased to communicate with; but I never designedly tried to puzzle people, as some of my critics have supposed. On the other hand, I never pretended to offer such literature as should be a substitute for a cigar or a game of dominos to an idle man." Dated, London, 27 Nov. 1868. [*Add. MS.* 33,610 C.] *Presented, in* 1890, *by P. Jenner Weir, Esq. Facsimile* in Ser. i. no. 30.

42. SIR EDWARD LYTTON BULWER-LYTTON, afterwards LORD LYTTON [b. 1803—d. 1873]. Letter to Macvey Napier, with reference to an article for the *Edinburgh Review* and to supposed neglect of his novels, and depreciatory allusions, in the Review. "The singleness with which, as a novelist, I have contended against all prejudice and all hypocrisy has of course gained me many enemies . . . and all envy and all scorn are vented more successfully on works like mine than those of a graver nature." Dated, 8 Sept. 1830. *Holograph.* [*Add. MS.* 34,614, f. 387.]

43. CHARLES DICKENS [b. 1812—d. 1870]. Letter written the day before his death to Charles Kent, appointing to meet him on the morrow: "To-morrow is a very bad day for me to make a call . . . . but I hope I may be ready for you at 3 o'clock. If I can't be—why then I shan't be. You must really get rid of those opal enjoyments. They are too overpowering. 'These violent delights have violent ends.' I think it was a father of your church who made the wise remark to a young gentleman who got up early (or stayed out late) at Verona." Dated, Gad's

Hill Place, 8 June, 1870. *Holograph.* [*Add. MS.* 31,022, f. 1.] Presented, in 1879, by Charles Kent, Esq. Facsimile in Ser. i. no. 27.

44. WILLIAM MAKEPEACE THACKERAY [b. 1811—d. 1863]. Letter to T. W. Gibbs, on some passages in Sterne's letters and his "Bramine's Journal" (see below, p. 70): "He wasn't dying, but lying, I'm afraid—God help him—a falser and wickeder man it's difficult to read of. . . . Of course any man is welcome to believe as he likes for me *except* a parson: and I cant help looking upon Swift and Sterne as a couple of traitors and renegades . . . with a scornful pity for them in spite of all their genius and greatness." Dated, 12 Sept. [1851]. *Holograph.* [*Add. MS.* 34,527, f. 75.] *Bequeathed, in* 1894, *by T. W. Gibbs, Esq.* Facsimile in Ser. i. no. 28.

45. THOMAS CARLYLE [b. 1795—d. 1881]. Letter to Macvey Napier, asking leave to review [Ebenezer Elliot's] *Corn Law Rhymes* for the *Edinburgh Review* : " His *Rhymes* have more of sincerity and genuine natural fire than anything that has come in my way of late years. . . . I would also willingly do the unknown man a kindness, or rather a piece of justice; for he is, what so few are, a *man* and no *clothes-horse*." He alludes also to his failure to find a publisher for his *Sartor Resartus* : " I have given up the notion of hawking my little Manuscript Book about any farther: for a long time it has lain quiet in its drawer, waiting for a better day. The Bookselling trade seems on the edge of dissolution; the force of Puffing can go no farther, yet Bankruptcy clamours at every door: sad fate! to serve the Devil, and get no wages even from *him!*" Dated, 6 Feb. 1832. *Holograph.* [*Add. MS.* 34,615, f. 202.] *Facsimile* in Ser. i. no. 29.

46. HENRY, LORD BROUGHAM AND VAUX [b. 1778—d. 1868]. Letter to Macvey Napier, on Macaulay's share in the *Edinburgh Review*: " As to Macaulay, I only know that he left his party which had twice given him seats in Parliament for nothing. . . and jumped at promotion and gain in India . . . But what think you of his never having called on me since his return? Yet I made him a Commissioner of Bankrupts in 1827 to the exclusion of my own brother. . . . As he is the second or third greatest bore in society I have ever known, and I have little time to be bored, I dont at all lament it, but I certainly know that he is by others despised for it." Dated, 6 July, 1838. *Holograph.* [*Add. MS.* 34,619, f. 199.]

47. THOMAS BABINGTON MACAULAY, afterwards LORD MACAULAY [b. 1800—d. 1859]. Letter to Macvey Napier, on Brougham's share in the *Edinburgh Review*: " As to Brougham's feelings towards myself, I know and have known for a long time that he hates me. If during the last ten years I have gained any reputation either in politics or in letters, if I have had any success in life, it has been without his help or countenance, and

often in spite of his utmost exertions to keep me down. . . . . .
I will not, unless I am compelled, make any public attack on
him. But . . . I neither love him nor fear him." Dated, 20
July, 1838. *Holograph.* [*Add. MS.* 34,619, f. 233.]

(*FOREIGN.*)

[In Case VIII. on the right of the entrance to the Students' Room.]

1. DESIDERIUS ERASMUS [b. 1467—d. 1536]. Letter, in *Latin*, to Nicholas Everard, President of Holland, on Luther's marriage, etc.: "Solent Comici tumultus fere in matrimonium exire, atque hinc subita rerum omnium tranquillitas . . . Similem exitum habitura videtur Lutherana Tragœdia. Duxit uxorem, monachus monacham . . . Luterus nunc mitior esse incipit, nec perinde sevit calamo." Dated, Basel, 24 Dec. 1525. *Holograph*; with signature "ERASMUS Rot[erodamus] vere tuus, ex tempore manu propria." [*Egerton MS.* 1863, f. 2.] *Facsimile* in Ser. iii. no. 30.
2. MARTIN LUTHER [b. 1483—d. 1546]. Letter, in *Latin*, to Thomas Cromwell, Secretary of State, excusing himself for not replying to a letter sent by Dr. Barnes on account of the sudden departure of the latter, and rejoicing in Cromwell's zeal for the cause of Christ and his power to advance it. Dated, Wittenberg, Palm Sunday, 1536. *Holograph*; with signature "T[uae] D[ominationi] deditus, Martinus Lutherus." [*Harley MS.* 6989, f. 56.] *Facsimile* in Ser. ii. no. 29.
3. PHILIP MELANCHTHON [b. 1497—d. 1560]. Letter, in *Latin*, to Henry VIII., sending him a book by the hands of Alexander Alesius, the Scotchman, and expressing admiration of his talent and virtue. Dated, Aug. 1535. *Holograph*; with signature "Regiae Maiestati tuae addictissimus, PHILIPPUS MELANTHON." [*Harley MS.* 6989, f. 54.]
4. JOHN CALVIN [b. 1509—d. 1564]. Letter, in *Latin*, to Guillaume Farel, pastor of the church of Neufchatel, in recommendation of the bearer as a school-teacher. Dated, Geneva, 8 Dec. 1551. *Holograph*: with signature "JOANNES CALVINUS, vere tuus." [*Add. MS.* 12,100, f. 6.]
5. MICHELANGELO BUONARROTI [b. 1474—d. 1564]. Letter, in *Italian*, to Lodovico di Buonarrota Simoni, his father, contradicting a rumour of his death, complaining that he has received no money from the Pope for 13 months, and referring to an action at law of Monna Cassandra, his aunt. [June, 1508.] *Holograph*; with signature "Vostro MICHELAGNIOLO in Roma." [*Add. MS.* 23,140, f. 6.] *Facsimile* in Ser. iii. no. 29.
6. TIZIANO VECELLI [b. 1477—d. 1576]. Letter, in *Italian*, to the Marquis [afterwards Duke] of Mantua, asking him to expedite a grant which had been promised to him: "Spero per lo avenire con quella poca virtu che mha dato Dio satisfare in qualche parte al singulare obligo chio tengo cum loptima cortesia del unico

Marchese de Mantoa." Dated, Venice, 17 Jan. 1530. The date, address, etc., *autograph*; with signature " TICIAN PITORE." [*Egerton MS*. 2015, f. 3.]
7. LUDOVICO ARIOSTO [b. 1474—d. 1533]. Letter, in *Italian*, to the Duke of Mantua, accompanying a copy of the second edition of his " Orlando Furioso," amended and enlarged, and recommending the bearer to the Duke's favour. Dated, Ferrara, 8 Oct. 1532. *Holograph*. [*Egerton MS*. 2015, f. 7.]
8. GALILEO GALILEI [b. 1564—d. 1642]. Letter, in *Italian*, to Michelangelo Buonarroti the younger, thanking him for his letter, hoping to be with him before St. John's day, and referring to his improvement in the construction of spectacles. Dated, Padua, 4 Dec. 1609. *Holograph*. [*Add. MS*. 23,139, f. 39.]
9. PETER PAUL RUBENS [b. 1577—d. 1640]. Letter, in *Italian*, to [— Dupuy?] on the defeat of the English at La Rochelle, thanking him for letters of J. L. Guez, Sieur de Balzac, criticising the latter's " Censor," etc. Dated, Antwerp, 30 Dec. 1627. *Holograph*; with the signature " PIETRO PAUOLO RUBENS." [*Add. MS*. 18,741, f. 101.]
10. ANTHONY VAN DYCK [b. 1599—d. 1641]. Letter, in *Dutch*, to Francis Junius the younger, in praise of his work " De Pictura Veterum," and requesting him to supply a Latin motto for an engraved portrait of Sir Kenelm Digby. Dated, 14 Aug. 1636. *Holograph*. [*Harley MS*. 4935, f. 45.]
11. PAUL REMBRANDT VAN RYN [b. 1608—d. 1669]. Letter, in *Dutch*, to [Constantine Huygens] Heer van Zuylichem, Secretary to the Prince of Orange, asking for payment of a sum due to him. Not dated. *Holograph*. [*Add. MS*. 23,744, f. 3.]
12. MICHEL DE MONTAIGNE [b. 1533—d. 1592]. Letter, written while Mayor of Bordeaux, during the civil wars in France, [to the Maréchal de Matignon, Lieutenant-Governor of Guyenne], giving him all the information and reports he can gather as to the movements of various persons of political importance in the neighbourhood, and assuring him of his activity in the public service: " Je vous dis ce que japrans et mesle les nouvelles des bruits de ville que je ne treuve vraisamblables aveq des verites .... nous n'espargnerons cepandant ny nostre souin ny s'il est besouin nostre vie pour conserver toutes choses en lobeissance du roy." Dated, Bordeaux, 22 May, 1585. *Holograph*. [*Egerton MS*. 23, f. 241].
13. JEAN BAPTISTE POQUELIN MOLIÈRE [b. 1622—d. 1673]. Notarial Certificate, in *French*, signed by him and Jacques Martin, relative to the disposition of the goods of Françoise Rousseau, deceased. Dated, 25 Jan. 1664. [*Add. MS*. 24,419, f. 2.]
14. PIERRE CORNEILLE [b. 1606—d. 1684]. Letter, in *French*, to C. Huygens van Zuylichem, Secretary to the Prince of Orange, accompanying a gift of two volumes of his poems: " Ce sont les peches de ma jeunesse et les coups d'essay d'une Muse de Province, qui se laissoit conduire aux lumieres purement

Naturelles, et n'avoit pas encore fait reflexion qu'il y avoit un Art de la Tragedie, et qu'Aristote en avoit laissé des preceptes. Vous n'y trouveres rien de supportable qu'une Médée qui veritablement a pris quelque chose d'asses bon a celle de Seneque," from which he proceeds to quote some lines. Dated, Rouen, 6 March, 1649. *Holograph*. [*Add. MS.* 21,514, ff. 20, 21.]

15. JEAN RACINE [b. 1639—d. 1699]. Letter, in *French*, to Nicolas Boileau Despreaux, the poet, on business matters, with news of the war [with England], the King's health, etc.: "Quelque horreur que vous ayez pour les meschans vers, je vous exhorte a lire Judith [a tragedy by the Abbé Boyer], et sur tout la preface dont je vous prie de me mander vostre sentiment. Jamais je n'ay rien veu si mesprisé que tout cela l'est en ce pays cy, et toutes vos predictions sont accomplies." Dated, Compiègne, 4 May, 1695. *Holograph*. [*Add. MS.* 21,514, f. 45.]

16. FRANÇOIS MARIE AROUET DE VOLTAIRE [b. 1694—d. 1778]. Letter, in *English*, to George Keate, F.R.S., expressing friendship and passing remarks on the literary position of England and France: "Had I not fix'd the seat of my retreat in the free corner of Geneva, I would certainly live in the free kingdom of England, for, tho I do not like the monstruous irregularities of Shakespear, tho I admire but some lively and masterly strokes in his performances, yet I am confident no body in the world looks with a greater veneration on your good philosophers, on the croud of your good authors, and I am these thirty years the disciple of your way of thinking. Your nation is at once a people of warriours and of philosophers. You are now at the pitch of glory in regard to publick affairs. But I know not wether you have preserv'd the reputation your island enjoy'd in point of litterature when Adisson, Congreve, Pope, Swift, were alive." Dated, Aux Délices, 16 Jan. 1760. *Holograph*. [*Add. MS.* 30,991, f. 13.] *Bequeathed, in* 1879, *by John Henderson, Esq. Facsimile* in Ser. ii. no. 30.

17. JEAN JACQUES ROUSSEAU [b. 1712—d. 1778]. Letter, in *French*, to ——, giving reasons for his refusal to write further in defence of the Protestants, and referring to what he had already written: "Quand un homme revient d'un long combat hors d'haleine et couvert de blessures, est-il tems de l'exhorter à prendre les armes tandis qu'on se tient soi-même en repos? .... Mes cheveux gris m'avertissent que je ne suis plus qu'un vétéran, mes maux et mes malheurs me prescrivent le repos, et je ne sors point de la lice sans y avoir payé de ma personne." Dated, Motiers, 15 July, 1764. *Holograph*. [*Add. MS.* 24,024, f. 72.] *Facsimile* in Ser. iii. no. 30.

18. VICTOR HUGO [b. 1802—d. 1885]. Letter, in *French*, to Charles Griffin, publisher, declining to correct the proof of the notice of his life in the *Dictionary of Contemporary Biography*: "Quelques petits faits inexacts sont moins graves à mes yeux que l'inexactitude des appréciations. Or, je comprends que sur ce point toute

liberté doit être laissée à l'auteur de la biographie, dont je reconnais du reste avec empressement la parfaite politesse et la parfaite bonne foi." Dated, Hautville House [Jersey], 1 March, 1860. *Holograph*. [*Add. MS*. 28,510, f. 269.]

19. GOTTFRIED WILHELM LEIBNITZ [b. 1646—d. 1716]. Letter, in *Latin*, to Sir Hans Sloane, Secretary to the Royal Society, complaining of a statement made by Dr. Keill in the Transactions of the Royal Society to the effect that Leibnitz had derived his method of differential calculus from Sir Isaac Newton's method of fluxions and had published it, with a mere change of name, as his own discovery; protesting his complete independence of Newton ("vir excellentissimus"), and asking for a public withdrawal of the calumny. Dated, Berlin, 4 March, 1711. *Holograph*. The controversy as to priority and independence in this great mathematical discovery lasted long after the death of both Leibnitz and Newton. [*Sloane MS*. 4042, f. 263.]

20. IMMANUEL KANT [b. 1724—d. 1804]. Letter, in *German*, to D. Biester, royal librarian at Berlin, apologising for delay in sending contributions to the *Berliner Monatsschrift*: "Bedenken Sie indessen, werthester Freund! 66 Jahre alt, immer durch Unpässlichkeit gestöhrt, in Planen, die ich nur noch zur Hälfte ausgeführt habe und durch allerley schriftliche oder auch öffentliche Aufforderungen von meinem Wege abgelenkt, wie schwer wird es mir alles, was ich mir als meine Pflicht denke, zu erfüllen, ohne hier oder da eine zu verabsäumen." Dated, Koenigsberg, 29 Dec. 1789. *Holograph*. [*Add. MS*. 28,167, f. 76.]

21. JOHANN WOLFGANG VON GOETHE [b. 1749—d. 1832]. Letter, in *German*, to ——, giving reasons for not entering at length upon a discussion of "die Windischmannische Recension," and returning his correspondent's manuscript. Dated, Weimar, 4 Aug. 1811. *Holograph*. [*Egerton MS*. 2407, f. 122.]

22. JOHANN CHRISTOPH FRIEDRICH VON SCHILLER [b. 1759—d. 1805]. Letter, in *German*, to [Karl Theodor Körner] on domestic matters, with remarks upon C. F. Zelte's satisfactory setting of his ballad "Der Taucher" to music, upon F. Schlegel's tragedy "Alarcos" and Goethe's support of it, and upon W. Schlegel's tragedy "Ion." Dated, Weimar, 5 July, 1802. *Holograph*. [*Add. MS*. 29,804, f. 3.]

23. HEINRICH HEINE [b. 1799—d. 1856]. Letter, in *French*, to ——, returning a volume of Goethe with adverse comments, and adding "Depuis 10 jours je suis ici, jouissant d'une parfaite solitude, car je suis entourré de la mer, de bois, et d'Anglais, qui sont aussi muet que le bois—je ne veux pas dire aussi *hölzern*." Dated, Boulogne, 15 July, 1834. *Holograph*. [*Add. MS*. 33,964, f. 433.] Bequeathed, in 1891, by *A. G. Kurtz, Esq*.

24. GEORGE FREDERICK HANDEL [b. 1685—d. 1759]. Letter to [the Keeper of the Ordnance Office], requesting him to deliver the artillery kettle-drums lent to him for use in his oratorios. Dated, 24 Feb. 1750. *Holograph*. [*Add. MS*. 24,182, f. 15.]

25. GEORGE FREDERICK HANDEL. Portion of the original manuscript of the anthem "As pants the hart." *Holograph.* [*Add. MS.* 30,308, f. 130.]
26. JOSEPH HAYDN [b. 1732—d. 1809]. Letter, in *German*, to William Forster, musical instrument maker, complaining of Artaria, the music publisher of Vienna, and mentioning the enhanced value of his compositions and that he had a contract for six pieces for upwards of 100 guineas. Dated, Esterhazy, 28 Feb. 1788. *Holograph.* [*Egerton MS.* 2380, f. 9.]
27. JOHANN CHRYSOSTOM WOLFGANG AMADEUS MOZART [b. 1756—d. 1791]. Score of the 130th Psalm ('De Profundis'), in *Latin*, for four voices with organ accompaniment. [1770?] *Holograph.* [*Add. MS.* 31,748, f. 1.]
28. LUDWIG VAN BEETHOVEN [b. 1770—d. 1827]. Sketch of music of "Adelaide," from a note-book containing rough drafts of several of his compositions. [1795?] *Holograph.* [*Add. MS.* 29,801, f. 44.]
29. LUDWIG VAN BEETHOVEN. Letter, in *German*, to Baron Ignaz von Gleichenstein, with reference to a change in the dedication of one of his works. [1808?] *Holograph.* [*Add. MS.* 29,804, f. 10.]
30. FELIX MENDELSSOHN-BARTHOLDY [b. 1809—d. 1847]. Setting of the 13th Psalm (in the version of C. B. Broadley, to whom it is dedicated) as a mezzo-soprano or alto solo, with organ accompaniment. Dated, Leipzig, 14 Dec. 1840. *Holograph.* [*Add. MS.* 31,801, f. 3.]
31. WILHELM RICHARD WAGNER [b. 1813—d. 1883]. Sketch of the People's Chorus, melody and bass only, from the end of the 2nd act of "Rienzi." [1839?] *Holograph.* [*Egerton MS.* 2746, f. 3.]
32. WILHELM RICHARD WAGNER. Authorisation, in *German*, to Theodor Uhlig, royal Kammermusikus at Dresden, to deliver to the director of the Stadttheater at Wurzburg, on payment of 50 thalers, a corrected copy of the music and words of "Tannhäuser." Dated, Zürich, 24 Aug. 1852. *Holograph.* [*Add. MS.* 29,999, f. 30.]

AUTOGRAPH LITERARY WORKS,

ETC.

Besides literary works proper, including five at the end by famous foreign authors (Nos. 44–48), a few other MSS. of personal interest, such as volumes with royal and other inscriptions, autograph note-books, etc., are here exhibited.

[In Cases IX. and X. on either side of the entrance to the King's Library.]

1. HENRY VII. AND VIII. Book of Hours, etc., in *Latin*; written late in the 15th century, and illuminated in Flemish style. The volume seems to have belonged to a lady in the court of the Tudor Kings, and contains *autograph* inscriptions by Henry VII. ("Madame I pray you Remembre me, your lovyng maistre, HENRY R.") and Elizabeth his Queen ("Madam I pray you forget not me to pray to God that I may have part of your prayers, ELYSABETH ye quene"), Henry VIII. ("HENRY R.") and Queen Katherine of Aragon ("I thinke the prayrs of a frend be most acceptable unto God, and because I take you for one of myn assured I pray you to remembre me in yours, KATHERINA the quene," the last two words having been subsequently obliterated). On f. 192 b is a prayer translated from Latin by Princess [afterwards Queen] Mary in her 11th year; and below, an *autograph* inscription by the Princess ("I have red that no body lyveth as he shulde doo but he that foloweth vertu, and I rekenyng you to be on of them I pray you to remembre me in your devocyons, MARYE the princesse," the last two words having been subsequently obliterated). [*Add. MS.* 17,012.] *Facsimile* in Ser. iii. no. 2.

2. HENRY VIII. Metrical version of the Penitential and other Psalms, in *English* [by John Croke, Clerk in Chancery]; written early in the 16th century. With a portrait of Henry VIII. Bound in gold, worked in open leaf-tracery, with remains of black enamel. At the top of the covers are rings to attach the volume to the girdle. Traditionally said to have been given by Queen Anne Boleyn, when on the scaffold, to one of her maids of honour. [*Stowe MS.* 956.]

3. EDWARD VI. Treatise on the Sacrament of the Body and Blood of Christ, in *French*, composed in 1549 by King Edward VI., and written with his own hand; with corrections by his tutor. [*Add. MS.* 29,432.]

4. EDWARD SEYMOUR, DUKE OF SOMERSET. A small volume containing the Calendar, and various tables for the moveable feasts, epacts, etc.; and having on the flyleaf some Scriptural verses written by the Duke of Somerset " frome the toware [the Tower] the day before my dethe, 1551." He was executed on 22 Jan. 1551½. The last sentence is " Be not wise in thyne owne conscyte, but fere the lord and fle frome evile." [*Stowe MS.* 1066.]

5. LADY JANE GREY. A small Manual of Prayers, written on vellum, with miniatures; believed to have been used by Lady Jane Grey on the scaffold, 12 Feb. 1553¾. It contains on the margins some lines in the handwriting of Lady Jane, addressed to Sir John Gage, Lieutenant of the Tower, and to the Duke of Suffolk, her father: to the former, "[The] Precher sayethe there is a tyme to be borne and a tyme to dye and the daye of deathe is better then the daye of oure birthe. youres as the lorde knowethe trew frende, JANE DUDDELEY"; and to the latter, " The Lorde comforte your grace and that in his worde whearein all creatures onlye are to be comforted, and thoughe it hathe pleased God to take awaye ii of youre children, yet thinke not, I moste humblye besoche your grace, that you have loste them, but truste that we by leasinge thys mortall life have wunne an immortal life, and I for my parte, as I have honoured youre grace in thys life, wyll praye for you in another life. youre gracys humble daughter, JANE DUDDLEY." [*Harley MS.* 2342.]

6. ELIZABETH, WHEN PRINCESS. Prayers or Meditations, composed originally in *English* by Queen Katherine Parr, and translated into *Latin, French,* and *Italian,* by Queen Elizabeth, when Princess. Entirely in her own hand, on vellum; with a dedication to her father, Henry VIII., dated, Hertford, 20 Dec. 1545. In silk binding, embroidered with silver. [*Royal MS.* 7 D. x.]

7. WILLIAM CECIL, LORD BURGHLEY [b. 1520—d. 1598]. Memorandum-book of public and private business, about 1592. The page exhibited contains a list of the ships of the Royal Navy, with their stations, tonnage, and crews. [*Royal MS.* App. 67.]

8. JAMES I. ΒΑΣΙΛΙΚΟΝ ΔΩΡΟΝ, or Book of the Institution of a Prince; written by King James for the instruction of his son, Prince Henry. Wholly in the King's hand; and in the original binding of crimson velvet, with the King's initials and the arms of Scotland, in gold. [*Royal MS.* 18 B. xv.]

9. CHARLES I., WHEN PRINCE. " FLORUM FLORES, sive Florum ex veterum Poetarum floribus excerptorum Flores ": a selection of passages from the classical Latin Poets, entirely in the hand of Prince Charles, and presented by him to his father James I. as a new year's gift. [*Royal MS.* 12 D. VIII.]

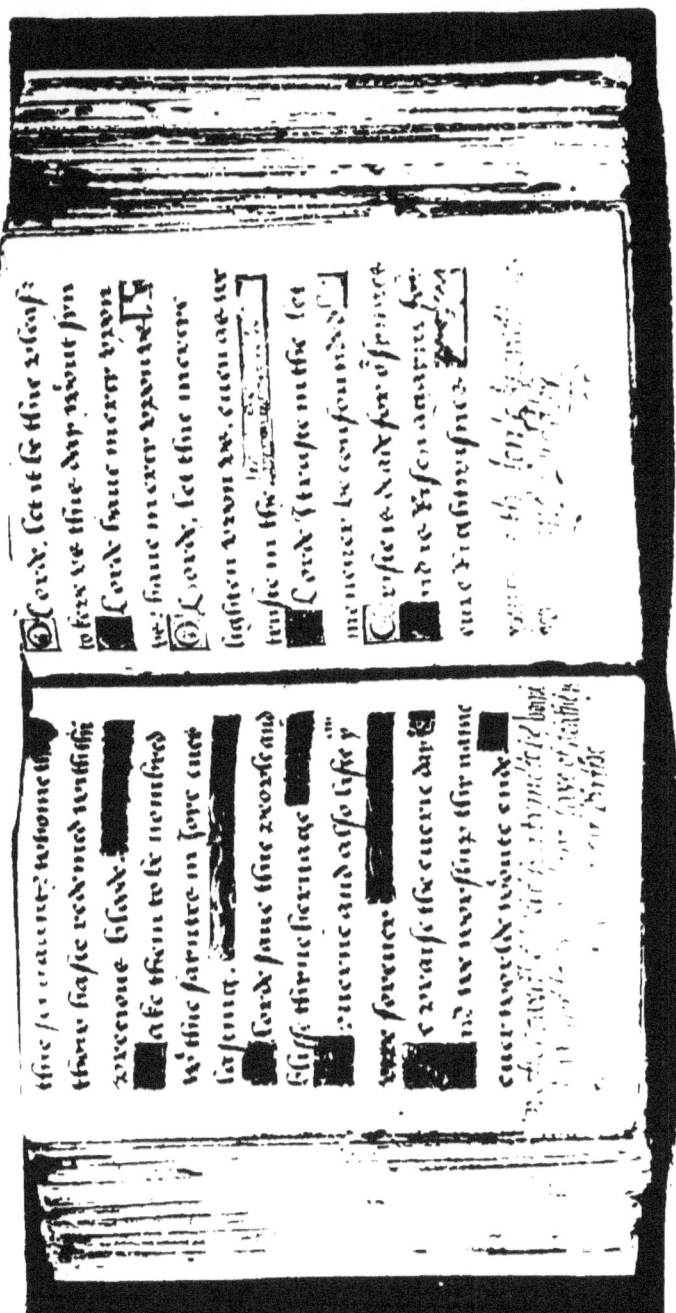

PRAYER BOOK OF LADY JANE GREY.

John Milton was born the 9th of December
1608 die Veneris half an howr after 6 in the
morning
Christofer Milton was born on Friday about
a month before Christmass at 5 in the morning
1615
Edward Phillips was 15 year old August 1645
John Phillips is a year younger about Octob.

My daughter Anne was born July the 29th
on the fast at eebning about half an houre
after six 1646.
My daughter Mary was born on Wedensday
Octob. 25th on the fast in the morning about
6 a clock 1648.
My son John was born on Sunday March the
16th about half an hower past nine at night 1650
My daughter Deborah was born the 2d of May
being Sunday somwhat before 3 of the clock in the
morning 1652.
It is my wife hir mother dyed about 3 days after. And my
son about 6. weeks after his mother.
Katherin my daughter by Katherin my second wife, was
borne ye 19th of October, between 5 and 6 in ye morning
and dyed ye 17th of March following, 6 weeks after her
mother, who dyed ye 3d of Feb. 1657/8

BIBLE OF JOHN MILTON.

10. CARDINAL WOLSEY [b. 1471—d. 1530]. The Life of Cardinal Wolsey, by George Cavendish, his Gentleman Usher. The original MS. [*Egerton MS. 2402.*]
11. SIR FRANCIS BACON [b. 1561—d. 1626]. Memorandum-book of Sir F. Bacon, afterwards Lord Verulam and Viscount St. Albans, containing memoranda for public and private business, literary notes, etc., entered in July and August, 1608. [*Add. MS. 27,278.*]
12. BEN JONSON [b. 1574—d. 1637]. "The Masque of Queenes," represented at Whitehall, 2 Feb. 1609. In the autograph of the author, with a dedicatory address to Prince Henry. [*Royal MS. 18 A. XIV.*] *Facsimile* in Ser. iii. no. 18.
13. SIR WALTER RALEGH [b. 1552?—d. 1618]. Journal of his second voyage to Guiana, from 19 Aug. 1617 to 13 Feb. 1618, in search of gold. From 30 Oct. to 11 Nov. he was disabled by fever, and the change of hand at f. 172, l. 11, shows where he resumed his Journal on his recovery. *Holograph.* The failure of this expedition, and the acts of hostility against Spain done in the course of it, led to his execution shortly after his return home [29 Oct. 1618]. [*Cotton MS. Titus B. viii.*] *Facsimile* in Ser. iv. no. 6.
14. WILLIAM HARVEY [b. 1578—d. 1657]. Original notes for Lectures on Universal Anatomy, delivered on 16, 17 and 18 April, 1616, containing the first public statement of his discovery of the circulation of the blood. One of the pages shown (f. 80 b) contains the conclusion of his demonstration of this discovery: "unde d[emonstratum est] perpetuum sanguinis motum in circulo fieri pulsu cordis." [*Sloane MS. 230.*]
15. JOHN MILTON [b. 1608—d. 1674]. Album Amicorum of Christopher Arnold, Professor of History at Nuremberg, containing autographs collected in the years 1649–1672; including a sentence in Greek, signed by the poet Milton, "JOANNES MILTONIUS," and dated, London, 19 Nov. 1651. [*Egerton MS. 1324.*]
16. JOHN MILTON. The Holy Bible: Printed by Robert Barker, London, 1612. The copy which formerly belonged to John Milton, who has entered, in his own hand, on a blank page, memoranda of the births, etc., of himself and members of his family; others being added by a different hand under Milton's direction. [*Add. MS. 32,310.*] *Facsimile* in Ser. ii. no. 18.
17. PERCY BALLADS. The volume of English Ballads and Romances from which Bishop Percy selected the poems published in 1765 under the title of "Reliques of Ancient English Poetry"; written in the middle of the 17th century. [*Add. MS. 27,879.*]
18. LUCY HUTCHINSON [b. 1620—d. 167-]. Narrative of the Civil War in Nottinghamshire, 1642–5; afterwards used as the basis of part of her Memoirs of her husband, Colonel John Hutchinson, M.P., Governor of Nottingham [d. 1664]. [*Add. MS. 25,901.*]
19. SAMUEL BUTLER [b. 1612—d. 1680]. Draft of a passage in "Hudibras" (iii. 3, l. 621), from a volume of autograph literary

remains in prose and verse, many of them unpublished. [*Add. MS.* 32,625, f. 139.]

20. JOHN LOCKE [b. 1632—d. 1704]. Original Diary and Note-book kept by John Locke during 1679, partly at Paris and partly in England. [*Add. MS.* 15,642.]

21. DANIEL DEFOE [b. 1661 ?—d. 1731]. The original MS. of "The Compleat English Gentleman"; written about 1729. [*Add. MS.* 32,555.]

22. ALEXANDER POPE [b. 1688—d. 1744]. A volume of the original draft of Pope's Translation of the Iliad and Odyssey, in his own hand and for the most part written upon the backs of letters addressed to himself. [*Add. MS.* 4808.] *Presented, in* 1766, *by Mrs. Lucy Mallet.*

23. LAURENCE STERNE [b. 1713—d. 1768]. The first part of the corrected draft of "A Sentimental Journey through France and Italy," by Laurence Sterne, M.A. [1767]; in the author's own hand. The page exhibited contains the mention of "Eliza" and her picture referred to in his Journal [see the next MS. exhibited, [no. 24]. [*Egerton MS.* 1610.] *Facsimile* in Ser. iv. no. 24.

24. LAURENCE STERNE. "The Bramine's Journal," being Sterne's Journal addressed to Mrs. Eliza Draper after her departure for India. It extends from 13 April [1767] to 4 Aug., with a postscript on 1 Nov., and is entirely in the author's hand. It is full of expressions of extreme devotion, and was discontinued on the arrival of Mrs. Sterne. At the beginning is a note (evidently prefixed with a view to publication) stating that the names are fictitious and the whole translated from a French manuscript. The page exhibited contains the entry for 17 June: "I have brought your name *Eliza!* and Picture into my work" [*The Sentimental Journey,* see the page exhibited above, no. 23]—"where they will remain—when you and I are at rest for ever. —Some annotator or explainer of my works in this place will take occasion to speak of the Friendship which subsisted so long and faithfully betwixt Yorick and the Lady he speaks of." See also the letter of W. M. Thackeray exhibited in Case VII., no. 44, written after reading the MS. [*Add. MS.* 34,527.] *Bequeathed, in* 1894, *by T. W. Gibbs, Esq.*

25. DR. SAMUEL JOHNSON [b. 1709—d. 1784]. Original draft of Dr. Johnson's Tragedy of "Irene," acted at Drury Lane in 1749; in the author's own hand. [*King's MS.* 306.]

26. EDWARD GIBBON [b. 1737—d. 1794]. Autobiographical Memoirs, being the six sketches of parts of his life from which the "Memoirs of My Life and Writings" were selected and put together after his death by Lord Sheffield. The pages exhibited belong to the fifth of these sketches, and contain the well-known narrative of his first conception of the idea of writing his history: "It was at Rome, on the fifteenth of October, 1764, as I sat musing amidst the ruins of the Capitol, while the bare-footed fryars

were singing Vespers in the temple of Jupiter, that I conceived the first thought of my history." *Holograph.* [*Add. MS.* 34,874.]

27. THOMAS CHATTERTON [b. 1752—d. 1770]. "Eclogues and other Poems, by Thomas Rowley, with a glossary and annotations by Thomas Chatterton"; being a portion of the literary forgeries of Chatterton, in his own hand, written about 1767-8. [*Add. MS.* 24,890.]

Case X.

28. THOMAS GRAY [b. 1716—d. 1771]. "Elegy written in a Country Churchyard"; a fair copy, enclosed in a letter to Dr. Thomas Warton. Dated, Cambridge, 18 Dec. [1750]. The poem had already circulated privately to some extent, but was not published until Feb. 1751. *Holograph.* [*Egerton MS.* 2400, f. 45.] *Facsimile* in Ser. iii. no. 22.

29. GILBERT WHITE [b. 1720—d. 1793]. Letters to T. Pennant, from 10 Aug. 1767 to 8 July, 1773, being the original form of most of the first part of the *Natural History of Selborne.* The pages exhibited contain his description of the sedge warbler, a reference to speculations as to the origin of species peculiar to America, and part of White's poem, "The Naturalist's Summer Evening Walk." [29 May, 1769.] *Holograph.* [*Add. MS.* 35,138.]

30. WILLIAM COWPER [b. 1731—d. 1800]. "The Entertaining and facetious History of John Gilpin, showing how he went farther than he intended and came home safe at last. To the tune of Chevy Chace." Copy in the poet's own hand, apparently sent by him to the Rev. W. Unwin. [1782.] [*Add. MS.* 24,155, f. 31.]

31. ROBERT BURNS [b. 1759—d. 1796]. The original MS. of the Autobiography of Robert Burns, contained in a letter to Dr. John Moore dated, Mauchline, 2 Aug. 1787; with a postscript dated, Edinburgh, 23 Sept. of the same year. [*Egerton MS.* 1660.]

32. GEORGE GORDON, LORD BYRON [b. 1788—d. 1824]. "Childe Harold's Pilgrimage: a Romaunt." The first and second cantos, as copied for the press for the first edition, London, 1812; with corrections and notes in the author's own hand. [*Egerton MS.* 2027.]

33. SAMUEL TAYLOR COLERIDGE [b. 1772—d. 1834]. Literary remains, in prose and verse. *Holograph.* The first page exhibited (f. 8 b) contains the conclusion of the "Hymn before Sunrise in the Vale of Chamouny," signed, and with the note "S. T. Coleridge intreats Mrs. Brabant to excuse the slovenly state into which this Copy has degenerated from Candles and Carelessness. . . . . It is however a correct Copy, and the only correct Copy in existence." *Facsimile* in Ser. i. no. 24. The second page (f. 2) is from a school exercise, entitled "Dura Navis," written in his 15th year, with a note added in his 51st:

"I well remember old Jemmy Bowyer, the plagose Orbilius of Christ's Hospital, but an admirable Educer no less than Educator of the Intellect, bad me leave out as many epithets as would turn the whole into 8-syllable Lines,—and then ask myself if the Exercise would not be greatly improved. How often have I thought of this proposal since then—and how many thousand bloated and puffing lines have I read that by this process would have tripped over the tongue excellently." [*Add. MS.* 34,225.]

34. CHARLES LAMB [b. 1775—d. 1834]. Extracts from the Garrick Plays in the British Museum, contributed by Lamb to Hone's *Table Book*. [1826.] One of the two original note-books into which the selected passages were copied, in Lamb's own hand throughout. The page exhibited contains a scene from "Arden of Feversham," a play supposed by some critics to have been written, at least in part, by Shakespeare. [*Add. MS.* 9956.] *Presented, in* 1835, *by Mr. E. Moxon.*

35. ROBERT SOUTHEY [b. 1774—d. 1843]. "Joan of Arc": a poem, in ten books, by Robert Southey. The original MS., with notes and corrections for the first edition [published in 1796] by the author and S. T. Coleridge. [*Add. MS.* 28,096.]

36. SIR WALTER SCOTT [b. 1771—d. 1832]. Autograph manuscript of the novel of "Kenilworth," by Sir Walter Scott, corrected for the press; written between Sept. 1820 and Jan. 1821. [*Egerton MS.* 1661.] *Facsimile* in Ser. iii. no. 27.

37. JOHN KEATS [b. 1795—d. 1821]. Note-book, containing autograph copies of "The Pot of Basil," an Ode ("Souls of Poets dead and gone"), and "The Eve of St. Mark," written 1818–19 and sent by the poet to his brother George in America; with transcripts, apparently by Mrs. George Keats, of "Saint Agnes' Eve" and several of the shorter poems, evidently from early autograph drafts. All the poems differ more or less from the printed copies. "The Eve of Saint Mark," here exhibited, is obviously the first draft of the poem, with corrections bringing it into the form in which it was subsequently published by Lord Houghton from a copy found among Keats' papers after his death. [*Egerton MS.* 2780.]

38. THOMAS BABINGTON MACAULAY, afterwards LORD MACAULAY [b. 1800—d. 1859]. Article on "Gladstone on Church and State," contributed to the *Edinburgh Review* in April, 1839: the original MS. as sent to press. It begins: "The author of this volume" [W. E. Gladstone, M.P., afterwards Prime Minister] "is a young man of unblemished character and of distinguished parliamentary talents, the rising hope of those stern and unbending Tories who deplore the necessity which compels them to follow, reluctantly and mutinously, a leader whose experience and eloquence are indispensable to them, but whose cautious temper and moderate opinions they abhor. It would not be at all strange if Mr. Gladstone were one of the most unpopular men in England But we believe that we do him no more than

O loyal to the royal in Thyself,
And loyal to thy land, as This to Thee —
Bear witness, that rememberable hour, morn
When pale from fever yet the goodly Prince,
Who scarce had pluck'd his flickering life again
From halfway down the shadow of the grave,
Past with thee Thro' thy people & their love,
And London roll'd one tide of joy thro' all
Her trebled millions, & loud leagues of man
And welcome: witness Too, the silent cry,
The prayer of many a people, creed & clime —
Thunderless lightnings striking under sea
From sunset & sunrise of all thy realms,
And that true North, whereof we lately heard
A strain to shame us "keep ye to yourselves;
So loyal is too costly! we sicken of your loyalty: deports
Your love is as a burthen; get you gone!"

ALFRED, LORD TENNYSON.

justice when we say that his abilities and his demeanor have obtained for him the respect and good will of all parties." [*Add. MS.* 34,629, f. 1.] *Facsimile* in Ser. iii. no. 28.

39. WALTER SAVAGE LANDOR [b. 1775—d. 1864]. Autograph Poems, etc., consisting mainly of the shorter pieces published in his "Heroic Idyls" (1863), written, according to his custom, on small scraps of paper. The page exhibited contains the lines addressed to Chaucer. [*Add. MS.* 35,070.] *Presented*, in 1896, by *A. de Noé Walker, Esq., M.D.*

40. JOHN HENRY NEWMAN, afterwards Cardinal [b. 1801—d. 1890]. "The Dream of Gerontius": the actual copy sent to the printers of the *Month* magazine, in which it first appeared, with *autograph* additions and corrections. On the page exhibited the last three lines, together with the signature, are *autograph*. [1865.] [*Add. MS.* 33,984.]

41. ALFRED, LORD TENNYSON [b. 1809—d. 1892]. Epilogue to the "Idylls of the King," addressed to the Queen; first published in 1872. *Holograph.* [*Add. MS.* 35,203, f. 1.] *Presented, in* 1898, *by Hallam, Lord Tennyson. Facsimile* in Ser. iv. no. 28.

42. CHARLOTTE BRONTË [b. 1816—d. 1855]. "The Spell, an Extravaganza. By Lord Charles Albert Florian Wellesley"; with other stories and fragments written in 1834-5, but never published. In a feigned hand; with signatures and dates in her natural hand. [*Add. MS.* 34,255.]

43. GEORGE ELIOT [pseudonym of MARIAN EVANS, b. 1819—d. 1880]. "Adam Bede": the original MS., with dedication at the beginning, "To my dear husband, George Henry Lewes, I give this MS. of a work which would never have been written but for the happiness which his love has conferred on my life. MARIAN LEWES, March 23, 1859." A note is appended, stating that the work was begun on the 22 Oct. 1857 and finished on 16 Nov. 1858. "A large portion of it was written twice, though often scarcely at all altered in the copying; but other parts only once." The page exhibited is from one of the passages specified as having been written only once. [*Add. MS.* 34,020.] *Bequeathed by the authoress. Facsimile* in Ser. iv. no. 27.

(FOREIGN.)

44. LEONARDO DA VINCI [b. 1452—d. 1519]. Book of observations and demonstrations, in *Italian*, on subjects chiefly of mixed mathematics, being unconnected notes entered at different times, beginning 22 March, 1508. Written in his own hand from right to left in reversed letters. [*Arundel MS.* 263.]

45. MICHELANGELO BUONARROTI [b. 1474—d. 1564]. Autograph draft of a poem [Madrigale lii., ed. Guasti], in *Italian*, differing from the five other forms in which it is known; on a sheet containing pencil drawings. [*Add. MS.* 21,907, f. 1.]

46. ALBERT DÜRER [b. 1471—d. 1528]. One of four volumes of sketches, with rough drafts of portions of the text in *German*, for various works on Art, especially on the Proportions of the Human Body, Fortification, and Architecture. The pages exhibited contain designs for roofs, with explanatory text, all in Dürer's hand. [*Sloane MS.* 5229.]

47. TORQUATO TASSO [b. 1544—d. 1595]. The autograph manuscript of his tragedy "Torismondo," with numerous corrections. From the library of Cardinal Cibo. [*Add. MS.* 23,778.]

48. LOPE FELIX DE VEGA CARPIO [b. 1562–d. 1635]. Comedies, in *Spanish*, in the author's own hand, 1624–1628. The volume is open at the end of the Third Act of "Sin secreto no ai Amor," showing the poet's signature, and the licence for the piece to be acted, dated, 13 Dec. 1626. [*Egerton MS.* 548.]

MANUSCRIPTS.

In Cases A—F, which occupy the middle of the room, is exhibited a series of MSS., which, apart from the interest of their contents, illustrate the progress of handwriting. Cases A and B contain Greek MSS., from the 3rd century before Christ to the 15th century, when hand-written books were superseded by the invention of printing. The material on which Greek books were written in classical times, and down to about the 4th century after Christ, was papyrus, a material resembling paper, made out of the stem of the papyrus plant, which grew in Egypt. This was made into large rolls, on which literary matter was written in columns, corresponding roughly in size to the pages in modern books. Specimens of papyrus MSS. are shown in Case A. For literary works the style of writing was properly that known as *uncial*, or capital letters seldom or not at all attached to one another [see Nos. 1, 3, 4, 5, 8, 9, 11, 35]; while for the ordinary purposes of every-day life a *cursive* or running hand was employed, as at the present day [see Nos. 12—34]. Occasionally a literary work was transcribed in a cursive, or non-literary, hand [see No. 7], but such copies were intended for private use, not for public circulation. About the 4th century vellum or parchment superseded papyrus as the material commonly used for literary purposes, and the modern book form, with pages, was adopted in place of the earlier roll form. Manuscripts on papyrus are occasionally found in book form; but these, belong only to the period of transition. For private purposes papyrus continued in use much later, till about the 8th century. Case B contains Greek MSS. on vellum and (from the 13th century onwards) on paper; the earlier MSS. (from the 4th to the 9th or 10th century) being written in uncials (larger and heavier than on papyrus, and wholly without ligatures), the later (from the 9th to the 15th century) in minuscule or cursive hands. In Cases C and D are arranged MSS., chiefly in Latin (Nos. 60-133), in which the development of the writing of Western Europe can be followed from about A.D. 600 to the end of the 15th century. The earliest specimens are written in *uncial*, or large, letters, which differ from ordinary capitals chiefly in the rounded forms of A, D, E, H, M (ᴀ, ᴅ, ᴇ, ʜ, ᴍ). To these succeed various specimens of national handwritings in *half-uncial*, or mixed large and small, letters, or *minuscules*, as practised in England, Ireland, France, Italy, and Spain, until in the 9th Century the Caroline or Carlovingian form of *minuscule* writing, which developed in the French schools established under the rule of Charlemagne, gradually superseded them, and became the common hand of Western Europe which survives to the present day; as may be seen in the specimens numbered 79 and onwards. Case E contains Anglo-Saxon and English MSS. (Nos. 134-159) from A.D. 1000 to the 15th century written in Saxon characters and the succeeding forms of English writing. In the octagonal Case F in the centre are Chronicles of England down to the 15th century.

I.—GREEK MSS.

Case A.—Papyri.

1. PLATO: portions of the *Phaedo*. *The oldest classical Greek manuscript in existence* (except a few very small fragments), written in the 3rd century B.C., in a small uncial hand. Discovered in

the cartonnage of a mummy-case, composed of fragments of papyrus covered with plaster. [*Papyrus* cccclviii.] *Presented, in* 1895, *by H. Martyn Kennard, Esq.*

2. HYPERIDES, Oration against Philippides. *The only extant manuscript of the oration*, but very imperfect, only the concluding portion of it being preserved. Brought from Egypt in 1890. Written in a delicate semi-uncial hand, probably in the 1st century B.C., with exceptionally narrow columns, leaning somewhat to the right. [*Pap.* cxxxiv.]

3. BACCHYLIDES, Triumphal Odes and Dithyrambs. *The only extant manuscript of the poet*, brought from Egypt in 1896. Written in a fine uncial hand, probably in the 1st century B.C. Twenty poems are preserved, whole or in part, of which six are contained in the portion here exhibited, which is the longest continuous part of the papyrus roll in its present mutilated condition. The subjects are "The Sons of Antenor," "Heracles," "Theseus and Minos," "Theseus at Athens," "Io," and "Idas." [*Pap.* dccxxxiii.]

4. HOMER'S ILIAD: fragments of books xxiii. and xxiv. Found in Egypt. The MS. when complete was a roll of about 20 ft. in length, containing 43 or 44 columns. The critical marks of Aristarchus have been added in some cases, and a few scholia. The part exhibited contains *Il.* xxiv., ll. 164–243. Written in a fine, square uncial hand, probably in the 1st century B.C. [*Pap.* cxxviii.]

5. HOMER'S ODYSSEY, book iii., ll. 283–497. *The earliest extant MS. of any portion of the poem.* Found in Egypt. Carefully written in a graceful uncial hand, early in the 1st century; with scholia in a small cursive hand, added about the end of that century. [*Pap.* cclxx.]

6. HYPERIDES: fragments of a roll (about 28 feet long when complete) containing the orations against Demosthenes and in defence of Lycophron and of Euxenippus. *The only extant MS. of these orations.* Found in a tomb at Gournou in the district of Western Thebes in Egypt, in 1847. Written in graceful rounded uncials, probably towards the end of the 1st century. [*Pap.* cviii.]

7. ARISTOTLE ON THE CONSTITUTION OF ATHENS. *The only extant MS. of the work*, brought from Egypt in 1890. Written about A.D. 100 in four rolls, in four different hands, on the back of papyrus which had already been used [in A.D. 78–79] for the accompts of a farm-bailiff named Didymus, near Hermopolis. The portion exhibited is the latter part of the first roll, written in a small cursive (*i.e.* running) hand with abbreviations. [*Pap.* cxxxi. *verso.*]

8. THE MIMES OF HERODAS: part of an incomplete roll, about 15 ft. in length, containing seven poems, with small portions of at least two more. *The only extant MS. of this author*, brought from Egypt in 1890. The part exhibited contains the dramatic sketch (in choliambic verse) entitled "The Schoolmaster,"

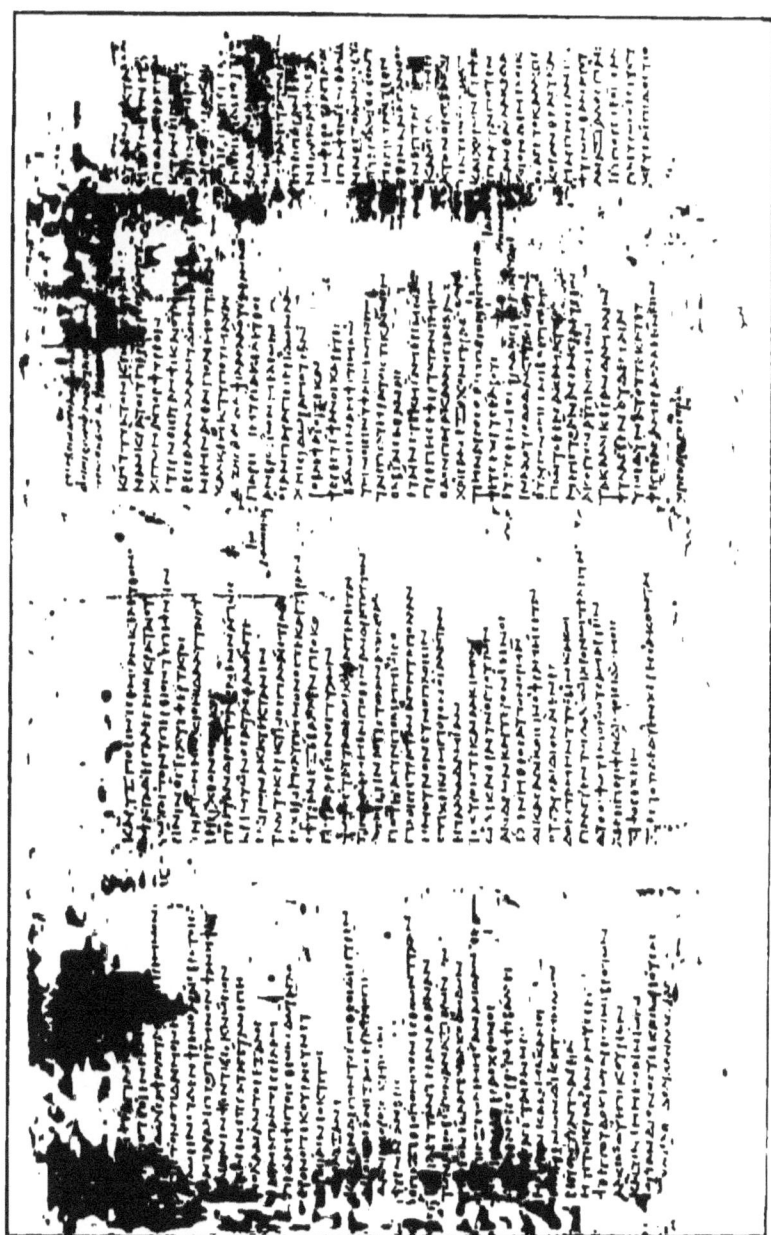

BACCHYLIDES.

describing the flogging of a scapegrace boy. Written in a small, clear uncial hand, in the 1st or 2nd century. [*Pap.* cxxxv.]
9. HOMER'S ILIAD: portions of books xiii. and xiv. Found in Egypt. The MS. when complete was a roll of about 16 ft. in length, containing 36 columns. The part exhibited contains *ll.* xiii., 11. 187–301. Written in a firm, well-formed uncial hand of medium size, in the 1st or 2nd century. [*Pap.* dccxxxii.]
10. PSALTER: fragment, containing Ps. xii. 7–xv. 4. *One of the earliest MSS. of any portion of the Bible at present known to be in existence.* Found in Egypt in 1892. Written stichometrically; and a second hand has marked off the syllables by a dot over the end of each, probably for the purpose of reading or singing in school. Written in a well-formed uncial hand. Late 3rd or early 4th century. [*Pap.* ccxxx.]
11. HESIOD: fragments of the *Theogonia*, including portions of ll. 210–238, 260–270. Written with very black ink, in a large and firm uncial hand. Probably 4th or 5th century, contemporary with the early MSS. on vellum, and so marking the transition from the one material to the other. [*Pap.* clix.]
12. WILL of Aphrodisius of Heraclea, a residence in Crocodilopolis [Arsinoë] in Egypt. Written in a fine semi-cursive hand. B.C. 226–5. Found (like no. 1) in the cartonnage of a mummy-case. [*Pap.* ccccxciii.]
13. PETITION addressed to Ptolemy [Energetes I.] by a soldier, complaining of an assault upon him by a person named Cephalon. Written in a very cursive hand. B.C. 222. [*Pap.* cvi.]
14. TAXING ACCOUNT, from the village of Ptolemaidis Hormus in the Fayum. Written in a clear semi-cursive hand. 3rd cent. B.C. [*Pap.* dlxxvii.]
15. LETTER from Ammonius, a Treasury clerk in the district of Oxyrhynchus, to Phaies, the Oeconomus, or principal revenue official of the district, reporting that he has been suddenly arrested and put in prison. 3rd cent. B.C. [*Pap.* dxxviii.]
16. PETITION from Ptolemy the Macedonian, a recluse in the Temple of Serapis at Memphis, to the strategus Dionysius, complaining of an assault made upon him by several of the Egyptian attendants in the temple, who disliked him because he was a Greek. Written in slightly cursive uncials. B.C. 161. [*Pap.* xliv.]
17. LOAN of 35 artabas of wheat from Apollonia, wife of Druton, to Apollonius and his wife Herais, to be repaid without interest after the next harvest. Written in a small, regular cursive hand. B.C. 132. [*Pap.* dexiii.]
18. LOAN of six measures of wine from Petearsemtheus to Psemmenches, without interest. From the Pathyrite nome in Upper Egypt. Written in a rather thick cursive hand. B.C. 106–5. [*Pap.* delviii.] *Presented, in 1896, by E. R. Bevan, Esq.*
19. ANNUAL RETURN, of the nature of a census-paper, addressed by Pnepheros, an agricultural labourer, to Apollonius, the village

secretary; written in a small cursive hand, with abbreviations. 28 Jan., B.C. 19. [*Pap.* dcxlvi.]

20. PETITION addressed to Gaius Tyrrhanius, Prefect of Egypt, by Satabous, an agricultural labourer, and his son, for redress of an injury done to them, and release from unjust imprisonment. Written very carefully, in a handsome uncial hand. About B.C. 10. [*Pap.* cccliv.]

21. PETITION addressed to Gaius Vitrasius Pollio, Prefect of Egypt, by Versenuphis for assistance to recover property left to him and his brothers by their father, which had been seized by their elder married sister. Written in a large, clear uncial hand. A.D. 40–41. [*Pap.* clxxvii.]

22. RECEIPT given by Chaeremon to three tenants of his land, for a portion of the produce of the land, paid to him as rent. Written in a strongly-marked semi-cursive hand. 23 Aug., A.D. 48. [*Pap.* cxxxix *a.*]

23. THREE CERTIFICATES granted to natives of the village of Socnopaei Nesus (in the Fayum), of having performed the statutory five days' labour on the embankments. Written in a very small cursive hand, with the signature of Dionysius, the official granting the certificate, in large, rather rough uncials. 2 Aug. A.D. 49. [*Pap.* clxv.]

24. RECORD of sale by Didymus, also named Diodorus, and Diodora his wife, to Miccalus, son of Ptolemy, of some olive-yards near the village of Karanis. Dated at Ptolemaïs Euergetis in the nome of Arsinoë [the Fayum], 3 June, A.D. 88. Written in a large, carefully-formed uncial hand, with cursive superscription. [*Pap.* cxli.]

25. RECEIPT given by Cephalas to Tapontos, natives of Karanis, for the sum of 160 drachmas, paid as an instalment of the purchase money of some land. Written in a small cursive hand, bearing some resemblance to that of the Aristotle [No. 7]. 2 March, A.D. 97. [*Pap.* cxliii.]

26. RECEIPT given by Dioscorus, a resident in the street of the Goose-pens in Heracleia, to Stotoëtis, a native of Socnopaei Nesus, for the sum of 148 drachmas, the price of an ass. Written by the scribe Alcimus, in a very cursive hand. 10 Aug. A.D. 142. [*Pap.* ccciii.]

27. RECEIPT given by Claudianus to Didymus and others for the repayment of a debt of 1124 drachmas. Written in a cramped cursive hand. 10 Sept., A.D. 166. [*Pap.* cccxxxii.]

28. ANNUAL RETURN by the priests of the god Socnopaeus [the crocodile-god] and the gods who share his temple, probably for the purpose of taxation. Imperfect; written in a large and clearly defined semi-cursive hand. 23 Aug. A.D. 221. [*Pap.* cccliii.]

29. RECEIPT given by Petechon to Aurelia Senosiris, natives of the village of Cusis in the Great Oasis, for the repayment of a loan of 1000 drachmas, with interest. Written in a small, rather thick, cursive hand. 7 Oct. A.D. 265. [*Pap.* dccix.]

30. LETTER from Demetrius, an official in charge of the revenue derived from the Government monopoly of natron (bitumen), to Abinnaeus, officer in command of a body of auxiliary troops in the camp of Dionysias (in the Fayum), requesting him to look out for smugglers importing natron into his district. Written in a good-sized semi-cursive hand. About A.D. 346. [*Pap.* ccxxxi.]

31. LETTER from Jovinus to Abinnaeus [see no. 30], begging him, in concert with the other officials concerned, to send him the ten artabas of vegetable-seed supplied to orphans; with friendly greetings to his wife and family. Written in a rather irregular cursive hand. About A.D. 346. [*Pap.* cccxix.]

32. LETTER from Flavius Macarius, steward of the imperial estates in Egypt, to Abinnaeus [see no. 30], requiring him, on pain of being reported for disaffection to the imperial house, to furnish soldiers to assist in the collection of the imperial dues. Written in a large semi-cursive hand. About A.D. 350. [*Pap.* ccxxxiv.]

33. LETTER from Victor, serving in the state galley of the governor of the Thebaid, to four other persons, complaining that they have compelled a certain Senuthes to undertake a public duty to which he is not liable, instead of serving in the galley, to which he is liable by hereditary custom, and threatening unpleasant consequences if they do not release him. Written in a large cursive hand. About A.D. 400. [*Pap.* dccxxii.]

34. CONTRACT for the lease of a farm from Phoebammon, *tabularius* of the town of Arsinoë, to John and Castous, agricultural labourers; the landlord to receive by way of rent two-thirds of the crops in general and five-sixths of the hay, but to be liable to perform the cutting of the hay and to provide the seed and animals for working the farm. Written in a clear, rather ornamental hand, of fair size. 8 June, A.D. 595. [*Pap.* cxiii (4).]

35. FESTAL LETTER from a Patriarch of Alexandria to his clergy, informing them of the date of Easter for the current year [25 April]; the information being accompanied by a theological disquisition and aspirations for the peace and unity of the Church. Imperfect, only the conclusion being preserved. Written in a large and handsome uncial hand of Coptic type. Probably A.D. 577. [*Pap.* dccxxix.]

[For a later Greek papyrus, of the 8th century, and for specimens of Coptic and Latin papyri, see p. 111].

Case B.—*Wax, Vellum, and Paper MSS.*

36. WAX-TABLET (such as the ancients used for note-books, letters, etc.), containing two lines of iambic verse, probably from Menander, written first by a schoolmaster in large capital letters and copied twice by a pupil. Probably 2nd cent. [*Add. MS.* 34,186.]

37. DEMOSTHENES: two leaves of the oration *De Falsa Legatione*. Written on vellum in double columns in a small uncial hand, resembling that found in some papyri. Probably the earliest extant vellum MS., dating from a time when vellum was regarded as inferior to papyrus. 2nd cent.(?) [*Add. MS.* 34,473 (1).]
38. GREEK-LATIN GLOSSARY. Written in uncials in the 7th century, in the West of Europe, being copied from a mutilated original. Vellum. [*Harley MS.* 5792.]
39. HYMNS used in the services of the Greek Church: fragments. Written in sloping uncials, in the 8th century. Vellum. [*Add. MS.* 26,113.]
40. EVANGELIARIUM, or lessons from the Gospels for services throughout the year. Written in sloping uncials of Sclavonic type, in the 9th or 10th century. Vellum. [*Harley MS.* 5787.]
41. BYZANTINE CHRONICLES, of Nicephorus, Patriarch of Constantinople [806–815, d. 828], etc. Written in minuscules, late in the 9th century. Vellum. [*Add. MS.* 19,390.]
42. THE FOUR GOSPELS. Written in finely-formed minuscules in the 9th or 10th century. Vellum. [*Add. MS.* 11,300.]
43. SCALA PARADISI, by St. John Climacus, Abbot of Mount Sinai. Written in minuscules, in the 10th century. Vellum. [*Add. MS.* 17,471.]
44. WORKS OF LUCIAN of Samosata. Written in fine minuscules [by Baanes, notary of Arethas, archbishop of Cæsarea, about A.D. 914]. Vellum. [*Harley MS.* 5694.]
45. THE BOOKS OF JUDGES AND RUTH in the Septuagint version, with part of the last chapter of Joshua. Written in elegant minuscules, in the 10th century. Vellum. [*Add. MS.* 20,002.]
46. THUCYDIDES; with the commentary of Marcellinus. Written in minuscules, in the 11th century. Vellum. [*Add. MS.* 11,727.]
47. THE FOUR GOSPELS. Written in minuscules by the priest Synesius, in December, 1033. Vellum. [*Add. MS.* 17,470.]
48. PSALTER, in *Greek*, *Latin*, and *Arabic*, in parallel columns. Written in minuscules, before A.D. 1153. Vellum. [*Harley MS.* 5786.]
49. THE FOUR GOSPELS. Written in minuscules, in the earlier half of the 12th century. Vellum. [*Egerton MS.* 2610.]
50. THE FOUR GOSPELS. Written in minuscules, in the 12th century. Vellum. [*Egerton MS.* 2783.]
51. THE FOUR GOSPELS. Written in fine minuscules, in the 13th century. Vellum. [*Egerton MS.* 2784.]
52. HOMER'S ILIAD, with copious marginal scholia; commonly known as the "Townley Homer." Written in minuscules, in the 13th century. Vellum. [*Burney MS.* 86.]
53. HOMER'S ODYSSEY, with marginal scholia. Written in minuscules, in the 13th century. Vellum. [*Harley MS.* 5674.]

54. THE ORATIONS OF ANDOCIDES, ISAEUS, DINARCHUS, ANTIPHON, LYCURGUS, etc. Written in minuscules, in the 13th century. Vellum. [*Burney MS.* 95.]
55. COMMENTARY on the Psalms, by Euthymius Zigabenus. Written in minuscules, with many abbreviations, by the monk Maximus, in July, 1281. Paper. [*Harley MS.* 5575.]
56. TREATISES OF ST. ATHANASIUS, Archbishop of Alexandria. Written in minuscules, with many abbreviations, by Romanus the Reader, A.D. 1321. Paper. [*Harley MS.* 5579.]
57. LEXICON of SUIDAS. Written in minuscules, by Georgius Bœophorus, A.D. 1402. Paper. [*Add. MS.* 11,892.]
58. HOMER'S ILIAD. Written in minuscules by a scribe named Christopher, in Italy, A.D. 1431. Vellum. [*King's MS.* 16.]
59. HOMER'S ODYSSEY. Written in minuscules, by the priest Johannes Rhosus, of Crete, A.D. 1479. Vellum. [*Harley MS.* 5658.]

II.—LATIN AND OTHER MSS.

Case C.

60. THE FOUR GOSPELS, in the *Latin* vulgate version. Written in uncials, probably in Italy, in the 6th or 7th century. Vellum. [*Harley MS.* 1775.]
61. HISTORY of PAULUS OROSIUS; fragments. *Latin*. Taken from the linings of the covers of a volume in the library of St. Remacle at Stabloo, or Stavelot, in Belgium. Written in uncials, late in the 7th century. Vellum. [*Add. MS.* 24,144.]
62. THEOLOGICAL TRACTS; with a Life of St. Furseus. *Latin*. Written in France, in uncials, in the 7th century; the Life of St. Furseus having been added in minuscules in the 9th century. Vellum. [*Harley MS.* 5041.]
63. ORIGEN'S Homilies on the Book of Numbers, in the *Latin* version of Rufinus. Belonged to the Abbey of Corbie, in France. Written in uncials, late in the 7th century. Vellum. [*Burney MS.* 340.]
64. THE FOUR GOSPELS, in the *Latin* vulgate version. Written in uncials for Abbot Atto, apparently of the monastery of St. Vincent, on the river Volturno, in the territory of Benevento in Italy, between A.D. 739 and 760. Vellum. [*Add. MS.* 5463.]
65. BEDE'S Ecclesiastical History. *Latin*. Partially injured by fire in 1731. Written in England, in pointed minuscules, in the 8th century. Vellum. [*Cotton MS.* Tiberius C. ii.]
66. THE FOUR GOSPELS, in the *Latin* vulgate version. Written in the north of England, in half-uncials, in the 8th century. Vellum. [*Royal MS.* 1 B. vii.]
67. THE FOUR GOSPELS, in the *Latin* vulgate version. From the monastery of St. Augustine at Canterbury. Written in half-uncials of English type, late in the 8th century. Vellum. [*Royal MS.* 1 E. vi.]
68. LIBER VITÆ, or lists of the names of benefactors of the church of St. Cuthbert at Lindisfarne, afterwards removed to Durham; together with the names of those who were entitled to the prayers of the monks by the ties of confraternity, etc. *Latin*. Written in half-uncials, in gold and silver, about A.D. 840. Vellum. [*Cotton MS.* Domitian vii.]
69. LESSONS and Prayers. *Latin*. Formerly belonged to Winchester. Written in round minuscules, in England, in the 8th century. Vellum. [*Harley MS.* 2965.]
70. LESSONS, Prayers and Hymns. *Latin*. Written in round minuscules, in England, in the 8th century. Vellum. [*Royal MS.* 2 A. xx.]

inuenietis infantem
pannis inuolutū
et positum in praesepi
et subito faciae(s)t cū
angelo multitudo
militiae caelestis
laudantium d(omi)n(u)m et
dicentium
gloria in altissimis d(e)o
et in terra pax in homi
nibus bonae uo
luntatis
et factum est ut dis
cesserunt ab eis
angeli in caelum
pastores loquebantur
 ad inuicem
transeamus usque
in bethleem
et uideamus hoc uer
bum quod fac
tum est
quod d(omi)n(u)s ostendit
nobis
et uenerunt festinantes

LATIN GOSPELS.

71. LITANY and Prayers. *Latin.* Written in round minuscules, probably in Ireland, in the 8th or 9th century. Vellum. [*Harley MS.* 7653.]
72. TREATISES of ST. JEROME and ST. CYPRIAN; with tracts on the paschal cycle, etc. *Latin.* Written in minuscules, in England, in the 9th century. Vellum. [*Cotton MS.* Caligula A. xv.]
73. COMMENTARY of THEODORE, Bishop of Mopsuestia, on the Pauline Epistles. *Latin.* Written in Italy, in Lombardic minuscules, in the 9th century. Vellum. [*Harley MS.* 3063.]
74. ST. GREGORY'S "Moralia," or commentary on the Book of Job. *Latin.* Written in France, in Merovingian minuscules, in the 7th century. Vellum. [*Add. MS.* 11,878.]
75. ST. GREGORY'S "Moralia," or commentary on the Book of Job. *Latin.* Written in France, in Merovingian minuscules, in the 8th century. Vellum. [*Add. MS.* 31,031.]
76. THEOLOGICAL TRACTS and excerpts. *Latin.* Written in minuscules, apparently in France, in the 8th century. Vellum. [*Cotton MS.* Nero A. ii.]
77. ORATIONALE GOTHICUM: containing prayers for the services in the early Mozarabic Liturgy. *Latin.* From the monastery of S. Domingo de Silos, near Burgos, in Spain. Written in Visigothic minuscules, in Spain, in the 9th century. Vellum. [*Add. MS.* 30,852.]
78. LIVES and Passions of Saints; with large ornamental initials. *Latin.* Written in Visigothic minuscules by the deacon Gomes, at the order of Damian, abbot of the monastery of S. Pedro de Cardeña, in the diocese of Burgos, in Spain, A.D. 919. Vellum. [*Add. MS.* 25,600.]
79. THE FOUR GOSPELS, in the *Latin* vulgate version. From the monastery of St. Geneviève in Paris. Written in gold Caroline minuscules, in the latter part of the 9th century. Vellum. [*Harley MS.* 2797.]
80. THE NEW TESTAMENT (wanting the Gospels), in the *Latin* vulgate version. Written at the monastery of St. Gall, in Switzerland, in Caroline minuscules, under the direction of Hartmut (abbot of St. Gall, 872–883), who has added in his own hand the apocryphal Epistle of St. Paul to the Laodiceans. Vellum. [*Add. MS.* 11,852.]
81. THE BIBLE, according to the *Latin* vulgate version of St. Jerome, revised [about 810] by Theodulf, Bishop of Orleans. From the monastery of St. Hubert, in the diocese of Liège. Written in a very small minuscule hand, in triple columns, in the 9th century. Vellum. [*Add. MS.* 24,142.]
82. THE FOUR GOSPELS, in the *Latin* vulgate version. From the monastery of Eller, near Cochem, on the Mosel. Written in small Caroline minuscules, in the 9th or 10th century. Vellum. [*Harley MS.* 2826.]
83. THE FOUR GOSPELS, in the *Latin* vulgate version. From the abbey of St. Martin of Tours. Written in Caroline minuscules, late in the 9th century. Vellum. [*Egerton MS.* 609.]

84. THE FOUR GOSPELS, in the *Latin* vulgate version. Written in Caroline minuscules, in red ink, in the 9th or 10th century. [*Harley MS.* 2795.]

85. THE FOUR GOSPELS, in the *Latin* vulgate version. From St. Petroc's Priory at Bodmin, in Cornwall. Written in Caroline minuscules, early in the 10th century. On the margins and blank leaves were entered, from time to time, records of the liberation of serfs publicly made at the altar of St. Petroc. Vellum. [*Add. MS.* 9381.]

86. PSALTER, in Tironian Notes, the shorthand characters invented by Marcus Tullius Tiro, the freedman of Cicero. *Latin.* From the abbey of St. Remy, at Reims. Written early in the 10th century. Vellum. [*Add. MS.* 9046.]

87. LEXICON TIRONIANUM: or explanations of the Tironian Notes, the shorthand characters invented by Marcus Tullius Tiro, freedman of Cicero. *Latin.* Written, probably in France, early in the 10th century. Vellum. [*Add. MS.* 21,164.]

88. CICERO'S "Aratea"; with drawings of the constellations filled in with explanations of the figures taken from the "Poeticon Astronomicon" of Hyginus. Written in Caroline minuscules, the extracts from Hyginus being in rustic capitals, in the 9th or 10th century. Vellum. [*Harley MS.* 647.]

89. VITRUVIUS "de Architectura." From the abbey of St. Pantaleon at Cologne. Written in Caroline minuscules, late in the 9th century. Vellum. [*Harley MS.* 2767.]

90. JUVENAL'S Satires. Written in Caroline minuscules, early in the 10th century. Vellum. [*Add. MS.* 15,600.]

91. HORACE'S Poems; with glosses and scholia. Written in Caroline minuscules, early in the 10th century. Vellum. [*Harley MS.* 2725.]

92. THE BIBLE, in the *Latin* vulgate version; with miniatures and initials. Written for the monastery of St. Mary de Parco, near Louvain, A.D. 1148. Vellum. [*Add. MS.* 14,790.]

93. THE BIBLE, in the *Latin* vulgate version; with miniatures and illuminated initials. Written for the abbey of Floreffe near Namur, in Belgium, about A.D. 1160. Vellum. [*Add. MS.* 17,738.]

94. ORIGEN'S Homilies in the *Latin* version of Rufinus and Jerome; with coloured initials. Written in the monastery of St. Mary at Cambron, in the diocese of Cambray, Belgium, A.D. 1163. Vellum. [*Add. MS.* 15,307.]

95. THE BIBLE, in the *Latin* vulgate version; with illuminated initials. Written in France, in the 13th century. Vellum. [*Add. MS.* 15,253.]

At the two ends of the Case:—

96. CICERO "De Oratore." Written in France, in the 10th century. Vellum. [*Harley MS.* 2736.]

97. CÆSAR's Commentaries "de bello Gallico." Written in France, in the 11th century. Vellum. [*Add. MS.* 10,084.]
98. RULE of St. Benedict. *Latin*. Written in the monastery of St. Gilles, in the diocese of Nîmes, in the south of France, A.D. 1129. Vellum. [*Add. MS.* 16,979.]
99. THE BOOK OF LEVITICUS and the Gospel of St. John, with commentary and glosses, in *Latin*. Written in the Abbey of St. Mary of Buildwas, in Shropshire, A.D. 1176. Vellum. [*Harley MS.* 3038.]

In the lower compartments of the Case:—

100. THE BIBLE, in the *Latin* vulgate version. Written probably in the north of France, in the 11th century. Vellum. [*Royal MS.* 1 E. viii.]
101. HOMILIES of St. Ambrose, St. Gregory, etc., and lessons from the Gospels and Epistles; with coloured initials. *Latin*. Written in Italy, early in the 12th century. Vellum. [*Harley MS.* 7183.]
102. THE BIBLE, in the *Latin* vulgate version; with illuminated initials. From the monastery of St. Mary at Worms, in Germany. Written in the 12th century. Vellum. [*Harley MS.* 2803.]
103. GRADUAL, or musical services for the Mass; with illuminated initials. *Latin*. Written in Italy, about A.D. 1400. Vellum. [*Add. MS.* 18,161.]
104. GRATIAN's "Decretorum discordantium Concordia"; with commentary. With miniatures and illuminated initials. Written in Italy, in the 14th century. Vellum. [*Add. MS.* 15,274.]
105. EARLY ENGLISH Poems and prose treatises; with illuminated initials and borders. Written about A.D. 1380–1400. Vellum. [*Add. MS.* 22,283.]
106. THE BIBLE, in the *Latin* vulgate version; with miniatures and illuminated initials and borders. Written in England, early in the 15th century. Vellum. [*Royal MS.* 1 E. ix.]
107. "CHRONIQUES D'ANGLETERRE": chronicle of the history of England, by Jehan de Wavrin; the third volume, containing the history of the years 1377–1387. With illustrations and illuminated initials and borders. Written and illuminated for the use of King Edward IV., probably at Bruges, in Belgium, about A.D. 1480. Vellum. [*Royal MS.* 14 E. iv.]
108. "CHRONIQUES DE ST. DENYS": chronicle of the history of France, carried down to A.D. 1461. With illustrations and illuminated initials and borders. Written in the latter part of the 15th century. Vellum. [*Royal MS.* 20 E. 1.]
109. ST. AUGUSTINE's Commentary on the Psalms; with illuminated initials and borders. *Latin*. Written in Italy for Ferdinand of Aragon, King of Naples, A.D. 1480. Vellum. [*Add. MS.* 14,779.]

Case D.

110. THE FOUR GOSPELS, in the *Latin* vulgate version; with coloured initials, of interlaced designs. Written by Mælbrigte Hua Maluanaigh, at Armagh, in Ireland, A.D. 1138. Vellum. [*Harley MS.* 1802.]
111. BREVIARY, of English use. *Latin.* Written, probably at St. Alban's, late in the 12th century. Vellum. [*Royal MS.* 2 A. x.]
112. MISSAL, of the use of the Church of St. Bavon of Ghent; with musical notation. *Latin.* With illuminated initials. Written at the end of the 12th century. Vellum. [*Add. MS.* 16,949.]
113. MARIALE: hymns to the Virgin, Penitential Psalms, etc. *Latin.* Written in England or Northern France, early in the 13th century. Vellum. [*Cotton MS.* Titus A. xxi.]
114. THE BIBLE, in the *Latin* vulgate version; with illuminated initials. Written, probably in England, in the 13th century. Vellum. [*Add. MS.* 15,452.]
115. HERBAL, compiled from Dioscorides, etc.; with coloured illustrations of plants. *Latin.* Written in England, early in the 13th century. Vellum. [*Sloane MS.* 1975.]
116. LIBER de natura Bestiarum: a treatise on the nature of beasts, birds and fishes, with coloured illustrations. Written in England, early in the 13th century. Vellum. [*Harley MS.* 3244.]
117. MISSAL, of the use of Amiens; with musical notation. *Latin.* Written in France, A.D. 1218. Vellum. [*Add. MS.* 17,742.]
118. MARTYROLOGY, founded on Usuardus, etc. *Latin.* Probably belonged to the Church of St. Bartholomew at Benevento. Written in Italy, in Lombardic minuscules, in the 13th century. Vellum. [*Add. MS.* 23,776.]
119. THE BIBLE, in the *Latin* vulgate version; with marginal commentary. With illuminated initials. Written in France, in the 13th century. Vellum. [*Harley MS.* 404.]
120. PSALTER, with illuminated initials and borders. *Latin.* Written in England, early in the 14th century. Vellum. [*Lansdowne MS.* 346.]
121. LAWS OF ALFONSO X., King of Castile and Leon [A.D. 1252–1284], known as "Las Partidas"; with small miniatures. *Spanish.* Written at the beginning of the 14th century. Vellum. [*Add. MS.* 20,787.]
122. "LE LIVRE DOU TRESOR": an encyclopædic treatise, by Brunetto Latini, the master of Dante; with illuminated initials. *French.* Written in the 14th century. Vellum. [*Add. MS.* 30,025.]
123. PSALTER, Litany, etc.; with illuminated initials and borders. *Latin.* Belonged to Philippa of Hainault [d. 1369], Queen of Edward III. Written in England, in the 14th century. Vellum. [*Harley MS.* 2899.]
124. THE BLACK BOOK of the Admiralty, with illuminated initials and borders. *French* and *Latin.* Written in England, early in the 15th century. Vellum. [*Cotton MS.* Vespasian B. xxii.]

125. MEDICAL Treatises, by John Arderne and others; with marginal illustrations. *Latin* and *English*. Written in England, early in the 15th century. Vellum. [*Add. MS.* 29,301.]
126. SELECT PSALMS; with illuminated initials and borders. *Latin*. Written in England for Humphrey, Duke of Gloucester [d. 1447], brother of Henry V., early in the 15th century. Vellum. [*Royal MS.* 2 B. i.]
127. LUCAN's "Pharsalia"; with illuminated initials. Written at Ferrara in Italy by "Jacobus Juliani de Portiolo" for Feltrino Boiardo, of Reggio, A.D. 1378. Vellum. [*Add. MS.* 11,990.]
128. VALERIUS MAXIMUS "de Romanorum exterorumque factis et dictis memorabilibus"; with coloured initials. Written in Italy by "Filipinus de Gandinonibus," A.D. 1412; and sold by him to Bertolino de' Medici on 22 Oct. 1440, for ten ducats. Vellum. [*Add. MS.* 14,095.]
129. LUCRETIUS "de Rerum Natura"; with illuminated initials. Written in Italy by "Joannes Rainaldus Mennius," in the 15th century. Vellum. [*Add. MS.* 11,912.]
130. JUVENAL's Satires; with illuminated initials and borders, and the arms of Este-Ferrara. Written in Italy, in the 15th century. Vellum. [*Add. MS.* 24,638.]
131. POEM in praise of, and dedicated to, Lodovico Maria Sforza-Visconti, Duke of Bari, who became Duke of Milan in A.D. 1494; by Bernardino de' Capitanei da Landriano. *Italian*. With illuminated border and initials. About A.D. 1480–1490. Vellum. [*Add. MS.* 14,817.]
132. ST. GREGORY's Dialogues; with illuminated initials. *Spanish*. Written in the middle of the 15th century. Vellum. [*Add. MS.* 30,039.]
133. ST. JEROME's Epistles, etc.; with miniatures and borders. *Latin*. Written in France, in the Italian style, late in the 15th century. Vellum. [*Add. MS.* 30,051.]

III.—ENGLISH MSS.

Case E.

134. BEOWULF: Epic poems in *Anglo-Saxon*. The unique manuscript of the oldest poem in the English language. Written in England, about A.D. 1000. Vellum. [*Cotton MS*. Vitellius A. xv.]
135. THE ANGLO-SAXON CHRONICLE, from the Invasion of Julius Cæsar to A.D. 1066. Written in the same hand to A.D. 1046, and afterwards in various hands. Vellum. [*Cotton MS*. Tiberius B. i.]
136. THE FOUR GOSPELS, in *English*, of the Anglo-Saxon or Wessex version, made in the 10th century; the earliest English version of the Gospels (apart from glosses in Latin MSS.). Written early in the 12th century. Belonged successively to the monastery of St. Augustine's, Canterbury, to Archbishop Cranmer, and to John, Lord Lumley. Vellum. [*Royal MS*. 1 A. xiv.]
137. THE CREED, Lord's Prayer, etc., followed by a Bestiary, in *English* verse; with other pieces, in *Latin*, *English*, and *French*. Written in England in the 13th century. Vellum. [*Arundel MS*. 292.]
138. LIVES of St. Katharine, St. Margaret, and St. Julian, with verses on the Passion of Christ, etc.; in *English*. Written in the first half of the 13th century. Vellum. [*Royal MS*. 17 A. xxvii.]
139. The "Ancren Riwle" [Rule for Anchoresses], Homilies, Lives of Saints, etc.; in *English*. Written in the first half of the 13th century. Vellum. [*Cotton MS*. Titus D. xviii.]
140. PSALTER, with Canticles, etc., in *Latin* and *English*, verse by verse; the English version attributed to William de Schorham [Shoreham], who was admitted vicar of Chart Sutton, near Leeds, co. Kent, A.D. 1320. Written in the middle of the 14th century. Vellum. [*Add. MS*. 17,376.]
141. The "Aȝenbyte of Inwyt" (i.e. Remorse of Conscience), by Dan Michel of Northgate, in Kent, a monk of St. Augustine's Abbey, Canterbury. The author's autograph manuscript, written A.D. 1340. Vellum. [*Arundel MS*. 57.]
142. THE LAY FOLKS' MASS-BOOK, or manner of hearing Mass: in verse. A translation, made at the end of the 13th century, probably from the French, the original author being one "Dan Jeremy" [Jeremiah, canon of Rouen and archdeacon of Cleveland, dioc. York, 1170-1175]. Late 14th century. Vellum. [*Royal MS*. 17 B. xvii.]

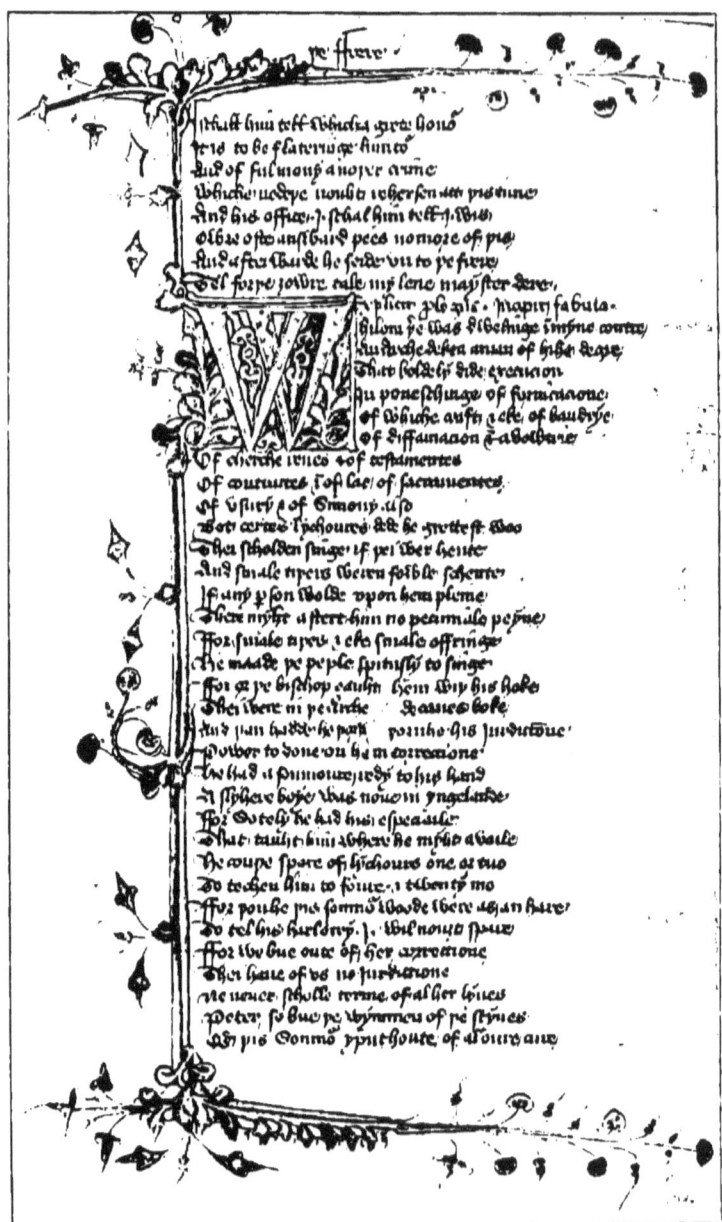

CHAUCER'S CANTERBURY TALES.

143. THE BIBLE, in the earlier Wycliffite version. Late 14th century. Vellum. [*Add. MS.* 15,580.]
144. TRACTS "of wedded men and wyves," and on the Lord's Prayer, attributed to Wycliffe; with other pieces. First half of the 15th century. Vellum. [*Harley MS.* 2398.]
145. THE NEW TESTAMENT, in the later Wycliffite version; with illuminated initials. First half of the 15th century. Vellum. [*Egerton MS.* 1171.]
146. THE CATHOLIC EPISTLES and Apocalypse, in the later Wycliffite version. Early 15th century. Vellum. [*Harley MS.* 5768.]
147. COMMENTARY on the Ten Commandments, attributed to Wycliffe; with other tracts. Middle of the 15th century. Vellum. [*Royal MS.* 17 A. xxvi.]
148. THE PRYMER, or Book of prayers, in *English*, containing the Hours of the Virgin, the dirge, penitential and other psalms, litany, etc.; with illuminated initials and borders. Early 15th century. Vellum. [*Add. MS.* 17,010.]
149. "PIERS PLOWMAN": a poem by William Langland, in *English* alliterative verse. Written before A.D. 1400. Vellum. [*Cotton MS.* Vespasian B. xvi.]
150. CHAUCER'S "Canterbury Tales." Early 15th century. Vellum. [*Lansdowne MS.* 851.]
151. CHAUCER'S "Troilus and Cressida." Early 15th century. Vellum. [*Harley MS.* 2280.]
152. GOWER'S "Confessio Amantis." Early 15th century. Vellum. [*Add. MS.* 12,043.]
153. THOMAS OCCLEVE'S poem, "De regimine Principum." With portrait of Geoffrey Chaucer. Early 15th century. Vellum. [*Harley MS.* 4866.]
154. JOHN LYDGATE'S poem, "The Storie of Thebes"; followed by Occleve's "De regimine Principum." Middle of the 15th century. Vellum. [*Add. MS.* 18,632.]
155. JOHN CAPGRAVE'S poem on the Life of St. Katharine. 15th century. Belonged to Campsey Priory, co. Suffolk, by the gift of Dame Katharine Babyngton, sub-prioress. Vellum. [*Arundel MS.* 396.]
156. MYSTERY-PLAYS, on subjects taken from the Old and New Testaments; said to have been represented at Coventry on the Feast of Corpus Christi. Written in 1468. Paper. [*Cotton MS.* Vespasian D. viii.]
157. METRICAL CHRONICLE of England to A.D. 1271, attributed to Robert of Gloucester. 15th century. Vellum. [*Harley MS.* 201.]
158. TRAVELS of Sir John Mandeville; *English* version. 15th century. The unique MS. of this version. Vellum. [*Cotton MS.* Titus C. xvi.]
159. TRAVELS of Sir John Mandeville: the only complete *English* version, formed by revision and completion of an earlier defective text, of which many copies exist. 15th century. The unique MS. Vellum. [*Egerton MS.* 1982.]

IV.—MS. CHRONICLES OF ENGLAND.

Case F.

A small typical selection of Chronicles and other MSS. intended to illustrate the manner in which the history of this country was recorded and handed down before the invention of printing, viz.:—

1. NENNIUS, *Historia Britonum*. The earliest history of Britain was written by Gildas, about the year 560, containing an account of the Roman conquest and occupation, the departure of the Romans (in 410), and the invasion and conquest of the island by the Saxons. Of this history there is no manuscript in the British Museum, except a badly burnt fragment of the 10th century. The next history to it in date is that of which a copy is here exhibited. It is attributed to Nennius on the authority of a prologue contained in one MS., which states that it was composed in the year 858; but there are some grounds for believing that it is really considerably older. In any case, nothing is known of the author's life. It contains the history of Britain in *Latin* from the Roman conquest to the year 687, but is so full of legendary matter that its authority can be but little depended on.

The manuscript here shown [*Cotton MS.* Vesp. D. xxi.] was written in the 12th century, and the passage exhibited describes the preaching of Christianity in Ireland by St. Patrick [§§ 53, 54]. The following is a translation of part of it:—

"From the creation of the world to the baptism of the Irish there are 5330 years; in the fifth year of King Loygare [A.D. 425] did St. Patrick begin to preach the faith of Christ. Thus St. Patrick preached the Gospel of Christ to foreign nations for forty years: he showed apostolical powers, he gave sight to the blind, he healed lepers, he made the deaf to hear, he cast devils out of the bodies of those who were possessed, he raised nine men that were dead to life, he redeemed many from captivity, both men and women, at his own expense. He wrote 365 manuals, or more, and founded the same number of churches. He ordained 365 bishops, or more, men in whom was the Spirit of God. Of priests he ordained as many as 3000, and in the region of Conachta (Connaught) alone he converted 12,000 persons to the faith of Christ, and baptised them. He fasted forty days and forty nights on the top of Mount Eile (that is, Cruachan Eile); on which mountain, overhanging the sea, he graciously made three petitions for all the Irish who received the faith. The first petition, as the Scots say, is that to everyone should be granted repentance, even though it were in the last extremity of life; the second, that they should not be utterly consumed

Hæc pdicto ppuitipicunda
opinio quae debatto
gregorio ipuadicome
maiorum ad nor urq pnti lacta ??
qua uidelicet pcauipa ad morcuy
cum regulam ipza palucum
norquae gnicar cupam ggr gut ?
Dicuno quia die quadam cum
ad uenibrab nupip mip accopub
multa uenalia In gopum puy pr
con lcca multa ad onfidum con
fluxippint. St ipprum gregorum
In cpi alios ad uinippe ac uidippe
In cpi alia pucnos uenulg poptur
candidi copporuy ac uenupa uultuy
capillorum qq forma gngia ;

by barbarians for ever; the third, that no Irishman should be alive at the Day of Judgment, since they will be destroyed in honour of St. Patrick seven years before the Judgment. Moreover, on that hill he blessed the peoples of Ireland, and indeed he ascended thither that he might pray for them, and that he might see the fruit of his labour; and there came to him innumerable birds of many colours, that he might bless them, signifying that all the saints of Ireland, of either sex, will come to him on the Day of Judgment, as to their father and master, that they may follow him to judgment. After this he passed away in a good old age to that place where he now liveth in joy for ever and ever. Amen."

2. BEDE, *Historia Ecclesiastica Gentis Anglorum.* The "Venerable" Bede is the first great historian of England, and most of our knowledge of the history of our country down to his time is derived from his work. He was born in 673, lived all his life as a monk at Jarrow in Northumberland, and died, in the act of translating the Scriptures into English, in 735. His *Ecclesiastical History of the English*, written in *Latin*, deals primarily with the English Church; but, owing to the intimate connection of Church and State in those days, it is also to a very great extent a general history of the country. It begins with a summary (taken from Gildas and other authors) of events from the invasion of Cæsar in B.C. 55 to the preaching of Christianity by Augustine in 597. From 597 to 731 the history is given in full detail, being based upon contemporary records collected by Bede and his own personal knowledge. It is the chief authority for the history of the introduction of Christianity into England, both in the south by Augustine from Rome, and in the north by Aidan from Iona.

More than 130 manuscript copies of Bede are known. The copy here shown [*Cotton MS.* Tiber. A. xiv.] is one of the earliest, having been written at the end of the 8th century or early in the 9th, and consequently not long after the lifetime of Bede himself. It belonged to Sir R. Cotton, and was considerably damaged in the fire among his books at Ashburnham House in 1731. A still older copy is exhibited in Case C, no. 65.

The passage exhibited, of which a translation follows, describes the origin of the mission of Augustine by Pope Gregory to England (Bk. II., Ch. i.).

"Nor should we pass over in silence the story concerning the blessed Gregory which has been handed down to us by our forefathers, as to the reason which encouraged him to take such zealous care of the salvation of our people. They say that on a certain day, when some merchants had lately arrived and many wares were brought together into the market for sale and a crowd of purchasers had assembled, Gregory too came with the rest and saw there, among other objects, some youths exposed for sale; they were of fair complexion and handsome countenance, with beautiful hair. When he saw them he asked, as the story goes, from what region or land they had been brought; and he was told they were from the island of Britain, and that all the inhabitants were of like appearance. Again he asked whether the islanders were Christians, or were still shrouded in pagan error; and he was told that they were pagans. Then, sighing from the bottom of his heart, he said: 'Alas, the pity, that the author of darkness should possess men of such bright countenance, and that such beauty of outward appearance should bear a mind void of internal grace!' He asked therefore again, what was the name of the people, and it was answered that they were called Angles [English]. 'Good,' said he, 'for they have an angelic face, and such should be co-heirs of the Angels in heaven. What is the name of the province from which they have been brought?' He was told that they were of the province of Deira. 'Good,' said he, 'De-ira; they are snatched from wrath [*de ira* in Latin], and called to the mercy of Christ. How is the king of that province named?' It was answered that he was called Ælla; whereupon, playing upon the name, he said, 'Alleluia, the praise of God the Creator must be sung in those parts.' Then going to the bishop of the Roman and apostolical see (for he was not yet bishop himself) he asked him to send some ministers of the word into Britain to the people of the Angles, by whom they might be converted to Christ."

3. THE ANGLO-SAXON CHRONICLE is the earliest history of this country in *English*. The first part of it, from the invasion of Cæsar [B c. 55] to the reign of Alfred [A.D. 871–901], is believed to have been compiled by order of King Alfred; and from that time it was carried on by successive chroniclers (whose names are not known) in various monasteries down to the year 1154, forming a sort of Annual Register of the most important events in each year. It is thus not only one of the most valuable authorities for the history of England, especially from the time of Alfred to the Norman Conquest, but also an unique record of the development of the language from its early Anglo-Saxon form until it approaches the character of English as we know it.

The copy here shown [*Cotton MS.* Tiber. B. iv.] was written towards the end of the 11th century; the Chronicle is brought down to the year 1016 in one hand, and continued in several others to 1079. It belonged to Sir R. Cotton, and suffered damage in the fire at Ashburnham House in 1731.

The passage exhibited [of which a translation into modern English from B. Thorpe's edition follows] contains a record of the war with the invading Danes in 871, including the great victory of Æthelred and Alfred at Ashdown, the site of which is commonly supposed to be marked by the well-known figure of a white horse cut in the chalk in the Vale of the White Horse, Berkshire.

"In this year [A.D. 871] the army [*i.e.* the Danes] came to Reading, in Wessex, and, three nights after, two jarls rode up, when the aldor-

Ħ. dccclxxi· Hēr cōm þe here to rēa
dingum on Westseaxe· 7 þæs ymbe ·iiii· niht þi don
twēgen eorlas up· þa gemette æþelwulf ealdor
man hie on Englafelda· 7 him þær wið gefeaht.
7 sige nam 7 heora oþer wearð ofslægen
þæs nama wæs Sidroc· Ða ymb ·iiii· niht æþered
cyning· 7 ælfred his broþor þær mycle fyrd
to Rēadingum gelæddon· 7 wið þone here ge
fuhton· 7 þær wæs mycel wæl geslægen on gehwæþere
hand· 7 eaðelwulf ealdorman wearð ofslægen·
7 þa deniscan ahton wælstowe geweald· 7 þæs
ymb ·iiii· nyht gefeaht æþered cyning 7 ælfred
his broþor wið ealne þone here on Æscesdune·
7 hi wærun on twam gefylcum on oðrum wæs
bag secg 7 healfdene þa hæðenan cyningas· 7 on
oþrum wæron þa eorlas· 7 þa feaht se cyning
æþered wið þara cyninga getruman· 7 þær
wearð se cyning bag secg ofslægen· 7 ælfred
his broþor wið þara eorla getruman· 7 þær

man Æthelwulf met them at Inglefield and there fought against them and gained the victory; and one of them was there slain, whose name was Sidroc. Four nights after this King Æthered and Ælfred his brother led a large force to Reading and fought against the army, and there was great slaughter made on each side; and the aldorman Æthelwulf was slain, and the Danes held possession of the battle-place. And four nights after, king Æthered and Ælfred his brother fought with all the army at Ashdown; and they were in two divisions; in one were Bagsecg and Hálfdán, the heathen kings, and in the other were the jarls; and then king Æthered fought with the kings' division, and there was the king Bagsecg slain; and Ælfred his brother fought against the jarls' division, and there was the elder jarl Sidroc slain, and the younger jarl Sidroc, and Asbiörn jarl and Fræna jarl and Harald jarl, and both divisions put to flight, and many thousands slain; and they were fighting until night. And fourteen nights after, king Æthered and Ælfred his brother fought against the army at Basing, and there the Danes gained the victory. And two months after, king Æthered and Ælfred his brother fought against the army at Merton; and they were in two divisions, and they put both to flight, and far in the day were victorious; and there was great slaughter on each side, but the Danes held possession of the battle-place; and there were bishop Heahmund slain and many good men."

4. WACE, *Roman de Rou.* Wace was a Norman, born in Jersey, and lived from about 1100 to 1170. He wrote a poetical history of the Norman Conquest, in *French,* which contains by far the fullest description of the Battle of Hastings. Wace had known many men who had fought in the battle, and his account is full of minute details of the fighting.

The copy here exhibited [*Royal MS.* 4 C. xi.] was written in the 13th century. The passage selected is part of the account of the Battle of Hastings. The following is Sir A. Malet's translation of the lines which describe the palisado formed by the English, and the arrangement of the English forces.

"Short Axes, sharp Bills, were the arms of offence
By the English Foot borne, and they made them a Fence
Of Bucklers, and wattle work well interlac'd;
Thus forming a Breastwork, in front of them plac'd.
The Barrier so form'd was a close Hurdle like,
Which the Normans must force, ere a stroke they could strike.
Thus fenc'd with their Shields, and a stout Barricade,
They deem'd,—and with reason,—defence might be made.
And if to this purpose they firmly had held,
Other issue that day had most surely beheld:
For no Norman Warrior that Barrier did force,
But met with disaster, and fell a dead Corse:
Hewn down by the Axe edge, or smote by Gisarme,
Or slain by the Club, or by some other arm.
Short close-fitting Hauberks those Englishmen wore,
And Helmets that join'd to their Hauberks they bore.

> The Kentish Men, claiming as matter of right
> To stand in the Van and strike first in the Fight,
> He caus'd to advance, and position to take,
> Where deeming the Normans their onset would make.
> They claim'd, when their Monarch to Battle should go,
> The right in that Battle to strike the first Blow.
> The Londoners' claim was His person to guard,
> That where'er He stood, they should keep watch and ward;
> They also to guard the King's Standard were bound,
> And where it was planted they took up their ground."

5. SIMEON OF DURHAM, *Historia Dunelmensis Ecclesiæ*. For several centuries after the Norman Conquest, the writing of history was carried on almost exclusively by monks. The greater monasteries trained a succession of writers, some of whom merely recorded in their chronicles such events as concerned the monasteries themselves, with occasional notices of outside occurrences of general interest; while others devoted themselves to the production of regular histories of the country from the earliest times down to their own day. One such flourishing school of historians is found in the north of England, carrying on the traditions of Bede. Simeon, a monk first of Jarrow and afterwards of Durham, was directed by his superiors, about the years 1104–1108, to write a History of the Church of Durham, which he brings from the establishment of Christianity in Northumbria by Aidan in 635 down to the year 1096. Like nearly all literary works down to the 15th century, it is written in *Latin*. It is principally occupied with religious matters, and is a valuable link in the history of the Church of England. He also wrote a general history, based largely upon Bede [see no. 2] and on Florence of Worcester, whose Chronicle comes down to 1116.

The copy here shown [*Cotton MS.* Faust. A. v.] was written in the 12th century, in or soon after the lifetime of Simeon himself, being copied from a manuscript at Durham, which may have been the author's own copy.

The passage exhibited, of which a translation follows, describes the wanderings of the monks of Lindisfarne with the body of St. Cuthbert during an invasion by the Danes [875–883], and the loss and recovery of a valuable copy of the Gospels, written in honour of St. Cuthbert. This identical MS. is now in the British Museum [*Cotton MS.* Nero D. iv.].

> [The monks endeavoured to cross over to Ireland, carrying the saint's body with them; but a storm drove them back.] "In this storm, while the ship was lying over on her side, a copy of the Gospels, adorned with gold and precious stones, fell overboard and sank into the depths of the sea. Accordingly after a little while, when they had in some degree recovered their senses and reflected who and where

they were, they bend their knees and prostrate themselves at full length before the feet of the sacred body, asking pardon for their foolish venture. Then they seize the rudder and turn the ship back to the shore and to their fellows, and immediately they arrive there without any difficulty, the wind blowing astern. . . . Amidst their lamentations in this distress at length the accustomed help of their pious patron came to their aid, whereby their minds were relieved from grief and their bodies from labour, seeing that the Lord is a refuge of the poor, a helper in times of trouble. For appearing in a vision to one of them, Hunred by name, he bade them seek, when the tide was low, for the manuscript which, as above related, had fallen from the ship into the midst of the waves; for perchance, beyond the utmost they could hope, they would, by the mercy of God, find it. For the loss of that book too had afflicted them with the most profound grief. . . . Accordingly they go to the sea and find that it had retired much further than it was accustomed; and after walking three miles or more they find the sacred manuscript of the Gospels itself, exhibiting all its outer splendour of jewels and gold and all the beauty of its pages and writing within, as though it had never been touched by water. . . . Further, the above-mentioned book is preserved to this day in this church [of Durham], which is honoured by the possession of the holy father's body, and, as we said before, no sign of damage by water is visible in it. And this is believed to be due to the merits of St. Cuthbert himself and of those who made the book, namely, bishop Eadfrid of holy memory, who wrote it with his own hand in honour of the blessed Cuthbert, and the venerable Ethelwold, his successor, who caused it to be adorned with gold and precious stones, and St. Bilfrid the anchorite, who, obeying with skilled hand the wishes of his superior, achieved an excellent work. For it was a splendid example of the goldsmith's art."

6. WILLIAM OF MALMESBURY, *Gesta Regum Anglorum*. This writer was born about 1095 and died about 1143. Nearly the whole of his life appears to have been spent in the monastery of Malmesbury, of which he ultimately declined the abbacy, preferring to retain the librarianship. He was an active historian, writing *The Acts of the Kings of England*, in which he summarises the early history from 449 to 731, where Bede had already covered the ground, and then continues it in greater detail down to 1125; *The Acts of the Bishops of England*, an ecclesiastical history from 597 to 1125; and the *New History*, a continuation of his earlier work from 1126 to 1142. He is the most important historian since the time of Bede, to whom he deliberately set himself to be a successor; and he had a high idea of a historian's duty, trying to trace causes and describe characters, as well as to record events.

The copy here exhibited [*Royal MS.* 13 D. ii.] was written in the 12th century, probably in the author's own life-time. It belonged to the Abbey of Margam, which was founded by Robert, Earl of Gloucester, to whom William of Malmesbury dedicated his history.

The passage selected for exhibition and translation [Bk. III. § 245] describes the character of the English at the time of the Norman Conquest.

"That day [of the battle of Hastings] was fatal to England,—the day of the miserable downfall of their beloved country and of submission to new masters. Submission had indeed long been familiar to the English, who had changed greatly in the course of time. In the first years of their arrival they had the appearance and bearing of barbarians, they were practised in war, their worship was savage; but afterwards, when they had adopted the Christian faith, the peace which they enjoyed led them gradually, as time went on, to regard the use of arms as of but secondary importance and to devote themselves entirely to religion. I am not speaking of the poor, whose lack of means generally restrains them within the bounds of right; and I pass over the clergy, who are deterred from error not only by the consideration of their profession, but often also by the fear of shame. I speak of the kings, who by reason of their power could indulge their desires as they chose; yet of them, some in their own country, and some at Rome, put off their kingly garb and gained the heavenly kingdom, making a blessed exchange, while many who to all appearance gave themselves to the world throughout their lives did so that they might scatter their treasures to the poor or distribute them to monasteries. What shall I say of the great army of bishops, hermits, abbots? Does not the whole island so shine with these relics of the old inhabitants, that you can scarcely pass a single village of any size without hearing the name of a new saint? And how many more are lost to memory for want of chroniclers? But as time went on the study of letters and of religion decayed, shortly before the arrival of the Normans. The clergy, content with a smattering of literary knowledge, could scarce stammer the words of the sacraments; one who knew grammar was a prodigy and marvel to the rest. . . . The custom of drinking together was universal, the night as well as the day being spent in this pursuit. They expended great sums, while living in small and contemptible dwellings; unlike the French and Normans, who live at a moderate rate in large and splendid buildings. Drunkenness was followed by the vices akin to it, which sap the vigour of a man. Hence it came about that they encountered William with rashness and headlong fury rather than military science, and after one battle, and that a very easy one [!], they surrendered themselves and their country into serfdom."

7. HENRY OF HUNTINGDON, *Historia Anglorum*. This work forms an exception to the rule that mediæval history was the work of monks. Its author was probably a native of Huntingdon, born about 1080, and brought up in the palace of Bishop Blouet of Lincoln; and between 1110 and 1120 he was made archdeacon of Huntingdon. The history begins with Cæsar's invasion, and in its first edition ended in 1129; subsequent additions brought it down to the death of Stephen in 1154. The greater part of it is derived from Bede and the Anglo-Saxon Chronicle. As a historian, Henry of Huntingdon is intelligent, but easy-going, and prefers moralisation to research.

The copy exhibited [*Arundel MS.* 48] was written about the end of the 12th century. It formerly belonged to the priory of Southwick, in Hampshire.

The passage selected [Bk. VI. § 38] contains a description of the character of the Normans at the time of the Conquest. It therefore forms a companion picture to the character of the English at the same time given by William of Malmesbury [see no. 6].

"In the 21st year of king William, since now the Normans had fulfilled the righteous will of God upon the people of England, and scarcely any prince of the English race was left in England, but all had been reduced to slavery and mourning, so that the very name of Englishman was become a reproach, William, the author of this punishment, ended his life. For God had chosen the Normans for the extermination of the English race, because He saw that they excelled all people in the quality of unrivalled savagery. Their nature is such that, when they have crushed their enemies so far that they can go no further, they turn to crush one another and reduce themselves and their lands to poverty and desolation; and always the Norman lords, when they have destroyed their enemies and can no longer vent their cruelty on them, destroy their own people as though they were enemies. This is continually more and more evident in Normandy and England, in Apulia, Calabria, Sicily and Antioch, in short, in all the lands which God has subjected to them. Hence in England unjust taxes and iniquitous customs have multiplied exceedingly in these days. All the princes were so blinded by greed of gold and silver that it could be truly said of them, 'None asks whence a man has money, but have it he must.' The more they talked of right, the greater the wrong that was done. Those who were called Justices were at the head of every injustice. The sheriffs and officers whose duty was to execute judgment and justice were worse than thieves and robbers and fiercer than the fiercest. The king himself, when he had leased all his lands at as high a rent as possible, would continually break his pledged word and give them to another who offered more, and then to another, caring for nothing except increase of gain."

8. ROGER OF HOVEDEN, *Chronica.* Roger of Hoveden, or Howden, in Yorkshire, had a very different training from that of most mediæval historians. He was not a monk, but a secular cleric, and, having obtained a post in the household of Henry II., was employed on the king's service in embassies and negotiations, and finally as an itinerant Justice. He is consequently a representative of the Civil Service of his day. After 1189 he retired, and died probably soon after 1201. His Chronicle provides an interesting example of the methods of the early historians, who incorporated their predecessors' works in their own with the utmost freedom. It begins where Bede ends, in 731, and ends in 1201. For the part from 731 to 1148 he simply copied an earlier Chronicle, written at Durham, called *The History of the English since the death of Bede*, which was itself compounded

from the histories of Simeon of Durham [see no. 5] and Henry
of Huntingdon [see no. 7]; while, to go still further back,
Simeon's history was largely derived from Florence of Worcester
and an early Northumbrian Chronicle coming down to 802.
From 1148 to 1169 Hoveden's narrative appears to be original,
though partly based on the Chronicle of the Abbey of Melrose,
and the lives and letters of Becket. From 1170 to 1192 his
work is merely a revision of the Chronicle ascribed to Benedict
of Peterborough. Finally, from 1192 to 1201, he is an original
and independent witness. Hoveden is the last of the line of
northern historians, and, as just shown, he incorporates much of
his predecessors' work. In style he is moderate and impartial.

The copy exhibited [*Royal MS.* 14 C. ii.] is contemporary with
the author; it is probably the original text as finally written
out, and has marginal notes which may be in the author's own
hand. It only contains the Chronicle as far as the year 1180;
the second volume, containing the rest, is in the Bodleian
Library at Oxford.

The passage selected is a description of a striking scene in
Becket's career, his appearance at the Council of Northampton
in 1164.

"So after the celebration of mass the archbishop [Becket] put on his
stole and black canonical cope and proceeded at once to the court of
the king. And immediately there was a great concourse of people
from all sides, to see the end. But he bore his cross in his right hand,
while with his left he held the reins of the horse whereon he rode.
And when he had come to the hall of the king he dismounted and
entered the king's house, carrying his cross. Then he entered the outer
chamber, bearing his cross, alone; for none of his people followed him.
And when he had entered he found much people there, and sat down
among them. The king meanwhile was in the inner chamber with his
intimate associates. Then came Gilbert, bishop of London, who was
of the king's party, to the archbishop, and rebuked him warmly because
he thus came armed with his cross to the court; and he tried to snatch
the cross from his hands, but the archbishop held it firmly. But
Henry, bishop of Winchester, said to the bishop of London, 'Brother,
let the archbishop hold his cross; for he ought rightly to bear it.'
Then the bishop of London was very angry with the bishop of Winchester, and said to him, 'You have spoken ill, brother, and therefore
evil shall befall you, because you have spoken against the king.' Then
came to him Roger, archbishop of York.

'How oft he thought to come with kindly words
And gently make request.'
[*Ovid*, Metam. III. 376.]

But the old fire of hatred came between, and would not let him speak
peaceably; on the contrary, he reproached him bitterly because he thus
came armed with his cross to the court, saying that the king had a

sharper sword, and if the king would be guided by his advice, he would take away the archbishop's cross. But one of the bystanders said:

'Trust me, if thou trust him thou'lt be deceived.
Sweet sings the bird-call till the bird be caught:
Under sweet honey deadly poison lurks.'
                                        [*Ovid*, Am. I. viii. 104.]

But the archbishop of Canterbury would not lay down his cross, and said, 'If the king's sword slays the fleshly body, yet my sword slays in the spirit, and sends the soul to hell.'"

9. RICHARD FITZ-NEAL, *Dialogus de Scaccario*. This work is not, strictly speaking, a history, but it contains very valuable material for the early constitutional history of England. It is a *Latin* treatise, in the form of a dialogue between a master and pupil, on the nature and procedure of the Court of Exchequer. In this court, under the Norman kings, "the whole financial business of the country was transacted, and as the whole administration of justice, and even the military organisation, was dependent upon the fiscal officers, the whole framework of society may be said to have passed annually under its review. It derived its name from the chequered cloth which covered the table at which the accounts were taken" (Stubbs). The author was Richard Fitz-Neal, Bishop of London and Treasurer of the Exchequer under Henry II., and the Dialogue was written in 1176-1178.

The copy here exhibited [*Cotton MS*. Cleop. A. xvi.] was written in the 14th century; and the selected passage is the opening of the work.

"In the 23rd year of king Henry II., as I was sitting in the window of a chamber overlooking the river Thames, I heard the voice of one speaking to me eagerly, saying, 'Master, hast thou not read that there is no value in hidden knowledge or in hidden treasure?' I answered, 'Yes,' and he at once proceeded 'Why then do you not teach to others the knowledge of the Exchequer which you are said to possess so plentifully? Why do you not commit it to writing, lest it perish with you?' Then I said,' Why, brother, you have long sat in the Exchequer yourself, and nothing can have escaped you, since you are so carefully observant; and probably the same is the case with the others who sit there.' He, however, replied, ' As those who walk in darkness and grope with their hands frequently stumble, so do many sit there who seeing see not, and hearing understand not.' . . . . Then said I, 'I see you are getting angry. But calm yourself; I will do what you urge me. Come, rise and sit down opposite me, and ask me of the matters which trouble you . . .'

Pupil. What is the Exchequer?

Master. The Exchequer is a rectangular table, about ten feet in length and five in width, placed like a dinner-table with persons seated at it. It has a ledge about four fingers high all round it, that nothing which has been placed upon it may fall off. Upon the table is placed a cloth, which is bought each year in Easter term. The cloth is not of any kind you please, but a black cloth marked out by lines, at a distance of a foot or a hand's-breadth apart. On the spaces thus marked out are counters, ranged in their proper order, as will be explained presently. And though the name of 'chequer' is properly applied to a table such as this, it is transferred also to the court which is held in the presence of the chequer. Accordingly, if any decision has been made by the common council of the realm on any matter, it is said to have been done at the Exchequer of such and such a year."

10. JOCELIN OF BRAKELONDE, *Chronica.* This is not a history of the country in the ordinary sense of the term, but is an example of the more domestic chronicles of a monastery, from which much may be learnt with regard to the ordinary life of the people. Jocelin of Brakelonde was an inmate of the great monastery of St. Edmund at Bury St. Edmunds, and his chronicle records the history of the monastery under the able and vigorous Abbot Samson [1182–1202], with a short sketch of his predecessor, Abbot Hugh. It gives a graphic picture of life in and around a monastery, and of the difficulties in which the monastery might be involved; and it has a special interest as having been taken by Carlyle as the basis of his *Past and Present.*

The manuscript here exhibited [*Harley MS.* 1005] is the only extant copy of the book, and was written in the 13th century. It belonged formerly to Bishop Stillingfleet of Worcester.

The passage selected describes the part taken by Abbot Samson, who, by virtue of his office, was summoned to the Great Council [the predecessor of Parliament] at the time of the imprisonment of King Richard Cœur de Lion in Austria. It also narrates an incident in the domestic life of the monastery.

> "When the report reached London of the capture of king Richard and of his imprisonment in Germany, and the barons had met to take counsel on the matter, the abbot sprang forward in the midst of them all and said that he was ready to go and seek his Lord the King, either in disguise or in any other way, until he found him and got certain news of him; by which saying he acquired great praise for himself. . . . When there was war in England, during the captivity of king Richard, the abbot in full convent solemnly excommunicated all makers of war and disturbers of the peace, not fearing Earl John, the king's brother, or any one else; whence he was called 'the magnanimous abbot.' After which he went to the siege of Windsor and bore arms, together with some other abbots of England, having his own standard and leading a large number of soldiers at great expense. We monks, however, thought it a dangerous thing to do, for fear of the consequences, lest perchance any future abbot should be compelled to go on warlike expeditions in his own person. . . .
>
> "On another occasion four and twenty young men, sons of noblemen, came with their followers to engage in a tilting match [in defiance of

an edict of the abbot]; and after it was over they returned to the town to seek lodging. The abbot, however, hearing of it, ordered the gates to be closed and the whole party shut in. The next day was the vigil of St. Peter and St. Paul. Accordingly, having given a pledge not to depart except by leave, they dined that day with the abbot; but after dinner, when the abbot had retired to his chamber, they all started up and began carolling and singing, sending into the town for wine, drinking, and afterwards howling, totally depriving the abbot and convent of their sleep; doing all this in derision of the abbot, and spending in such fashion the whole day until the evening, nor would they desist at the abbot's order. Night coming on, they broke the bolts of the town gates, and went off by violence. The abbot, however, solemnly excommunicated them all, by the advice of archbishop Hubert, who at that time was Justiciar; and many of them came in for repentance, begging for absolution."

11. WILLIAM OF NEWBURGH, *Historia Anglicana*. William, surnamed Petit, or the Small, was born in 1136 and entered the abbey of Newburgh in Yorkshire. He became famous in the neighbourhood as a student of history, and undertook his principal work, the *English History*, at the special request of the Abbot and Convent of Rievaulx. It begins with a short summary from the Conquest to 1135, but from the accession of Stephen to 1198, where it ends, it is a detailed and contemporary history, written with judgment and impartiality, but generally in a rather dry style.

The copy exhibited [*Stowe MS.* 62] was written in or soon after the author's life-time, and belonged to the abbey of Newburgh.

The selected passage [Bk. IV., Ch. xxxviii.] describes the extraordinary efforts made to raise the sum necessary to ransom Richard I. from his captivity, in 1193.

"At that time the king of the English, being very weary of his long imprisonment, frequently urged the administrators of his kingdom and all his adherents who seemed to have any influence to provide the sum necessary for his ransom, and so expedite his release. Accordingly the royal officers pressed the matter forward in all the borders of England, sparing none. No distinction was made between layman and cleric, secular and monastic clergy, town and country; all alike, according to the amount of their property or of their revenues, were compelled to pay for the ransom of the king. Privileges, prerogatives, and immunities of churches and monasteries were null and void. Rank and exemption were reduced to silence. None might say, 'I am such an one,' or 'I am of such a position; have me excused.' Even the monks of the Cistercian order, who had hitherto been exempt from all royal imposts, were now charged with a greater load in proportion to their previous escape from public burdens; for the wool of their flocks, which is notoriously the chief item of their property, and which supplies the place of all other revenue for general uses and necessary expenditure, they were now forced and compelled to give up. It was supposed that the masses of money thus swept together would exceed the total of the king's ransom; but when the separate collections were united at London, it was found not to reach that amount. This was believed to be due to fraud on the part of the collectors. Then, on account of the insufficiency of the first collection, the royal officials made a second and a third, despoiling all the richer persons and cloaking barefaced plunder with the honourable pretext of the king's ransom. Lastly, that no resource might be left untried, and that what the palmerworm had left the locust might eat, and what the locust had left the cankerworm might eat, and what the cankerworm had left the caterpillar might eat, hands were laid upon the sacred vessels themselves."

12. MATTHEW PARIS, *Historia Anglorum*. The greatest of all the monastic schools of history was that of St. Albans, and the greatest of the St. Albans historians was Matthew Paris. The Scriptorium, or literary department, of this abbey was established between 1077 and 1093; and the office of historiographer, or writer of history, was created between 1166 and 1183. The first St. Albans chronicle was probably the work of John de Cella, abbot of St. Albans from 1195–1215. This extends from the Creation to 1188, and is a compilation from the Bible and earlier historians and romancers, of an entirely uncritical character. Roger of Wendover, historiographer of the abbey early in the 13th century, continued this compilation from 1189 to 1201, and carried on the history from 1201 to 1235 as an original historian. The whole work down to 1235 frequently passed under Wendover's name, and with the title of *Flores Historiarum*. In 1236, on Wendover's death, Matthew Paris, who had entered the monastery in 1217, succeeded him as historiographer. He then transcribed Wendover's work with additions and corrections of his own, and continued it as far as 1259. This entire work constitutes the *Greater Chronicles* which pass under Paris's name, being partly his own, and partly a re-editing of his predecessor's work. But he also wrote an independent *History of the English*, or *Lesser History*, extending from 1067 to 1253, rehandling his materials according to his own judgment instead of simply adopting the records of his predecessors. As a contemporary historian Matthew Paris is invaluable. He had ample means of collecting information and material, he was acquainted with the leading men of the day, including King Henry III., who even invited him to be present on an important occasion that he might be able to record it accurately. He is a lively and vigorous writer, criticising freely and with much independence, and supporting the popular cause against the king's misgovernment, and especially against the aggressions and extortions of the Pope's legates. He died in 1259.

The copy here exhibited [*Royal MS.* 14 C. vii.] is in all probability Matthew's own copy of his *Lesser History*, written by himself. It belonged successively to Humphrey, Duke of Gloucester, John Russell, Bishop of Lincoln, Henry VIII., Henry Fitz-Alan, Earl of Arundel, and John, Lord Lumley, after whose death, in 1609, it was bought with the rest of his library for Henry, Prince of Wales, and so passed into the Royal Library, presented to the nation by George II. in 1757.

The passage selected describes the death of King John in 1216. The translation is slightly condensed in a few places.

"King John then marched rapidly northwards, all the inhabitants fleeing before his face, as at the approach of a hurricane. Arriving at the place called Well-stream, which is a mixture of sea and river water, he was foolhardy enough to cross without a guide; and, while he himself escaped with difficulty, his carriages, containing his plunder and booty and all his treasure and furniture, were irrecoverably lost. For there is open ground in the midst of the water, of the kind called a quicksand, which sucked in everything, men, horses, arms, tents, victuals, and all that the king held dearest on earth, next to his life. The next night he slept at the Abbey of Swineshead, very melancholy and depressed, and so much afflicted at his loss as to fall into an acute fever, much increased by his habitual over-eating and drinking..... [A litter was made for him, but it jolted him severely.] And being now overtaken by the pains of death, he was compelled to descend from the litter, saying 'That confounded, that accursed litter has shaken all my bones to pieces; nay, it has nearly killed me.' .... [After the administration of the Sacrament] one of those that sat near said 'Our Lord Jesus, when about to die for us, prayed for his persecutors, leaving us a good example. You should likewise abandon all your anger and bitterness against those who owe you ought.' To which he answered with a sigh, 'It is very hard for me to abandon my anger against those who try to drive me from my throne and to aid my chiefest enemy, and who still follow me with their persecution.' .... And his friend who had spoken first pressed the king urgently, lest his soul should be in peril, urging him for the love of Christ and for the safety of his soul to abandon his ill-will towards all the barons. Then the king, who was now at the last gasp, groaning from the depth of his heart with a lamentable sigh, said 'If I may not be saved otherwise, be it as you have persuaded me.'"

13. ADAM MURIMUTH, *Continuatio Chronicarum.* Adam Murimuth, born in 1275, was Doctor of Civil Law at Oxford, and acted for his University and for the Chapter of Canterbury in legal matters. He was also frequently employed on diplomatic service by King Edward II., and was Canon successively of Hereford and St. Paul's. His *Continuation of the Chronicles* (which he began to write after 1325) starts from the year 1303, but until 1337 it is very meagre in its information. In 1337 Murimuth retired to the rectory of Wraysbury, and from this point his history becomes full and interesting. He continued it year by year down to his death in 1347. It is of particular value for the campaigns of Edward III. in France.

The copy exhibited [*Royal MS.* 13 A. xviii.] was written about the middle of the 14th century, very soon after Murimuth's death.

The passage selected describes the Battle of Sluys in 1340, the first great victory of the English navy.

> "And on the Thursday [22 June] before the feast of the Nativity of St. John the Baptist the wind was good, and the king made a favourable start on his voyage. And on the Friday following, that is, on the eve of St. John, he saw the French fleet drawn up in the port of La Swyne, as it were in order of battle; and for the whole of that day he considered what would be best to do. And on the feast of St. John the Baptist [24 June], early in the morning, the French fleet, dividing itself into three divisions, moved out the distance of one mile towards the fleet of the king of England. When the king of England saw this, he exclaimed that he would wait no longer, but at once prepared himself and his men for battle. Accordingly, shortly after the ninth hour, having the wind and the sun behind him and the tide in his favour, he divided his fleet similarly into three divisions and attacked the French. Then was fought a great sea fight, for the ships furnished by Spain and France for the battle were great and strong. Nevertheless the English defeated the French and boarded the ships of their first division, to wit, one very great ship called the St. Denis, and another called the St. George, and others, such as the Christopher and the Black Cog, which the French had previously captured by treachery in the port of La Swyne, as narrated above. In this first engagement fought the Earl of Gloucester, the Earl of Northampton, the Earl of Huntingdon, who was chief and admiral of the ships of the Cinque Ports, Sir Robert de Morley, who was admiral and chief of the northern ships, to wit, those of Yarmouth and Lynn and the other ships from the north, and many other noblemen. When then the first division of the French had been defeated, though with great difficulty, they attacked the second division, which they defeated more easily, many of the crews leaping into the sea of their own accord; and they captured their ships in the twilight. Night now coming on, they resolved, partly on account of the darkness, partly from excessive fatigue, to rest till day. But the ships of the third French division resolved to make their escape under cover of night; and about thirty of them actually escaped. One, however, called the James de Depe, thought in its flight to capture a ship of Sandwich, belonging to the prior of Christ Church, Canterbury; but her crew resisted, with the help of the Earl of Huntingdon. The combat lasted till morning, but finally the English defeated the Normans and took their ship, in which they found over four hundred men killed.

14. CHRONICLE OF ST. ALBANS, 1328–1388. After the death of Matthew Paris [see no. 12], the St. Albans chronicle was carried on from 1259 to 1272 by a writer who, from diffidence at following so great a historian as Matthew, conceals his name. William Rishanger [born 1250] seems to have been the next historiographer, and continued the history from 1272 to 1306. From 1307 to 1323, John de Trokelowe was the chronicler, and

for 1323 and 1324 Henry de Blaneforde. For the next few years there is a gap, and then comes the present chronicle, the author of which is unknown. It has a special value as containing by far the fullest account of the important years 1376 and 1377. The author bitterly attacks John of Gaunt, who was the patron of Wycliffe; and when Henry IV., son of John of Gaunt, came to the throne, this chronicle was suppressed, and a much toned-down version substituted, which is preserved in the Royal MS. 13 E. ix. This latter chronicle extends from 1272 to 1392, thus re-covering all the ground worked over by the historians mentioned above, and is believed to be the work of Thomas Walsingham, who was chief copyist at St. Albans in 1396, and lived till 1420 or later. He may perhaps have had some share in the original chronicle of 1328–1388, but of this it is impossible to be certain. The *Historia Anglicana*, which passes under Walsingham's name, is a compilation from this chronicle and other sources, notably Higden's *Polychronicon* [see no. 16], extending from 1272 to 1422. This is the last of the great series of St. Albans Chronicles which is also a general history of England.

The copy exhibited [*Harl. MS.* 3634] was written in the 14th century. Some leaves from it have been incorporated in the Bodleian MS. 316 at Oxford. It formerly belonged to Archbishop Matthew Parker.

The passage selected is from the description of the trial of Wycliffe at St. Paul's in 1377. It is part of the narrative which is suppressed in the revised version by Walsingham.

"Accordingly, on the Thursday before the feast of the Chair of St. Peter [19 Feb. 1377], the son of perdition, John Wycliffe, was to appear before the Bishops, that a decision might be had concerning the marvels which proceeded out of his mouth, by the teaching, as was believed, of Satan, the adversary of the whole Church. Then after the ninth hour, attended by the Duke [John of Gaunt] and Lord Henry Percy and some others, who by their rank might overawe the weak-hearted, and followed by the aforementioned Mendicants, that if any crumb should fall from the rich men's table,—that is, if any unrefined words should escape from the Bishops' mouths,—they might gather it up and gnaw it by way of scandal, that offering of abomination, the above-mentioned John, was brought in with great pomp. Nor could he be satisfied with common officers, except he were ushered by Lord Henry Percy, the Marshal of all England. . . . At this point the devil astutely found a way for bringing off his pupil, who should escape through the deaths of many from the hands of the Bishops; for he created a dissension between the great lords and the Bishops, that so the trial might be delayed. As the people thronged together and obstructed the passage of the lords and this same John, Lord Henry Percy, by an abuse of the power committed to him, miserably attacked the people in the church [St. Paul's]. The Bishop of London, seeing this, forbad him to exercise such authority in the church, and affirmed that, if he had known he intended to behave in such a manner there he would not have allowed him to enter the church. Then the Duke, hearing these words, gnashed his teeth and swore he should exercise authority there, whether the Bishop liked it or not. . . . Thus the Duke and the Bishops were greatly excited, alike by the insults which they hurled at one another and by the fury of the people which had been aroused. This happened, as we believe, by the device of the Enemy of mankind, who hoped that by an occasion of this kind that lying scoundrel might escape for that day from being confounded for his innovations. For he perceived that he [Wycliffe] would be useful to him in every way; and therefore he took care that such a champion of his party should not perish silently or without a struggle."

15. THOMAS ELMHAM, *Vita Henrici Quinti*. Thomas Elmham was a monk of St. Augustine's, Canterbury, and was treasurer of the monastery in 1407, and Prior of Lenton, in Nottinghamshire, in 1414. He wrote a history of the monastery of St. Augustine's and a Life of Henry V. The latter, which is here exhibited, is one of the chief authorities for the events of that reign, though written in a diffuse and pretentious style.

The copy exhibited [*Cotton MS.* Jul. E. iv.] was written in the 15th century. The passage selected [ch. 27] is part of the description of the battle of Agincourt.

"When the hostile lines had approached within twenty paces, not far from Agincourt, and the sound of the trumpets, rending the air with tremendous clamour, summoned the courage of the warriors to the battle, the enemy's force first moves forward, and advances against the English. At once the terrible fury of war arises greater and greater. On the one side, huge armed forces charge, in the ancient manner of conflict, with deadly spear-thrusts and eager sword-strokes and all other madnesses of war; the strong fastenings of armour are violently rent asunder; and noble warriors inflict on one another fatal wounds. On the other side, the warlike wedges of archers, covering the sky with clouds by their dense and powerful discharges, hurl forth, like stormdrops from a cloud of rain, an intolerable swarm of piercing arrows, breathing all their strength into the service of war and death. At the first conflict of the armies, the French cavalry, who had been posted with the object of charging down the archers and assailing the English in the rear, were met with a reiterated discharge of arrows, which wounded their horses and cast the riders to the earth or forced them to retreat, and so this great and formidable scheme was shattered to pieces at the beginning of the fight. . . . In this deadly struggle, it must be recorded, above all things, how that brilliant star of kings, the light and lamp of chivalry [Henry V.], exposed that precious treasure of his person to all the chances of war, and with the pre-eminent valour of his rank thundered with sudden panic and irresistible assault upon the enemy, in unslackening and noble war. Nor did the madness of battle so far respect the royal dignity as that he should escape the enemy's attacks and the heavy burden of wounds; for a part of the iron coronet which crowned his royal helmet was struck off by an enemy's blow. Verily if he had been but a chief of inferior rank among the fighting knights, he would yet have deserved the crown of honour above them all, for the excellent greatness of his noble valour."

16. RANULPH HIGDEN, *Polychronicon*. This work was the most popular history extant in the 14th and 15th centuries and even later. The author was a monk of the abbey of St. Werburgh, in Chester, and died in 1363. His chronicle is an universal history of the world in *Latin*, from the Creation to the time of Edward III., and it is preceded by a geographical description of the world, especially of Great Britain. In its first form the history closed at 1326, but the author subsequently brought it down to 1342; and continuations of it beyond this date were frequently made by other writers. As an independent authority it is not of much value; but it was the standard history of its day, and shows the condition of historical and geographical knowledge at that time. Its popularity is proved by the fact that, besides circulating largely in Latin, it was translated into English. The translator was John de Trevisa, chaplain to Lord Berkeley, who completed his work in 1387. On the invention of printing, Trevisa's translation was printed by Caxton, in a slightly modernised form, in the year 1482.

The copy exhibited [*Add. MS.* 24,194] is a manuscript of Trevisa's translation, written early in the 15th century. It was written for Richard Beauchamp, Earl of Warwick, who died in 1439, and whose wife was daughter and heiress of Thomas, Lord Berkeley, for whom Trevisa executed his translation. It belonged subsequently to Archbishop Tenison.

The passage selected [Bk. I., ch. 60] is from a description of the character of the English in Higden's time. The language is somewhat modernised, for the sake of intelligibility, Caxton's version being adopted whenever possible.

> "The Englische men that dwellen in Engelond and ben medled [= intermingled] in the island, that ben [= are] far from the places that they sprung of first, will lightly, without enticing of any other men, by their owne assent turn to contrary dedes; and so uneasy, also full impatient of peace, eager for business, and hating sloth, that when they have destroyed their enemies all to the ground, then they fighte with them selves and slay each other, as a void and an empty stomach worketh in itself. Nevertheless men of the south ben easier and more mylde; and men of the north be more unstable, more cruel, and more uneasy. The middle men be somdele [= to some extent] partners with bothe. Also they give themselves to gluttony more than other men, and be more costly in mete and in drynke and in clothinge. . . . These men ben speedy both on horse and on foote, able and ready to all manner of dedes of armes, and they be wont to have the victorie and the masterie in every fight, where no treason is walkyng. And they ben curious and can well telle dedes and wonders that they have seen. Also they go in dyvers landes; unnethe [= hardly] ben any any men richer in their own land or more gracious in far and in strange landes. They can better win and get new things than keep their owne heritage; therefore it is that they be spred so wide and ween [= think] that every land is their owne. The men ben able to do all manner of sleight and

wit, but before the dede blundering and hasty, and more wise after the dede; and they leave lightly what they have begonne. . . . These men dispise their owne and praise other men's, and unnethe [= hardly] be pleased with their owne estate; what befalleth and becometh other men, they gladly take to themselves; therefore it is that a yeoman arrays him as a squire, a squire as a knight, a knight as a duke, and a duke as a king."

17. THE CHRONICLE OF THE BRUT. This was one of the most popular histories of England in the 15th and 16th centuries. It was first written in *French* by an unknown author in the reign of Edward III., and took its name from the fact that it begins with the legendary colonisation of England by the Trojans under Brut or Brutus. In its earliest form it ends in 1332. A revised edition, in which the accounts of the reigns of Edward II. and Edward III. were enlarged, appeared shortly afterwards; and in 1435 this was translated into *English* by John Maundeville, rector of Burnham Thorpe in Norfolk. The history was then brought down to the year 1418, and in this shape it became very popular and was largely circulated. A further continuation was added to it, bringing the narrative down to 1436; and finally, on the invention of printing, Caxton continued it to the year 1460 and printed it in 1480. This edition, with additions and alterations, was frequently reprinted in the course of the next fifty years, but since then the chronicle has never been reprinted. The early part of the history is based upon the romance of Geoffrey of Monmouth (the source of most of the legends concerning early English history), and has no historical value; from the reign of Edward I. it has some original matter, but its chief interest is as the first popular history of England which circulated in the English language.

The copy exhibited [*Add. MS.* 33,242] was written in the 15th century. The passage selected is a criticism of English fashions of dress in the reign of Edward III. In the following transcript the spelling has been modernised.

"In this time Englishmen so much haunted and cleaved to the woodness [= madness] and folly of the strangers [that] from the time of the coming of the Hainaulters eighteen years passed they ordained and changed them every year divers shapes and disguising of clothing, of long, large and broad and wide clothes, destitute and dishert [= far removed] from all old honest and good usage; and another time short clothes and strait waisted, jagged and cut on every side, slatenyd [slashed] and buttoned with sleeves and tippets of surcoats and hoods over long and large and over much hanging, that, [if] I sooth shall say, they were [more] like to tormentors and devils in their clothing and showing and other array than to men. And the women more nicely yet passed the men in array and curiosity. . . . The which disguising and pride peradventure afterwards brought forth and caused many mishaps and mischiefs in the realm of England."

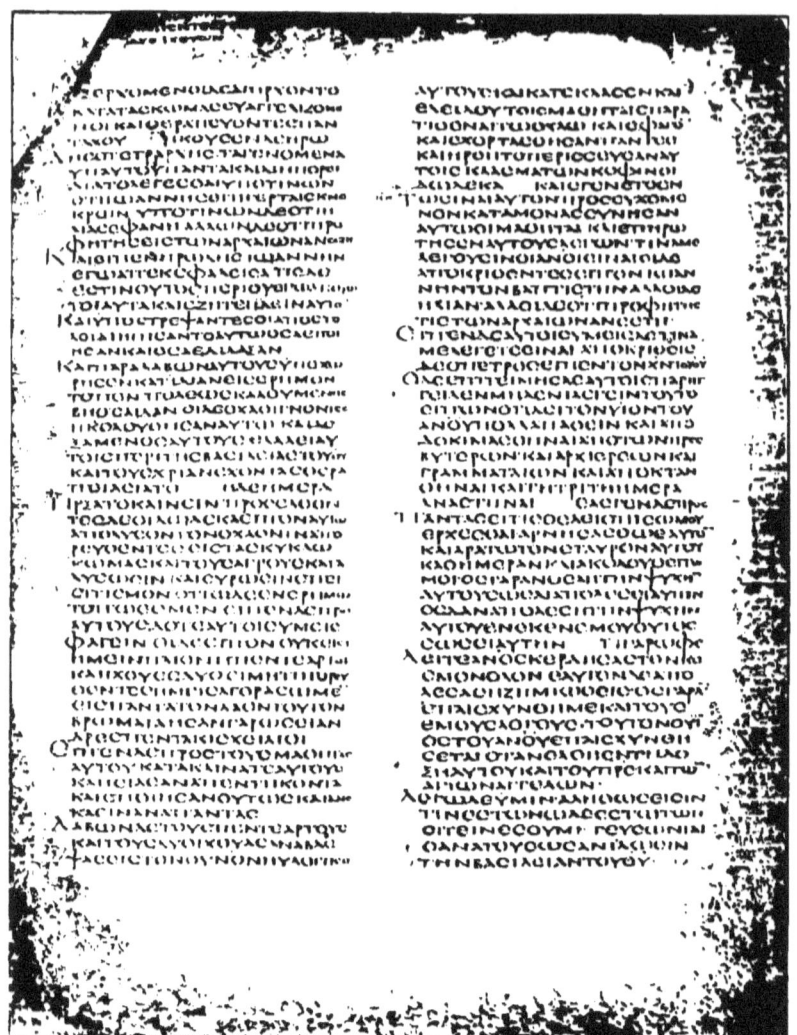

CODEX ALEXANDRINUS.

EARLY BIBLICAL MSS.

[Exhibited in Cases G—K, against the pilasters, beginning on the right of the entrance to the King's Library.]

Case G.

1. THE BIBLE, in *Greek*: a volume of the celebrated "CODEX ALEXANDRINUS," written in uncial letters, in double columns, on very thin vellum, probably in the middle of the 5th century. One of the three earliest and most important MSS. of the Holy Scriptures, containing both Old and New Testaments and the Epistles of St. Clement of Rome. It formerly belonged to the Patriarchal Chamber at Alexandria (whence its name), and was presented in 1628 to King Charles I. by Cyril Lucar, Patriarch of Constantinople, and previously of Alexandria. [*Royal MS.* 1 D. viii.]

In the same case are exhibited, for the sake of comparison, photographs of the only two MSS. of the Greek Bible which are older than the Codex Alexandrinus, viz. (1), Codex Vaticanus (B), in the Vatican Library at Rome, originally containing the whole Bible, but now wanting most of Genesis, the Pastoral Epistles, and the Apocalypse; (2) Codex Sinaiticus (ℵ), discovered by Tischendorf at Mount Sinai in 1844, of which some leaves are in the Hof-Bibliothek at Leipzig, and the rest (including the whole of the New Testament, the Epistle of Barnabas, and the Shepherd of Hermas) in the Imperial Library at St. Petersburg. These two MSS. are assigned to the 4th century.

In the lower division of the case is:—

2. THE GOSPEL OF ST. LUKE, in *Greek* (CODEX NITRIENSIS). A *palimpsest* manuscript (one, that is, in which the original writing has been partially washed out, and another work written above it), containing portions of St. Luke's Gospel, with a *Syriac* treatise by Severus of Antioch written above it. The original writing is in large uncials of the 6th century, written in double columns, with enlarged initials projecting into the margin; the Syriac is of the beginning of the 9th century, written in double columns in a direction at right angles to the Greek. The MS. formerly belonged to the Syrian convent of St. Mary Deipara in the Nitrian Desert in Egypt. Vellum. [*Add. MS.* 17,211.]

Case II.

3. THE BIBLE, in *Latin*, of St. Jerome's version (commonly known as the Vulgate), as revised by Alcuin of York, then Abbot of Tours, by command of the Emperor Charlemagne, between A.D. 796 and 801. The present copy was probably written about A.D. 840, and is adorned with large miniatures and numerous initial letters in gold and silver. Vellum. [*Add. MS.* 10,546.]

Case I.

4. THE BIBLE, in *Latin*, of St. Jerome's version. Written by Goderannus and Ernestus, monks of the Abbey of St. Remacle at Stabloo or Stavelot, in Belgium, and illuminated and bound within four years ending in A.D. 1097. Vellum. Two volumes, both exhibited, one in the lower division of the case. [*Add. MSS.* 28,106, 28,107.]

Case K.

5. THE BIBLE in the earlier *English* version of Wycliffe, beginning with the Book of Proverbs; with illuminated initials and borders. Late 14th century. The MS. belonged to Thomas of Woodstock, Duke of Gloucester, youngest son of Edward III., who was put to death by his nephew, Richard II., in 1397. His shield of arms is introduced into the illuminated border of the first page. Vellum. [*Egerton MS.* 617.]

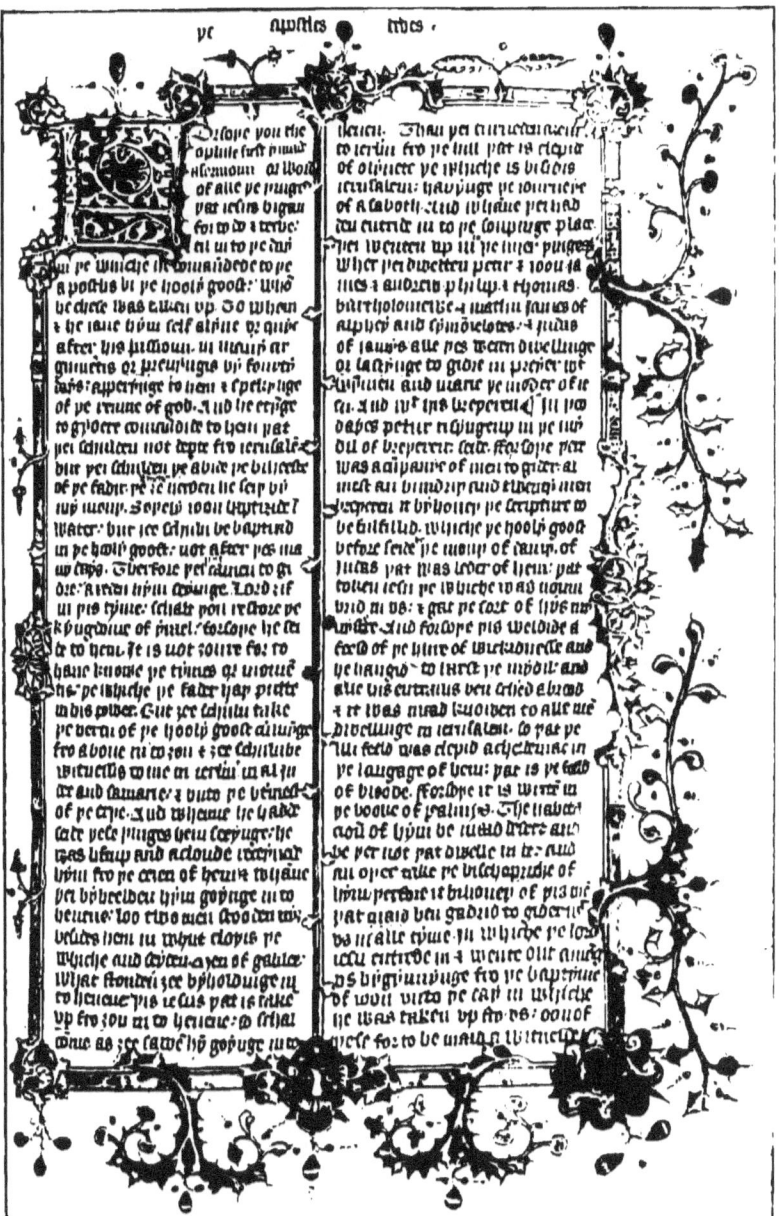

WYCLIFFE'S ENGLISH BIBLE.

HISTORICAL DEEDS AND PAPYRI.

[In frames fixed against the wainscot on either side of the entrance to the King's Library.]

On the East Side.

A series of PAPYRI, four of which are written in *Coptic*, and one in *Greek*, relating to the Monastery of St. Phœbammon, near Hermonthis in Egypt; of the 8th and 9th centuries. [*Papyri* lxxvi–lxxix, lxxxi.]

On the West Side.

1. Instrument written in *Latin*, on papyrus, 8½ feet in length by 1 foot in width, containing a deed of sale of a house and lands in the territory of Rimini; dated at Ravenna, 3 June, in the 7th year of the reign of Justin the Younger [A.D. 572]. [*Add. MS.* 5412.]
2. Deed of sale of a slave-boy, in *Latin*, whereby C. Fabullius Macer, an officer on the vessel "Tigris," in the Misenatian squadron of the Roman fleet, purchases a boy named Abbas or Eutyches, aged seven years, of Eastern nationality, from Q. Julius Priscus, a soldier on the same vessel, for 200 denarii. Dated at Seleucia Pieria, in Syria, 24 May, A.D. 166; with autograph signatures of the parties and witnesses, whose seals are ranged along the top of the document. Written on papyrus in a large cursive hand of early type; the signatures in similar hands, but generally smaller. [*Pap.* ccxxix.]
3. Charter of the Emperor Conrad III., granting to Corbey Abbey, in Westphalia, the adjacent Nunnery of Keminada. Dated at Frankfort, 1147. *Latin.* A contemporary copy, written in gold upon purple vellum. [*Egerton Ch.* 620.]
4. Photograph of the MAGNA CHARTA of KING JOHN. Dated at Runnymede, 15 June, in the 17th year of his reign [A.D. 1215]. A fragment only of the Great Seal remains, and the document itself was so much damaged by the fire of 1731 at Ashburnham

House as to be almost illegible. The original was given to Sir Robert Cotton, probably by Sir Edward Dering, in 1630, and is now in the Department. [*Cotton Ch.* xiii. 31.]

5. Collotype facsimile of a contemporary and official copy of the MAGNA CHARTA, which was given to Sir Robert Cotton by Humphry Wyems in 1628, and is now in the Department.* [*Cotton MS.* Augustus ii. 106.]

6. Original Act constituting a Municipal Council for the city of Cologne; and having appended the seals of the various Guilds. Dated, 14 Sept. 1396. [*Add. Ch.* 13,946]. *Presented, in* 1858, *by Octavius Morgan, Esq., M.P.*

7. Original Bull of POPE LEO X., conferring on King Henry VIII. the title of Defender of the Faith; dated at Rome, 5 id. [11] Oct., in the 9th year of his pontificate [A.D. 1521]. Signed by the Pope and many of the Cardinals. It was much damaged in the fire of 1731. [*Cotton MS.* Vit. B. iv. f. 226.]

8. Grant by Mahomet II., Sultan of the Ottoman Turks, to the Genoese inhabitants of Galata (the suburb of Constantinople) of special privileges for residence and trade; the origin of the "Capitulations" regulating the position of foreign residents in Constantinople. *Greek.* With the monogram of the Sultan at the top, and the signature of the vizier Saganos at the bottom, in *Arabic.* Dated in the week following the capture of Constantinople by the Turks [29 May, 1453]. [*Egerton MS.* 2817.]

[On the pilaster by the side of Case H, facing south.]

9. Counterpart of a deed of conveyance of land at PORT PHILIP, now the site of MELBOURNE, VICTORIA, from the native chiefs to John Batman, Founder of VICTORIA COLONY, for 20 pair of blankets, 30 tomahawks, 100 knives, 50 pair of scissors, 30 looking-glasses, 200 handkerchiefs, and 100 pounds of flour, with a yearly rent of 100 pair of blankets, 100 knives, 100 tomahawks, 50 suits of clothing, 50 looking-glasses, and 50 pair of scissors. Dated, 6 June, 1835. [*Add. Ch.* 37,766.]

* Copies of the collotype and printed text are sold in the Museum.

p. 113, no. 20.

GREAT SEAL OF EDWARD III.

SEALS.

[In the table-cases on either side of the entrance to the Department of Prints and Drawings.]

Case L.

Great Seals of the Sovereigns of England.

1. 2. Edward the Confessor. 1st seal, obv. and rev.* [1053–65 and 1041–66.]
3. William I. 1st seal, obv. [1066–87.]
4. William II. [1087–1100.] Cast of rev.
5. Henry I. 4th seal, obv. [About 1100–23.]
6. Stephen. 2nd seal, obv. [1139–44.]
7. Henry II. [1171–74.] 1st seal, obv.
8. Richard I. 1st seal, obv. 1189.
9. Richard I. 2nd seal, obv. 1198.
10. John. Only seal, obv. 1200.
11. 12. Henry III. 1st seal, obv. and rev. 1230, 1243.
13. Henry III. 3rd seal, obv. [About 1259.]
14. 15. Edward I. Only seal, obv. and rev. 1276, 1285.
16. 17. Edward II. Only seal, obv. 1307–27, and rev. 1323.
18. Edward III. 2nd seal, obv. 1331.
19. Edward III. 3rd seal, obv. 1338.
20. Edward III. 6th seal, obv. [1340–1372.]
21. Edward III. 7th, or "Bretigny," seal, obv. [1366–1375.]
22. Richard II. [1377–99.] 1st seal, obv. No date.
23. Richard II. 2nd seal, obv. No date.
24. Henry IV. [1399–1413.] 1st seal, obv.
25. Henry IV. 2nd seal, obv. 1411.
26. Henry V. 2nd seal, obv. 1415.
27. Henry VI. 1st seal, obv. 1442.
28. 29. Edward IV. 2nd seal, obv. and rev. [1461–71], 1462.
30. 31. Edward IV. 5th seal, obv. and rev. 1471, [1471–83.]
32. Richard III. Only seal, obv. 1484.
33. 34. Henry VII. Only seal, obv. and rev. 1507, 1486.
35. Henry VIII. 2nd seal, obv. 1536. (The last great seal of England exhibiting gothic architecture.)
36. Henry VIII. 3rd seal, obv. 1544.
37. 38. Edward VI. Only seal, obv. and rev. 1548, 1553. (The latter used by Queen Mary.)
39. 40. Mary I. Only seal, obv. and rev. No date, and 1554.
41. Philip I. and Mary I. [1554–58.] Only seal, obv.; bronze cast.
42. 43. Elizabeth. 1st seal, obv. and rev. [1558–85], and 1559.

* On the obverse of a Great Seal the sovereign is generally represented enthroned, on its reverse mounted on horseback.

44. 45. Elizabeth. 2nd seal, obv. and rev. [1585–1603], and 1598.
46. James I. 1st seal, obv. [1603–5.]
47. James I. 2nd seal, obv. 1605–25.
48. 49. Charles I. 3rd seal, obv. and rev. 1633, 1627.
50. 51. Commonwealth. "The great seal of England. 1651," obv. in wax and rev. in sulphur. Used in 1656.
52. Commonwealth. Seal used during the Protectorate of Oliver Cromwell, rev. [1658.]
53. Commonwealth. [1658 – 60.] Second Seal, used during the Protectorate of Richard Cromwell, rev.
54. Charles II. [1649–85.] 3rd seal, rev. [1664–74.]
55. 56. Charles II. Seal for Ireland, obv. and rev. Dated "1660."
57. James II. Only seal, rev. 1686.
58. William III. and Mary II. [1689–94.] Original design on stone for rev. of a great seal.
59. William III. and Mary II. Only seal, rev. 1689.
60. Anne. 2nd seal, rev. 1704.
61. Anne. 3rd seal, obv.; cast. [Matrix made in 1707.]
62. 63. George I. Only seal, obv. and rev. 1720; no date.
64. 65. George II. Only seal, obv. and rev. No date; 1748.
66. George III. [1760–1820.] 4th seal, obv. No date. (Not used after 1800.)
67. George III. 7th seal, obv. No date.
68. George IV. Only seal, obv. 1824
69. 70. William IV. [1830–37.] Only seal, obv. and rev.; proofs.
71. 72. Victoria. [1837.] 2nd seal, obv. and rev.; proofs.

Case M.

a.

SEALS OF ECCLESIASTICAL DIGNITARIES.

1. Anselm, Archbishop of Canterbury. [1093–1109.]
2. Alexander, Bishop of Lincoln. 1145.
3. Theobald, Archbishop of Canterbury. [About 1144.]
4. Robert de Chesney or de Querceto, Bp. of Lincoln. 1152.
5. Richard Fitz-Neal, Bp. of London. [1189–98.]
6. Geoffrey Plantagenet, Bp. of Lincoln. [About 1173.]
7. William de Salso Marisco, Bp. of Llandaff. 1190.
8. Hugh, Bishop of Lincoln. [1191–95.]
9. Hubert, Archbp. of Canterbury. 1198.
10. Henry, Prior of Abergavenny, Bp. of Llandaff. [1193–1218.]
11. William of Blois, Bp. of Lincoln. [1203–6.]
12. Stephen Langton, Archbp. of Canterbury. 1226.
13. Elias de Radnor, Bp. of Llandaff. [1230–40.]
14. Chapter of Llandaff. [1230–40.]
15. Walter de Suthfield, Bp. of Norwich. [1245–57.]
16. Henry Lexington, Bp. of Lincoln. [1254–58.]
17. Hugh Balsam, Bp. of Ely. 1266.
18. Lawrence de S. Martin, Bp. of Rochester. 1268.
19. William Middleton, Bp. of Norwich. [1278–88.]
20. William Fraser, Bp. of St. Andrews. 1281.
21. William de Luda, Archdeacon of Durham. 1286.
22. Anthony Bek, Bp. of Durham. 1286.
23. John Romayne, Archbp. of York. 1293.
24. John Salmon, Bp. of Norwich. 1308.
25. John de Aldreby, Bp. of Lincoln. 1305.
26. Robert Winchelsey, Archbp. of Canterbury. 1309.
27. Richard de Kellawe, Bp. of Durham. [1311–16.]

Seals. 115

28. John de Eglescliffe, Bp. of Llandaff. [1323-47.]
29. William de Melton, Archbp. of York. 1328.
30. Stephen de Gravesend, Bp. of London. 1337.
31. Ralph Stratford, Bp. of London. 1340.
32. William Bateman, Bp. of Norwich. [1344-55.]
33. John Thoresby, Archbp. of York. [1353-73.]
34. Simon Sudbury, Archbp. of Canterbury. [1380-81.] Seal "ad causas."
35. William Courtney, Archbp. of Canterbury. [1381-96.]
36. John Bokyngham, Bp. of Lincoln. 1386.
37. Chapter of Lincoln. 1386.
38. Henry Spencer, Bp. of Norwich. 1392.
39. Henry Beaufort, Bp. of Lincoln. 1403. Seal "ad causas."
40. Richard Clifford, Bp. of London. 1409.
41. Philip Repingdon, Bp. of Lincoln. 1415. Seal "ad causas."
42. John Stafford, Archbp. of Canterbury. [1443-52.] Seal "ad causas."
43. Richard Beauchamp, Bp. of Salisbury. 1470.
44. William Smith, Bp. of Lincoln. 1496.
45. William Warham, Archbp. of Canterbury. [1504-32.] Seal of Prerogative Court.
46. Thomas Cranmer, Archbp. of Canterbury. 1540.
47. Edward Lee, Archbp. of York. 1540.
48. Thomas Thirleby, Bp. of Westminster. (Design on wood.) [1540-50.]
49. Nathaniel, Lord Crewe, Bp. of Durham. [1674-1722.] "Palatine seal," rev.

b.

Seals of Abbots, Abbeys, etc.

1. Wilton, co. Wilts. [1372.] [11th cent. matrix.]
2. St. Mary's, York. [11th cent.]
3. Westacre, co. Norf. [About 1231-36.] [12th cent. matrix.]
4. Selby, co. York. 1282. [12th cent. matrix.]
5. 6. Robert, Bp. of Bath, and Priory of St. Peter's, Bath. [1159-66.] [The latter from 10th or 11th cent. matrix.]
7. St. Alban's, co. Hertf. 1435. [12th cent. matrix.]
8. Nun Kelynge, co. York. [13th cent. charter, 12th cent. matrix.]
9. Newstead, co. Notts. [12th cent.]
10. Kilburn, co. Midd. 1402. [12th cent. matrix.]
11. Ankerwyke, co. Bucks. 1194.
12. Battle, co. Suss. [About 1212.]
13. St. John's Redcliffe, Bristol, co. Somers. [14th cent.] [Matrix early 13th cent.]
14. Lees Priory, co. Essex. [About 1230-50.]
15. Merton, co. Surr. [About 1240-52.]
16. Simon, Abbot of St. Edmund's Bury, co. Suff. [1257-79.]
17. John, Abbot of St. Alban's. 1258.
18. Holy Trinity, Norwich. 1321. [Matrix made in 1258.]
19. Greenfield, co. Linc. [About 1260.]
20. John de Medmeham, Abbot of Chertsey. 1269.
21. Chertsey, co. Surr. 1269.
22. St. James, Northampton. [About 1270.]
23. Nun Appleton, co. York. 1272.
24. Simon, Abbot of Kirkstead, co. Linc. 1278.
25. Newhouse, co. Linc., 3rd seal. 1283.
26. St. Bartholomew, London. 1533. [13th cent. matrix.]
27. Peterborough, co. Northt., 2nd seal. [13th cent.]
28. Lesnes, co. Kent. [13th cent.]
29. Selborne, co. Southt. [13th cent.]
30. Southwick, co. Southt., 2nd seal. [13th cent.]
31. Evesham, co. Worc., 1st seal. [13th cent.]

116   Seals.

32. St. Paul's, London, 2nd seal. [13th cent.]
33. Hagneby, co. Linc. 1392. [13th cent. matrix.]
34. Bromholme, co. Norf. 1421. [13th cent. matrix.]
35. Christ Church, Canterbury, 3rd seal. 1452. [13th cent. matrix.]
36. Waltham, co. Essex. 1537. [13th cent. matrix.]
37. Boxgrave, co. Sussex. [13th cent.]
38. Daventre, co. Northt. 1295.
39. Thornholm, co. Linc. 1297.
40. Oseney, co. Oxon. 1300.
41. Barlings, co. Linc. 1310.
42. Bridlington, co. York. 1327.
43. Bardney, co. Linc., 2nd seal. 1347.
44. Henry, Abbot of St. Werburgh, Chester. 1394.
45. Bissemede, co. Bedf. 1523. [14th cent. matrix.]
46. Elsing Spittle, London. 1405.
47. St. Edmund's Bury. 1517. [14th cent. matrix.]
48. John, Abbot of the above. 1517.
49. Dean and Chapter of Ely, co. Cambr. 1822. [16th cent. matrix.]

c. d.

BARONIAL SEALS.

1. Milo de Gloecestria, afterwards 3rd Earl of Hereford. [1140-43.]
2. Waleran de Bellomonte, Count of Mellent, Earl of Worcester. [1144–66.]
3. Richard de Humetis, King's Constable of Normandy. [1154-80.]
4. Robert, son of Turketin, Knt. [1155-68.]
5. Conan Le Petit, Duke of Brittany, 5th Earl of Richmond. [1165-71.]
6. Geoffrey Plantagenet, son-in-law of the above, 6th Earl of Richmond. [1168-86.]
7. Robert de Bellomonte, Count of Mellent. [1170-78.]
8. Helyas de Albeni. [Late 12th cent.]
9. Roger de Lacy, Constable of Chester. [1179-1211.]
10. Hugh de Beauchamp. [12th cent.]
11. Simon de la Tour, Knt. [12th cent.]
12. Ralph, son of Stephen de Oiland, or Hoiland. [12th cent.]
13. Roger de Mowbray, of co. York. [12th cent.]
14. Adam, son of Roger de Sumeri. [1186-91.]
15. John, Count of Mortain (King John). [About 1188.]
16. Stephen de Turnham, Knt. [About 1200.]
17. Gilbert Prudhomme. [Early 13th cent.]
18. Patrick, 5th Earl of Dunbar. [About 1200.]
19. Alan, Count of Penthièvre and Goello, son of Henry, Count of Tréguier. 1202.
20. Baldwin, Count of Flanders. [Early 13th cent.]
21. Leisanus filius Morgani, of co. Glamorgan. [Early 13th cent.]
22. Thomas de St. Waleric. [Early 13th cent.]
23. Richard, Earl of Cornwall, son of King John. [1225-1272.]
24. The same, as King of the Romans. 1257.
25. Brianus filius Radulphi, of co. Essex. [Early 13th cent.]
26. Peter de Brus III. [13th cent.]
27. Sir Robert de Ghisnes, Knt. [1245-1250.]
28. Roger de Quincy, 2nd Earl of Winchester. [About 1250.]
29. William de Fortibus, 7th Earl of Albemarle. 1251.
30. Simon de Montfort, 2nd Earl of Leicester. 1258.
31. Geoffrey de Geynville, of Ireland. 1259.
32. John, son of Hubert de Burgh. [About 1269.]

33. Robert, son of William de Ferrers, Earl of Derby. 1262.
34. Guillaume, Avoué of Arras, Lord of Béthune and Tenremonde. [13th cent.]
35. John Fitz-Alan, of co. Warwick. [About 1272.]
36. Hugh de Neville. [1211-23.]
37. Robert, son of Walter de Daviutre, of co. Northampton. [13th cent.]
38. Peter de Montfort. [Middle of 13th cent.]
39. Gilbert de Clare, Earl of Hertford. [1262-95.]
40. Edmund Plantagenet, Earl of Cornwall. 1275.
41. Sir John de la Hay, Knt. 1281.
42. Gerard de Furnivall. [Late 13th cent.]
43. Patrick, 8th Earl of Dunbar. [About 1289-1309.]
44. Henry de Laci, 3rd Earl of Lincoln. 1290.
45. The same — a different seal. [1300.]
46. John, Duke of Lorraine and Brabant. 1295.
47. The same, 2nd seal. 1300.
48. Thomas, 2nd Earl of Lancaster. [1295-1321.]
49. Theobald de Verdoun, Constable of Ireland. 1313.
50. John de Mowbray, Lord of the Island of Axholme [co. Linc.]. 1331.
51. William de Clinton, Earl of Huntingdon. 1340.
52. Hugh de Courtenay, 2nd Earl of Devon. 1349.
53. John Darcy, Lord of Knayth, co. Lincoln. 1349.
54. John Plantagenet "of Gaunt," Duke of Lancaster, Seneschal of England. (Privy seal.) 1363.
55. The same, as King of Castile and Leon. 1392.
56. 57. Sir Robert de Marny, Knt., and Alice Brun, his wife. 1365.
58. Walter, 4th Baron Fitz-Walter. 1368.
59. Ingelram de Coucy, Earl of Bedford. 1369.
60. Henry Percy, 1st Earl of Northumberland. 1390.
61. Edmund Plantagenet, Duke of York, 5th son of Edward III. 1391.
62. William de Beauchamp, 1st Baron Abergavenny. 1396.
63. Michael de la Pole, 4th Earl of Suffolk. 1408.
64. Thomas Plantagenet, Duke of Clarence, second son of Henry IV. 1413.
65. Humphrey Plantagenet, Duke of Gloucester, fourth son of Henry IV., seal for chancery of Pembroke. 1426.
66. William de Hoo, Knt. 1427.
67. Sir Maurice de Berkeley, Lord of Beverstone. 1428.
68. Sir James Ormond, Captain of Gournay, France. 1441.
69. Jasper Tudor, Earl of Pembroke. 1459.
70. John de la Pole, Earl of Lincoln. [1467-87.]
71. John de Vere, 13th Earl of Oxford, Lord Great Chamberlain and Lord High Admiral. 1496.
72. Richard Grey, Earl of Kent, Baron Grey of Ruthyn. [1506-7.]
73. Sir Robert Dudley, K.G., Earl of Leicester. 1566.
74. The same—another seal. 1577.
75. Charles Howard, 1st Earl of Nottingham, Lord High Admiral. 1601.

SEALS OF QUEENS CONSORT AND LADIES OF RANK.

76. Alice of Brabant, 2nd wife of Henry I. [After 1135.]
77. Mary, daughter of Lawrence of Rouen. [12th cent.]
78. Liece, daughter of the preceding and of Ralph of Rouen. [12th cent.]
79. Ydonia de Herste, Lady of Promhill, co. Kent. [Late 12th cent.]
80. Margaret de Quincey, Countess of Winchester. [About 1220.]
81. Ela, Countess of Salisbury. [1226-40.]

I

82. Margaret de Lacy, Countess of Lincoln and Pembroke. [After 1245.]
83. Maud, daughter of William Luvetot, widow of Gerard, Baron Furnival. [About 1260.]
84. 85. Sir Hugh de Coleworthe, Knt., and Elizabeth his wife. [Late 13th cent.]
86. Agnes de Percy, of co. Lincoln. [About 1300.]
87. Joan de Stuteville. [1265-75.]
88. Mabel de Gatton. [13th cent.]
89. Isabel de Beaumont, widow of Sir John de Vesey. [1289-1311.]
90. Isabella of France, wife of Edward II. [1307-1357.]
91. Alice de Lacy, Countess of Lincoln, daughter of the Marquis of Saluces. 1310.
92. Margaret de Neville. 1315.
93. Elizabeth de Burgh, Lady of Clare. 1335.
94. Elizabeth de Multon, wife of Walter de Bermyngham. 1341.
95. Matilda of Lancaster, Countess of Ulster. 1347.
96. Euphemia de Lucy, widow of Sir Walter de Heselarton, Knt. 1369.
97. Anne of Bohemia, wife of Richard II. 1390.
98. Anne, Countess of Stafford, daughter of Thomas, Duke of Gloucester, youngest son of Edward III. 1434.
99. Margaret, Countess of Shrewsbury, daughter of Richard, Earl of Warwick. 1456.
100. Elizabeth Wydevile, wife of Edward IV. 1467.
101. Margaret, Countess of Salisbury, daughter of George, Duke of Clarence. 1514.
102. Jane Seymour, wife of Henry VIII. 1537.
103. Henrietta Maria, wife of Charles I. [1625-69.]
104. Catharine of Braganza, wife of Charles II. 1662.

ILLUMINATED MANUSCRIPTS.

[In Cases 1-7 in the Grenville Library, beginning on the left as the visitor enters from the Hall.]

An illuminated MS. is one enriched with gold and colours, in miniatures, in borders wholly or partially surrounding the text, and in ornamental initials. Of the selection here shown, Nos. 1-9 are examples of the Byzantine school dating from the 10th to the 13th century, and characterised by a rigid conventionalism, most apparent in the stereotyped figures and attitudes of the Four Evangelists in copies of the Gospels. The colours are opaque and sombre, and the backgrounds are of gold or in monochrome. A marked feature of Greek MSS. is the rectangular headpiece, the designs of which have often a striking resemblance to oriental carpet-patterns. A freer style of Byzantine work may be seen in the delicate marginal illustrations in No. 3. The same case also contains a few English MSS. of the 10th and 11th centuries (Nos. 10-15). They illustrate the two styles of book-decoration practised at the time in the south of England, in one of which thick body-colours and gold are employed, with elaborate borders of foliage and interlaced work, while in the other style borders are absent and the figures are sketched freely in outline and only lightly touched or washed with colour. The curious fluttering appearance of the drapery and the unnatural length of the limbs, hands, and feet will also be noticed.

In the other cases, illuminated MSS. of different countries are brought together for comparison, and the progress of the art may be traced from the 12th century to its final decline in the 16th. Generally speaking, in the 12th century the figure-drawing is bold, the colours thickly laid on, and the background of highly burnished gold. The initials are often of large size, and are filled with intricate masses of foliage, amid which figures of various kinds are sometimes introduced. In the 13th century a minuter and more refined style came into use. The features, hair, and drapery are more carefully treated, and latterly the body becomes more flexible; delicate little miniatures occupy the interior of the initials, and plain gold grounds begin to give place to diapers and other patterns in gold and colours. This style reached its perfection in the 14th century, the finest period of the art in Western Europe. English and French MSS. may be chiefly distinguished by the colouring, the English preferring lighter tones, especially of blue and green, the French a deep blue and other more brilliant colours, together with a ruddy, copper-like gold. Flemish work is recognisable by its heavy outlines and generally dark colours.

Meanwhile the border also developed. At first a mere prolongation of a limb of the initial, terminating in a simple volute or bud, it gradually extends the whole height of the text, turns the corners along the top and bottom, and ultimately surrounds the page on all four sides, branching out more and more in the process into foliage, flowers, scroll-work, and other ornamentation. French borders of the 15th century (see Cases 4-6) are largely of the so-called "ivy-leaf" pattern, which in its simpler form dates from the century preceding.

It consists of delicate thread-like sprigs, with small tri-dentate leaves, generally richly gilt. This pattern frequently overruns the whole of a wide margin, and is latterly combined with gaily-painted flowers, birds, grotesques, etc., small miniatures also being sometimes inserted at intervals. A typical example of the form taken by a border of the English school just before its extinction is shown in Case 6, No. 59, and may be usefully compared with the earlier border in Case 3, No. 35, and with that in the large English Bible in the MS. Saloon (Case K). A different style was evolved by Flemish artists, the border, consisting of a broad band of colour or flat gold, serving as a ground for minutely realistic flowers, fruit, insects, jewels, etc.

In miniatures of the 15th century, among other changes in the direction of realism, diapered and other ornamental backgrounds were gradually supplanted by landscape. This was at first rude and conventional, with impossible rocks and trees, and no attempt at perspective; but as the century drew near its end the drawing became more accurate and the scenery truer to nature. In England, largely owing, no doubt, to the Wars of the Roses, miniature art was practically dead soon after the middle of the century, and before 1500 the productions of the French school, now become hard, tasteless and overladen, were surpassed by those of Flemish artists. The latter are remarkable for depth and softness of colour, power of expression, and fine landscape effects.

The Italian school of illumination is less well represented, and the few examples available fail to do it anything like justice. The revival of the art began later in Italy than further north, and the earliest MS. exhibited (Case 3, No. 36) is of the 14th century, and shows a strong Byzantine influence. No. 37 is more distinctively Italian; the somewhat stunted figures, greenish flesh-tints, and heavy drapery, together with the peculiar red and other colours, being marked characteristics. The elementary border consists of foliated scrolls springing from the initial, surrounded by exterior spots or studs of gold. Developments of this style may be seen in Cases 4 and 5 (No. 50). In illumination, as in other branches of art, the Italians advanced rapidly in the 15th century, and eventually they proved successful rivals of the Flemings, the best of their miniatures being exquisitely finished works of art, and the borders frequently marvels of invention, richness and grace. A familiar type of ornamentation is formed of a twining vine-pattern, generally in white or gold upon a coloured ground. This is used both in borders and initials, and seems to have been a revival of the interlaced Lombardic work of the 11th and 12th centuries (see in MS. Saloon, Case C, No. 101, Case D, No. 129). Beautiful borders were also composed of the most delicate flower and scroll work, studded with glittering spots of gold (No. 68); and in another style the text was enclosed within rectangular panels, richly painted in crimson, blue and green, and covered with floreated and other designs in gold and colours (No. 66). Both these styles were afterwards much elaborated, the artists availing themselves of the resources of the classical renaissance, and adding graceful candelabra, trophies and vases, medallions with portrait-busts and copies of antique gems, Cupids, fawns, sphinxes, etc., and wonderfully realistic pearls, rubies and other jewels. This brilliant period, however, was of brief duration. Not long after 1500 the art declined in Italy, as it had done elsewhere, and illuminated MSS. became a mere vehicle for the display of technical skill without refinement or good taste.

Case 1.

1. Evangeliarium, or Gospel-Lessons throughout the year, in *Greek*. Miniatures of the Four Evangelists, in colours on a gold ground, and ornamental head-pieces and initials. 10th century. [*Arundel MS*. 547.]

2. The Gospels, in *Greek*. Miniatures of the Evangelists and head-pieces. 11th century. [*Burney MS*. 19.]

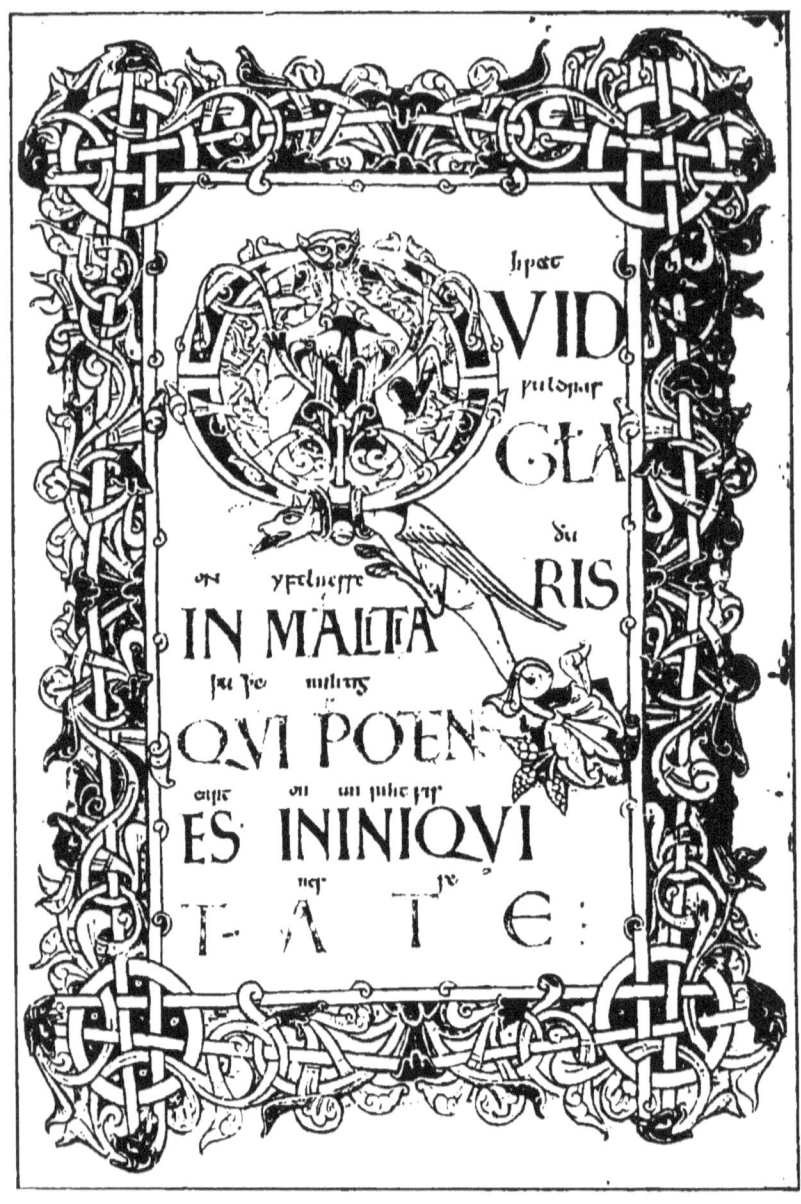

LATIN PSALTER, WITH ENGLISH GLOSS.

3. Psalter and Canticles, in *Greek*. Written by the arch-priest Theodorus of Caesarea, in A.D. 1066. The margins covered with illustrations of Bible-history, Lives of Saints, etc., in gold and colours. [*Add. MS.* 19,352.]
4. Martyrology or Lives of Saints, by Simeon Metaphrastes, in *Greek*. Beautiful miniatures of Saints, and elaborately designed head-pieces. 11th–12th century. [*Add. MS.* 11,870.]
5. The Gospels, in *Greek*. Figures of the Evangelists and numerous finely-executed miniatures. 12th century. [*Harley MS.* 1810.]
6. The Gospels, in *Greek*. Miniatures of the Evangelists and head-pieces. 12th century. [*Add. MS.* 4949.]
7. The Gospels (that of St. John now missing), in *Greek*. Miniatures of the Evangelists. 12th century. [*Add. MS.* 22,740.]
8. The Gospels, in *Greek*. Miniatures of the Evangelists and head-pieces. 12th–13th century. [*Add. MS.* 5112.]
9. The Gospels, in *Greek*. Miniatures of the Evangelists and head-pieces. Written in A.D. 1285. [*Burney MS.* 20.]
10. Charter of Foundation of Newminster at Winchester, by King Edgar, in *Latin*; A.D. 966. Written in gold; with a full-page miniature and elaborate border in gold and colours. [*Cotton MS.* Vesp. A. viii.]
11. The Gospels, in *Latin*; probably written at Newminster, Winchester. Miniatures of the Evangelists (that of St. Mark now lost), and fine initials and borders, in gold, silver and colours, at the beginning of each Gospel. Early 11th century. [*Add. MS.* 34,890.]
12. Paraphrase, in *English*, of the Pentateuch and Book of Joshua, by Ælfric, Archbishop of Canterbury [d. 1006]. Outline and coloured drawings. Early 11th century. [*Cotton MS.* Claud. B. iv.]
13. The "Psychomachia" of Aurelius Prudentius: a *Latin* poem on the conflict between the virtues and vices in the soul, with glosses and notes in *English*. Outline drawings, tinted. 11th century. [*Cotton MS.* Cleop. C. viii.]
14. The Gospels, in *Latin*; with a copy of a charter of King Cnut. Initials and borders in gold and colours, in the Winchester style. Early 11th century. [*Royal MS.* 1 D. ix.]
15. Psalter, in *Latin*, with interlinear glosses in *English*. Miniatures, initials and borders, in colours. Late 11th century. [*Arundel MS.* 60.]

Case 2.

16. Psalter, in *Latin*. Finely-executed miniatures and initials, apparently by English artists under foreign influence. 12th century. [*Lansdowne MS.* 383.]
17. Exposition by Smaragdus of the Rule of St. Benedict, in *Latin*. A full-page miniature of St. Dunstan, on a rich gold ground. English work, of the end of the 12th century. [*Royal MS.* 10 A. xiii.]

18. Diurnale, in *Latin*. Fine initials enclosing miniatures, of Flemish work. End of the 12th century. [*Harley MS.* 2895.]
19. Life of St. Guthlac of Croyland: a series of eighteen beautiful outline drawings, in ink, slightly tinted, enclosed within circular plaques and accompanied by explanatory sentences. English work, late 12th century. Vellum Roll, 9 ft. × 6½ in. [*Harley Roll* Y. 6.]
20. Psalter and Prayers, in *Latin*. Initials in gold and colours, by English artists. Late 12th century. [*Royal MS.* 2 A. xxii.]
21. Bible, in *Latin*. Written and illuminated with initials and borders at Canterbury. 13th century. [*Burney MS.* 3.]
22. Psalter, in *Latin*. Miniatures and initials, by English artists. Late 13th century. Belonged to John Grandison, Bishop of Exeter [1327-1369], who bequeathed it to Isabella, daughter of Edward III. [*Add. MS.* 21,926.]
23. Psalter, in *Latin*. Miniatures, initials and borders, by French artists. Late 13th century. [*Add. MS.* 17,868.]
24. Bible, in *Latin*. Miniature-initials by French artists. Late 13th century. [*Add. MS.* 27,694.]
25. Psalter, in *Latin*. Miniatures, initials and borders, by Flemish artists. End of 13th century. [*Add. MS.* 30,029.]
26. Psalter, in *Latin*. Miniatures, initials and borders, by Flemish artists. Late 13th century. Belonged to Queen Mary I. [*Royal MS.* 2 B. iii.]
27. Psalter, in *Latin*. Miniatures, initials and borders, by Scandinavian artists. Belonged to Jacobus, son of Suno, brother and father of two bishops of Roeskilde in Denmark [d. 1246]. Early 13th century. [*Egerton MS.* 2652.]
28. Psalter, in *Latin*. Miniatures, initials and borders, by French artists. Early 14th century. [*Add. MS.* 29,923.]
29. Bible-History, in *Latin*. Outline drawings by French artists. End of 13th century. [*Add. MS.* 18,719.]

Case 3.

30. The Apocalypse, in *Latin*. Miniatures by English artists. Late 13th century. [*Add. MS.* 35,166.]
31. The Apocalypse, in *French*. Miniatures by English artists. Early 14th century. [*Royal MS.* 19 B. xv.]
32. The Apocalypse, in *Latin* and *French*. Miniatures by French artists. Early 14th century. Belonged to Vaudieu Abbey, near Liège. [*Add. MS.* 17,333.]
33. The Apocalypse, in *Latin* and *French*. Miniatures by English artists. Early 14th century. [*Add. MS.* 18,633.]
34. Missal, in *Latin*. Miniatures, initials and borders, by French artists. 14th century. [*Harley MS.* 2891.]
35. Breviary, in *Latin*. Miniature-initials and borders, by English artists. A.D. 1322-1325. [*Stowe MS.* 12.]

APOCALYPSE.

36. Breviary, in *Latin*. Miniature-initials and borders, by Italian artists, closely following Byzantine models. Early 14th century. [*Add. MS.* 15,205.]
37. Lives of Saints, in *Italian*. Miniatures and initials, by Italian artists of the school of Giotto. 14th century. [*Add. MS.* 27,428.]
38. Ancient History, in *French*. Miniatures by artists of the south of France. Early 14th century. [*Add. MS.* 15,268.]
39. Ancient History, in *French*. Outline drawings, tinted, by artists of the south of France. Early 14th century. [*Royal MS.* 20 D. i.]

Case 4.

40. Bible, in *Latin*. Miniatures, initials and borders, by Italian artists. Early 14th century. [*Add. MS.* 18,720.]
41. Durandus "de divinis officiis." Miniatures, initials and borders, by Italian artists. Early 14th century. [*Add. MS.* 31,032.]
42. Poems, in *Latin*, by Convenevole da Prato, the tutor of Petrarch, written for Robert of Anjou, King of Naples [1334–1342]. Miniatures by Italian artists. 14th century. [*Royal MS.* 6 E. ix.]
43. Treatise on Virtues and Vices, in *Latin*, by a member of the family of Cocharelli of Genoa. Miniatures and coloured drawings of objects of natural history, executed probably by one of the family of Cibo, known as the Monk of Hyères. 14th century. [*Add. MS.* 28,841.]
44. The "Divina Commedia" of Dante. Miniatures by Italian artists. 14th century. [*Egerton MS.* 943.]
45. Epistle, in *French*, of Philippe de Mezières, for peace and friendship between Charles VI. of France and Richard II. of England. A miniature containing a portrait of Richard II., and borders by French artists. End of 14th century. [*Royal MS.* 20 B. vi.]
46. Hours of the Virgin, in *Latin*. Miniatures, initials and borders, by French artists. Beginning of 15th century. [*Add. MS.* 32,454.]
47. Bible History, in *French*. Miniatures, initials and borders, by French artists. 14th century. Belonged to John II. of France, and taken, with him, at the Battle of Poitiers, A.D. 1356. [*Royal MS.* 19 D. ii.]
48. Hours of the Virgin, in *Latin*. Miniatures, initials and borders, by Italian artists. 14th century. [*Add. MS.* 15,265.]

Case 5.

49. "Histoire des Rois de France." Miniatures by French artists. Early 15th century. [*Royal MS.* 20 C. vii.]
50. Hours of the Virgin, in *Latin*. Miniatures, initials and borders, by Italian artists. Early 15th century. [*Add. MS.* 17,043.]

51. "Roman do la Rose." Miniatures, initials and borders, in *camaïeu-gris*, by French artists. 15th century. [*Egerton MS.* 2022.]
52. Romances, in *French*. Miniatures, initials and borders, by French artists. 15th century. [*Cotton MS. Nero D. ix.*]
53. Hours of the Virgin and Psalter, in *Latin*. Miniatures, initials and borders by English artists. Early 15th century. [*Royal MS. 2 A. xviii.*]
54. Hours of the Virgin and Psalter, in *Latin*. Miniatures, initials and borders, by English artists. 15th century. [*Harley MS.* 3000.]
55. Bible-History, in *French*. Miniatures, initials and borders, by French artists. Executed for John, Duke of Berri, son of King John II. of France. Beginning of 15th century. [*Harley MS.* 4382.]
56. Romances of chivalry, in *French*. Miniatures, initials and borders, in French style. 15th century. Presented by John Talbot, Earl of Shrewsbury, to Margaret of Anjou, on her marriage to Henry VI. in 1445. [*Royal MS.* 15 E. vi.]
57. Froissart's Chronicle, in *French*. Miniatures, initials and borders, by French artists. Arms of Comines in the borders. Late 15th century. [*Harley MS.* 4380.]

Case 6.

58. Lectionary, in *Latin*. A miniature of the artist, John Siferwas, offering the MS. to John, Lord Lovel, of Tichmersh [d. 1408]; with initials and borders. English work of the beginning of 15th century. [*Harley MS.* 7026.]
59. Missal, in *Latin*. Miniature-initials and borders, by English artists. Bequeathed by William Melreth, alderman of London, to the church of St. Lawrence, Old Jewry, in Jan. 1445[6]. 15th century. [*Arundel MS.* 109.]
60. Hours of the Virgin, in *Latin*. Miniatures, initials and borders, by French artists. 15th century. [*Add. MS.* 18,192.]
61. Hours of the Virgin, in *Latin*. Miniatures, initials and borders, by French artists. 15th century. [*Harley MS.* 2971.]
62. Hours of the Virgin, in *Latin*. Miniatures, initials and borders, by French artists. 15th century. [*Harley MS.* 2952.]
63. Psalter, in *Latin*. Miniature-initials and borders, in a rather unusual style. Apparently executed at or near Metz. 15th century. [*Add. MS.* 16,999.]
64. Bible-History, to the death of Joshua, in *Italian*. Coloured drawings by Italian artists. Beginning of the 15th century. [*Add. MS.* 15,277.]
65. Hours of the Virgin, etc., in *Latin*. Miniature-initials and borders, with a few small miniatures at the foot of the page, by Italian artists; also numerous borders of great delicacy in

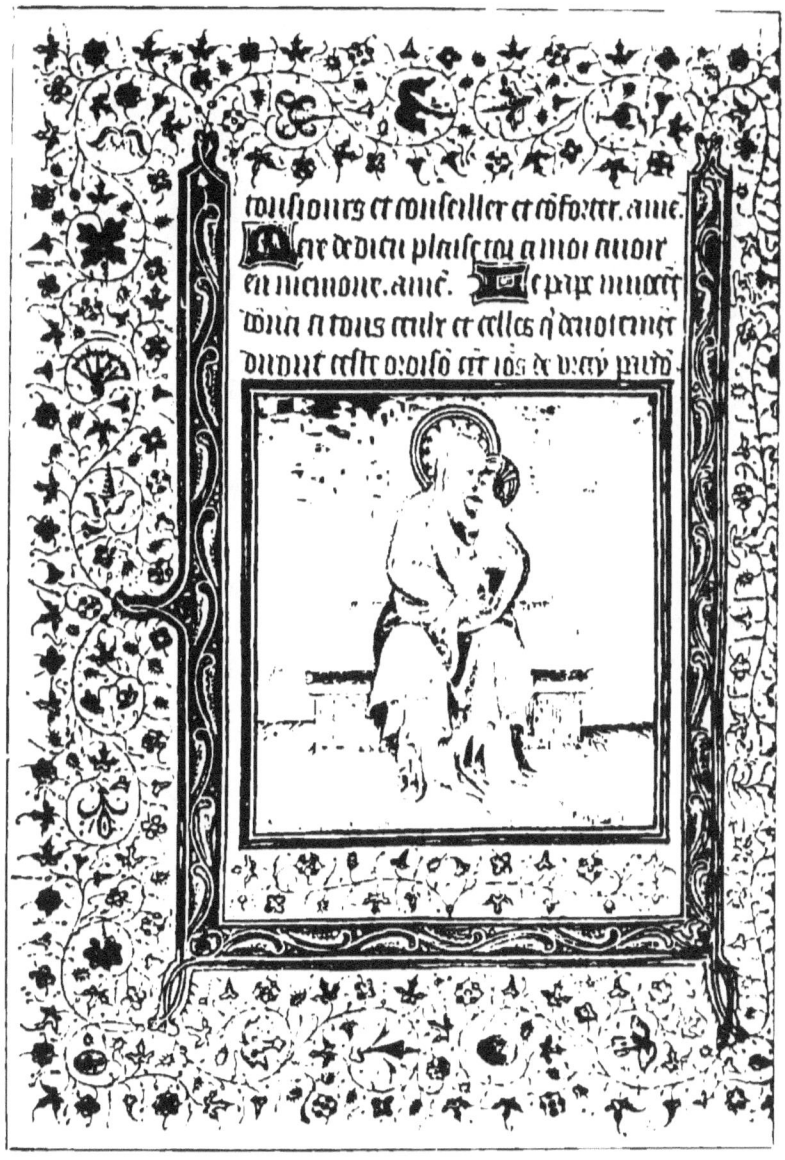

HOURS OF THE VIRGIN.

HOURS OF THE VIRGIN.

monochrome of red or blue, slightly touched with gold. 15th
century. [*Add. MS.* 34,247.]
66. Hours of the Virgin, etc., in *Latin*. Miniature-initials and
borders, by Italian artists; executed for a lady named Smeralda,
probably of Perugia. Late 15th century. [*Add. MS.* 33,997.]
67. Hours of the Virgin, in *Latin*. Miniatures, initials and borders,
by Italian artists. Late 15th century. [*Add. MS.* 19,417.]
68. Breviary, in *Latin*. Initials and borders, by Italian artists.
Late 15th century. Belonged to a member of the family of
Medici. [*Add. MS.* 25,697.]

Case 7.

69. Plutarch's Lives of Great Men, in *Latin*. Miniatures, initials
and borders, by Italian artists. 15th century. [*Add. MS.* 22,318.]
70. The Ethics of Aristotle, in *Spanish*; translated by Charles,
Prince of Viana, for his uncle, Alphonso V. of Aragon. Initials
and borders, by Spanish artists. A.D. 1458–1461. [*Add. MS.*
21,120.]
71. Hours of the Virgin, in *Latin*. Initials and borders by Spanish
artists. Late 15th century. [*Add. MS.* 28,271.]
72. Hours of the Virgin, in *Latin*. Miniatures, initials and borders,
by Spanish artists. Late 15th century. [*Add. MS.* 18,193.]
73. Hours of the Virgin, in *Dutch*. Miniatures, initials and borders,
by Dutch artists. Late 15th century. [*Add. MS.* 15,267.]
74. Hours of the Virgin, in *Dutch*. Miniatures, initials and borders,
by Dutch artists. Late 15th century. [*Add. MS.* 17,524.]
75. Breviary, in *Latin*. Miniatures, initials and borders, by Dutch
artists. Late 15th century. [*Harley MS.* 2975.]
76. Breviary, in *Latin*. Initials and borders, by Italian artists.
Late 15th century. [*Add. MS.* 15,260.]
77. Hours of the Virgin, in *Latin*. Miniatures, initials and borders,
by Flemish artists. Late 15th century. [*Add. MS.* 15,677.]
78. Alexander the Great; a *French* version of the romance of
Alexander. Miniatures, initials and borders, by French artists.
15th century. [*Royal MS.* 20 B. xx.]
79. Hours of the Virgin, in *Latin*. Miniatures, initials and borders,
by Flemish artists. Late 15th century. [*Egerton MS.* 2125.]
80. Travels of Sir John Mandeville, illustrated by twenty-eight
miniatures in grisaille, partly coloured, on pale green vellum;
executed by Flemish or German artists. 15th century. [*Add.
MS.* 24,189.]
81. "Mystère de la Passion." Miniatures by French artists. Late
15th century. [*Royal MS.* 19 B. vi.]
82. Hours of the Virgin, in *Latin*. Miniatures, initials and borders,
by Flemish artists. End of the 15th century. [*Egerton MS.*
1149.]
83. Hours of the Virgin, in *Latin*. Miniatures, initials and borders,
by French artists. End of the 15th century. [*Harley MS.* 2863.

84. Caesar's Commentaries, in *French*; the first of three volumes containing an adaptation of the history of the Gallic War, written in 1519–20 for Francis I. of France, by Albertus Pighius, and ornamented with miniatures in *camaïeu-gris*, by Godofredus Batavus. [*Harley MS.* 6205.]
85. Hours of the Virgin, in *Latin*. Miniatures, initials, and borders, by French artists. Written and illuminated, A.D. 1525, for François de Dinteville, Bishop of Auxerre. [*Add. MS.* 18,854.]
86. "Le Trésor" or "Les sept articles de la Foi," by Jehan de Meung. Miniatures by French artists. Early 16th century. [*Egerton MS.* 940.]
87. Hours of the Virgin, in *Latin*. Miniatures, initials and borders, by Flemish artists. Beginning of the 16th century. Belonged to Henry VIII. [*King's MS.* 9.]
88. "Splendor Solis," an alchemical work, in *German*. A.D. 1582. Miniatures and borders in Flemish style, by German artists. [*Harley MS.* 3469.]

In the lower divisions of Cases 1, 4, 5 and 7 are the following illuminated MSS. of large size:—

89. Genesis and Exodus, with gloss, in *Latin*. Large initials, enclosing miniatures on a dark blue ground diapered. English work of 13th century. [*Royal MS.* 3 E. i.]
90. Exposition of the Apocalypse, in *French*. Miniatures and figure-initials of English work. 14th century. [*Royal MS.* 15 D. ii.]
91. Romance of the Graal, in *French*. Illuminated borders, initials, and small miniatures, rather coarsely executed, by French artists. Early 14th century. [*Royal MS.* 14 E. iii.]
92. St. Augustine "De Civitate Dei," in *Latin*. Miniatures, initials, and borders of French work. Late 14th century. [*Add. MS.* 15,244.]
93. Bible-History, in *French*, translated by Guiart des Moulins from Petrus Comestor. Miniatures, initials and borders, of French work. Early 15th century. [*Royal MS.* 15 D. iii.]
94. Bible-History, in *French*, translated from Petrus Comestor. Miniatures and borders of French work. Written by Thomas Du Val, canon of Clerefontaine Abbey in the diocese of Chartres, in A.D. 1411. [*Royal MS.* 19 D. iii.]
95. Boccaccio's Fall of Princes, in *French*. Fine miniatures and border on the first page, and smaller miniatures throughout, of French work. Middle of the 15th century. [*Royal MS.* 18 D. vii.]
96. "Livre de la Boucachardière," by Jean de Courcy: a universal history to the time of the Maccabees, begun in A.D. 1416. A large miniature before each of the six books, and illuminated initials, of French work. About 1460–70. [*Harley MS.* 4376.]

97. Valerius Maximus, translated into *French* by Simon de Hesdin and Nicholas de Gonesse. Large miniatures and illuminated borders, of French work. 15th century. [*Harley MS.* 4372.]
98. "L'Histoire Tripartite": a universal history, in *French*, to the time of Constantine. Miniatures and borders, of French work. A.D. 1473. [*Royal MS.* 18 E. v.]
99. Valerius Maximus, in *French*, as above. Miniatures, and borders containing the arms of Edward IV. and the White Rose. Executed in Flanders for Edward IV. in A.D. 1479. [*Royal MS.* 18 E. iii.]
100. Bible-History, in *French*. Miniatures, and borders containing the arms of Edward IV. Flanders, late 15th century. [*Royal MS.* 18 D. ix.]
101. Romuleon: a Roman History, in *French*. Miniatures, and borders containing the arms of Edward IV. and the White Rose. Flanders, late 15th century. [*Royal MS.* 19 E. v.]
102. Treatise on Agriculture, etc., in *French*; translated from Petrus de Crescentiis. Miniatures, and borders containing the arms and badge of Edward IV. Written by Jehan du Ries (*cf.* no. 105), late 15th century. [*Royal MS.* 14 E. vi.]
103. St. Augustine "De Civitate Dei," translated into *French* by Raoul de Praelles. Miniatures, and borders containing the arms and badge of Edward IV. Flanders, late 15th century. [*Royal MS.* 17 F. iii.]
104. History of Godfrey de Bouillon, King of Jerusalem, in *French*. A fine miniature (a king and his court, with buildings and landscape), and a border of flowers and gilded scrolls on a black ground. Arms of Edward IV. Flanders, late 15th century. [*Royal MS.* 17 F. v.]
105. "Le Livre des propriétéz des choses," translated by Jehan Corbechon from the Latin of Bartholomew de Glanville. Miniatures, and borders of flowers, birds, etc., on a dark back-ground. Written at Bruges, by Jehan du Ries in 1482. [*Royal MS.* 15 E. iii.]
106. Chronicles of Great Britain, in *French*, by David Aubert. A large miniature of the author presenting his book to a patron, and border of flowers, birds, etc., on a yellow ground. Flanders, late 15th century. [*Royal MS.* 15 E. v.]
107. St. Augustine "De Civitate Dei," translated into *French* by Raoul de Praelles. Miniatures, some in tints of grey, and borders of flowers, strawberries, etc., on a white ground. France, late 15th century. [*Royal MS.* 14 D. i.]
108. "Eracles": a history of the Conquest of Jerusalem by Godfrey de Bouillon, in *French*. Miniatures, and borders of flowers, strawberries, etc., on a white ground, with the arms, banner and Red Rose of Henry VII. Flanders, late 15th century. [*Royal MS.* 15 E. i.]
109. Boccaccio's Fall of Princes, translated into *French*, by Laurent de Premierfait. One large and many small miniatures, and

borders with the Red and White Roses of Henry VII. Flanders, late 15th century. [*Royal MS.* 14 E. v.]

110. "La Forteresse de la Foi": a *French* translation of a treatise against the Saracens and Jews by Alphonsus de Spina. Large miniatures, and borders of flowers, scrolls and grotesques on a light ground. Written at Lille, by Johan Duquesne, late 15th century. [*Royal MS.* 17 F. vi.]

111. Psalter and Antiphonary, in *Latin*. Small miniatures, initials, and borders of flowers, birds, jewels, etc., on coloured grounds. Written by Franciscus Weert for Tongerloo Abbey, in Brabant, in 1522. [*Add MS.* 15,426.]

BINDINGS OF MSS.

[In Case 8 in the middle of the Grenville Library, to the left.]

1. The Four Gospels, in *Latin*; probably written in N. W. Germany, late 10th century. Bound in thick wooden boards, covered with leather. In the upper cover is a sunk panel, which, together with the surrounding frame, is overlaid with copper-gilt; the frame is also studded with large crystals. The metal in the panel has a scale pattern repoussé, the sunk edges being covered with small leaves, etc. In the centre is a seated figure of Christ, in high relief, the eyes formed by two black beads; and at the four corners are small squares of champlevé enamel, in blue, green and red, added not earlier than the 14th century. [*Add. MS.* 21,921.]

2. The Four Gospels, etc., in *Greek*: 10th century. Byzantine binding, 12th century (?), of wooden boards, covered with (tarnished) crimson velvet and lined with fine canvas richly embroidered in coloured silks. Round the upper cover are nailed thin plates of silver-gilt, with figures in relief, probably contemporary with the MS. The plates along the top and bottom contain half-lengths of the Four Evangelists, St. Peter and St. Paul, with their names. The plates at the sides apparently represent the overthrow of the heresiarchs Nestorius and Noetus in three designs, with inscriptions. A central plate, of much later work, represents Christ between the Virgin and St. John, all with enamelled nimbi. [*Add. MS.* 28,815.]

3. Gospels of SS. Luke and John, in *Latin*; written in Germany, 13th century. Bound in thick wooden boards, covered with leather stained red. In the upper cover is a sunk panel of Limoges enamel on copper-gilt, of the end of the 13th century: Christ in glory, within a vesica, with the symbols of the Evangelists at the corners, the figures gilt, with heads in relief. Plates of enamel, of leaf-and-flower pattern, are attached to the outer frame. The colours used are shades of blue, light green, yellow, white and red. The shelving sides of the sunk recess are covered with thin plates of copper-gilt, worked in diamond pattern. [*Add. MS.* 27,926.] *Presented, in* 1868, *by the executors of Felix Slade, Esq.*

4. The Four Gospels, in *Latin*; written, probably in Western Germany, 9th century. Bound in wooden boards, covered with silver plates, showing traces of gilding, of the 14th century. In a sunk panel on the upper cover is a seated figure of Christ, in high relief, the hollow beneath filled with relics; the borders have a scroll-and-flower pattern repoussé, and, as well as the panel, are set with gems, renewed in 1838. Attached to the two outer corners are the symbols of SS. Luke and John, set in translucent enamel of deep blue, the nimbi green. The sunk panel on the under cover has a fine ivy-leaf pattern repoussé, with an embossed Agnus Dei in the centre; the borders similar to those on the upper cover, but without the gems and enamels. [*Add. MS.* 11,848.]

5. Psalter, in *Latin*; written and illuminated for Melissenda, daughter of Baldwin, king of Jerusalem [1118–1131], and wife of Fulk, count of Anjou, and king of Jerusalem [1131–1144]. Inserted in the wooden covers are two fine Byzantine ivory-carvings of the 12th century. On the upper cover are six scenes from the life of David, enclosed within circles, the figures in the intervening spaces symbolizing the triumph of the Virtues over the Vices; the whole surrounded with an elaborate interlaced and floriated border. The general design of the under cover is similar, with six scenes representing the works of Mercy, and figures of birds and beasts. At the top is the name Herodius, probably that of the artist. Both covers jewelled with small rubies and turquoises. [*Egerton MS.* 1139.]

6. Liber Sapientiæ: early 13th century. English binding of thick wooden boards, covered with brown leather, blind-tooled: archaic stamps forming a central panel, with border; the designs including, on the upper cover, a bishop in pontificals, a lion, a mounted warrior with lance, a half-length warrior with sword and shield, rosettes, and a honeysuckle device, and, on the under cover, a church, a centaur shooting, a stag, a crowned king mounted, a winged lion with nimbus, and a saltire between four human heads. [*Add. MS.* 24,076.]

7. Historia Evangelica, by Petrus Comestor, 13th century. English binding of wooden boards covered with dark-brown leather, blind-tooled: a panel, with border, the stamps bearing king David, a lion, a griffin, a dragon, etc. [*Egerton MS.* 272.]

8. Hours of the Virgin, in *Latin*; written in the Netherlands, about A.D. 1300. Binding of brown leather, blind-tooled: a panel formed by impressions of a single stamp in three squares, containing two birds, a griffin, and a pelican respectively; with border of oblong dragon-stamps. [*Add. MS.* 17,444.]

9. Medical Treatises, in *Latin*; written in the Netherlands, 13th century. Binding, 14th century, of brown leather, blind-tooled: a panel of square stamps bearing a fleur-de-lis and a cross moline voided; with border of rosettes within ruled lines, and small dragon-stamps. [*Add. MS.* 26,622.]

10. Psalter, in *Latin*; written in England, end of the 13th century. Embroidered binding (now let into modern leather covers), probably worked by, or for, Anne, daughter of Sir Simon Felbrigge, K.G., a nun of Bruisyard, co. Suffolk, who owned the MS. in the latter half of the 14th century. On the upper cover, the Annunciation, on the lower, the Crucifixion, worked on fine canvas in coloured silks. [*Sloane MS.* 2400.]

11. Prayers, in *Latin*; written in Germany, 12th century. Binding, 15th century, of dark brown leather, blind-tooled: a panel of lozongo-stamps bearing severally a pierced heart, an eagle, and a fleur-de-lis; in the borders, rosettes and a long leaf-pattern stamp. [*Add. MS.* 15,301.]

12. "Livre des Quatre Dames," by Alain Chartier; written in France, early 15th century. Binding of brown leather, blind-tooled: a panel of nine narrow vertical bands of small stamps, bearing severally a lion, a quatrefoil, a serrated quatrefoil, and a stag; with borders of fleur-de-lis and larger serrated quatrefoils. [*Add. MS.* 21,247.]

13. Poems by Cristoforo di Fano, etc., in *Latin*; written in Italy, late 15th century. Binding of brown leather, blind-tooled; a panel of a diaper pattern, on either side two rows of small stamps bearing an Agnus Dei and an open flower; with borders of beaded lattice-work and intersecting segments. [*Add. MS.* 17,812.]

14. Small Manual of Prayers, in *German*; written by Johann vom Wald, A.D. 1485. Binding of brown leather, ruled, and stamped with rosettes; with brass corners and central boss. The leather is continued at the bottom in a long hanging strip tapering to a point and finishing with a plaited button for attachment to the girdle or dress. [*Add. MS.* 15,700.]

15. Commonplace-book of theology, in *Latin*; written in Germany, 15th century. Binding of deer-skin; having a short iron chain with ring attached, for the purpose of securing the volume to the fixed rod of the shelf or desk. [*Add. MS.* 30,049.]

16. Letters, etc., of Gasparino Barzizza and others, in *Latin*; written at Milan, A.D. 1438. Binding of brown leather, blind-tooled: a panel of a diaper pattern between two rows of stamps on either side bearing an Agnus Dei and a double scroll; with three narrow borders of different designs, a running flower, zigzag ribbon, etc., divided by ruled spaces. Brass bosses and fittings for clasps. [*Add. MS.* 14,786.]

17. Bible Glossary, in *Latin*; written in Italy, late 15th century. Binding of brown leather, blind-tooled: a panel of stamps bearing severally the biscia (or serpent devouring a child) of the family of Visconti, an Agnus Dei, and a small rose; with borders of a small lozenge with the biscia, and a large stamp with a shield of arms, similar to that painted on the first page of the MS. [*Add. MS.* 17,397.]

18. Chartulary of the Church of St. Bavon at Ghent; 12th century,

with additions. Flemish binding, 15th century, of light brown leather, blind-tooled: a panel, latticed with double cross lines and set with stamps bearing a fleur-de-lis, a flint and steel (the device of Philip, Duke of Burgundy, d. 1467), a floriated-lozenge, and a bee; in the border, the same lozenge and a rosette. Brass-mounted clasps. [*Add. MS.* 16,952.]

19. Breviary, in *Latin*; written in the Netherlands, 15th century. Binding of vellum stained red and impressed with a single stamp: a panel in three vertical bands containing various birds, beasts, etc., with a border of trailing vine. Brass clasps and fittings. Belonged to Roode Clooster near Brussels. [*Add. MS.* 11,864.]

20. History of the German Empire to A.D. 1450, by Thomas Ebendorffer, of Haselbach; dedicated and presented to the Emperor Frederic III. Binding of dark-brown leather, with designs cut in outline and brought into low relief by stippling the background. On the upper cover are the emperor's arms (the eagle black), with the inscription "Fridericus rex, etc., 1451," and below, his motto "A E I O U" [*i.e.*, Austriæ est imperare orbi universo]; the whole surrounded by foliage, with the binder's name, "Petrus ligator," at the base. On the under cover is a boldly treated design of foliage, with shield of arms at the top. Brass corner-pieces, central boss, etc. [*Add. MS.* 22,273.]

21. The "Phænomena" of Aratus; written in Italy, late 15th century. Binding of brown leather, blind-tooled: a panel and border of interlaced cable pattern, set with bead-like dots and minute rings, the last of metallic lustre; in the centre a star within a circle, both thickly beaded. [*Add. MS.* 15,819.]

22. Church-services in *Latin*; written in Germany, probably at Regensburg, end of the 15th century. Binding of brown leather, gilt-tooled: a panel of rich floreated pattern, with border of flowing-leaf and roses. Brass corner-pieces, central boss, etc. [*Add. MS.* 17,337.]

23. Ordo Missæ, etc.; written in Italy, late 15th century. Binding of brown leather, gilt-tooled; a panel having a floreated circular design in the centre, with broad arabesque border. [*Harley MS.* 2912.]

24. Sarum Breviary, in *Latin*; written in Flanders, about A.D. 1500. Binding of brown leather, blind-tooled: at the corners four panels from the same single stamp, of trailing vine pattern, with eagle, stag, etc., together with a border inscribed, "Ob laudem Christi librum hunc ligani Anthonius de Gauere" [*i.e.* Gavere, S. W. of Ghent]. Between the panels are impressions of two long stamps containing respectively three angels playing on trumpets and triangle, and a piper and four peasants dancing. [*Royal MS.* 2 A. xii.]

25. Description of the Holy Land, in *French*, by Martin Brion; dedicated to Henry VIII. Binding of crimson velvet, with the arms of England, Lancaster roses, etc., embroidered in coloured silks, gold thread and seed-pearls. [*Royal MS.* 20 A. iv.]

26. Commentary, in *Latin*, on the campaign of the Emperor Charles V. against the French in A.D. 1544; addressed by Anthonius de Musica, of Antwerp, to Henry VIII. Binding of dark-brown leather, gilt-tooled: in the centre the arms of England, with the initials H. R., flanked by medallions of Plato and Dido, etc.; above and below, tablets inscribed, " Vero defensori fidei," etc.; the whole within a light tooled border. [*Royal MS.* 13 B. xx.]
27. "Le Chappellet de Ihesus": prayers, with miniatures of French work, 16th century. Belonged to Anna, wife [1521–1547] of Ferdinand, king of the Romans, and afterwards to Margaret Tudor [d. 1539], wife of James IV. of Scotland. Binding of green velvet, having silver-gilt clasps with the letters ANNA on the sides; Tudor roses of silver-gilt added at the corners and in the centre, each bearing one of the letters MARGUERITE. [*Add. MS.* 25,693.] *Presented, in 1864, by the Earl of Home.*
28. Lists of cities, etc., named in Trogus Pompeius and in the epistles of Cicero; addressed by Petrus Olivarius to Edward, Prince of Wales, A.D. 1546. Binding of light-brown leather, gilt-tooled: a panel having the Prince of Wales's feathers, motto and initials E. P., surrounded by a circle of rays, in the centre; with scrolls, rosettes, and stars in the field, and a border of arabesque. [*Royal MS.* 15 C. i.]
29. Travels of Giosafat Barbaro, of Venice, to Tana and Persia; translated by William Thomas, and dedicated to Edward VI. Binding of light-brown leather, gilt-tooled: scroll-work with the arms of England in the centre within a circle, flamed. The circle, as well as a surrounding interlaced oblong and lozenge, and an outer border, coloured black. [*Royal MS.* 17 C. x.]
30. Collects, etc., of the Evangelical Church at Regensburg, in *German*; written in Germany, 16th century. Binding (apparently Italian) of dark-brown leather, covered with very rich and delicate gilt-tooling arranged in panel and borders; in the centre, the cross-keys, the arms of Regensburg. Narrow clasps of iron. [*Add. MS.* 18,312.]
31. Commission from Francesco Venerio, Doge of Venice, to Hieronymo Michiel as captain of galleys, A.D. 1554. Binding of crimson leather, gilt-tooled in panel and border, one cover having in the centre the name "Hieronimi Michael," the other the date "MDLIIII." [*Add. MS.* 17,373.]
32. Carta de Hidalguia, or grant of nobility, from Philip II. of Spain to Diego de la Guardia Espino, A.D. 1589. Spanish binding of light-brown leather, covered with elaborate tooling arranged in panel and three borders; with brass clasps. [*Add. MS.* 18,166.]
33. Gospels for Lent and Easter, in *German*; late 15th century. Binding, 16th century, of white skin, blind-tooled: borders with emblematical figures of Faith, Hope and Charity, and medallions

of Erasmus, Luther, Huss and Melanchthon, inscribed with names and inserted among foliage, etc.; in the centre, a shield of arms originally gilt. [*Egerton MS.* 1122.]

34. Acts of Guidobaldo II., Duke of Urbino, investing Count Pietro Bonarelli and Hippolita his wife with the territories of Orciano and Torre, A.D. 1559–1568. Oriental-pattern binding of papier-mâché, with sunk compartments; the latter gilt and stippled, the raised surface blue, the whole covered in scroll-work in colours and gold respectively. In the centre, a shield of arms painted in oils. [*Add. MS.* 22,660.]

35. Hours of the Virgin, in *Latin*; written in France, 15th century. Binding, 16th century, of olive leather, tooled with small ovals, each containing one of various designs, as a sun, bee, acorn, pink, etc. Among the designs in larger ovals on the back is the letter S. [*Add. MS.* 29,706.]

36. Commission from Jeronimo Priolo, Doge of Venice, to Benetto Semiteccolo as captain of galleys, A.D. 1564. Binding of crimson leather, gilt-tooled with scroll-work, etc.; in the centre, the arms of Semiteccolo in colours. [*Add. MS.* 18,846.]

LIST OF BENEFACTORS TO THE DEPARTMENT OF MANUSCRIPTS.

The following are the principal donations which have been made to the Department since the foundation of the British Museum in 1753 :—

1753. **Sir John Cotton, Bart.** The Cottonian Library of MSS. and Charters formed by his grandfather, Sir Robert Cotton, Bart. *Presented to the nation in 1700; incorporated in the Museum in 1753.*

1753. **Henrietta, Countess of Oxford, and Margaret, Duchess of Portland.** The Harley Collection of MSS. and Charters, formed by Robert Harley, Earl of Oxford, and his son Edward, second Earl.

1753. **Sir Hans Sloane, Bart.** The Sloane Collection of MSS. and Charters. *By bequest.*

1757. **His Majesty King George II.** The Royal Library of MSS. and Charters.

1765. **The Rev. Thomas Birch, D.D.** Historical and other MSS. *By bequest.*

1785. **The Rev. William Cole.** Collections for the History of Cambridgeshire. *By bequest.*

1790-99. **Sir William Musgrave, Bart.** MSS., chiefly biographical.

1796. **Sir William Burrell, Bart.** Collections for the history of Suffolk. *By bequest.*

1807-14. **Lord Frederick Campbell.** Collection of Charters.

1809. **The Very Rev. Sir Richard Kaye, Bart., Dean of Lincoln.** Autographs and Drawings. *By bequest.*

1822-30. **Hudson Gurney, Esq.** Collections for the history of Suffolk, by H. Jermyn.

1826. **Adam Wolley, Esq.** Collections, chiefly relating to Derbyshire. *By bequest.*

1829. **Francis Henry, fourth Earl of Bridgewater.** The Egerton MSS. and Charters, with an annual income for their maintenance and augmentation. *By bequest.*

1835. **Maj.-Gen. Thomas Hardwicke.** Correspondence and papers. *By bequest.*

1838. **Charles, Baron Farnborough.** Stock in the public Funds, as an addition to the Bridgewater Bequest. *By bequest.*

1842. **The Executors of Richard, Marquess Wellesley.** Official Papers of the Marquess Wellesley, Governor-General of India, 1798-1805.

1844. **The Governors of the Welsh School and the Cymmrodorion Society.** Two large collections of Welsh MSS.

1849. **Vincent Novello, Esq.** Music by various English composers.

1855-79. **Sir Walter Calverley Trevelyan, Bart.** Charters and papers of the family of Calverley, and other papers.

1857. **William Haldimand, Esq.** Correspondence of Brigadier-Gen. Bouquet and of Gen. Sir Frederick Haldimand, K.B., during their commands in North America, 1757-85.

1858. **The Rev. Lord John Thynne, Sub-Dean of Westminster.** Correspondence of John, Lord Carteret, afterwards Earl Granville.

1860. **Anne Florence, Countess Cowper.** Correspondence of Thomas Robinson, afterwards Lord Grantham.

1864. **Coventry Patmore, Esq.** Collection of Plays.

1870. **Sir Charles Wentworth Dilke, Bart., M.P.** Papers and deeds of the family of Caryll.

1873. **Mrs. Lina Balfe.** English Operas by her husband, M. W. Balfe.

1873. **Hugh, third Marquess of Westminster.** Charters of Reading Abbey.

1877. **The Hon. Maria Otway-Cave.** Papers of Henry Stuart, Cardinal York, and papers relating to the Sobieski family.

1879. **William White, Esq.** A sum of money, partially expended on additional rooms for the Department of MSS. *By bequest.*

1881. **William Burges, Esq., A.R.A.** Illuminated MSS. *By bequest.*

1884. **Sir Michael Costa.** Original scores of his compositions. *By bequest.*

1885. **Thomas A. E. Addington, Esq.** Rubbings from English Monumental Brasses.

1886-9. **Walter John, fourth Earl of Chichester.** Correspondence of Thomas Pelham-Holles, Duke of Newcastle, and of the first and second Earls of Chichester, with other papers relating to the Pelham family.

1887. **Jesse Haworth, Esq., and Henry Martyn Kennard, Esq.** Greek Papyri from Egypt.

1890. **Mrs. Hannah Streatfeild.** Collections for the history of Kent, by the Rev. T. Streatfeild.
1891. **Señorita Llanos-Keats.** Letters of John Keats.
1891. **Mrs. Cross ("George Eliot").** Original Manuscripts of her works. *By bequest.*
1891. **Miss Elizabeth Moreton.** Papers of the family of Moreton.
1893. **John Malcolm, Esq., of Poltalloch.** The Sforza Book of Hours.
1893. **Miss Mary Augusta Gordon.** The Khartoum Journal and other papers of General C. E. Gordon. *By bequest.*
1894-6. **Samuel Butler, Esq.** Correspondence of Dr. S. Butler, of Shrewsbury School, Bishop of Lichfield.
1894. **Thomas Washbourne Gibbs, Esq.** Autograph Journal of Laurence Sterne, etc. *By bequest.*
1896. **Sir A. Wollaston Franks, K.C.B.** Rubbings of Monumental Brasses.
1896. **Miss Eliza Wesley.** Autograph Music of Samuel Wesley, Bach, etc. *By bequest.*
1896. **A. de Noë Walker, Esq.** Autograph Poems of Walter Savage Landor.
1896-7. **George C. Boase, Esq.** Journals of travels, by J. J. A. Boase, etc.
1897. **F. C. Miers, Esq.** Papers of Francis Place.
1897. **Robert Barrett Browning, Esq.** Letter of Elizabeth Barrett Browning.
1898. **Miss Christian Maclagan.** Rubbings of Sculptured Stones of Scotland.
1898. **Hallam, second Lord Tennyson.** Epilogue to "Idylls of the King," by Alfred, Lord Tennyson.
1898. **Miss Helen Lindsay.** Illuminated MSS.
1898. **Sir George Grove, C.B.** Correspondence of Dean Stanley with Sir G. Grove.
1898. **Baron Ferdinand Rothschild, M.P.** Illuminated MSS. and Book of Funeral Processions. *By bequest.*

FACSIMILES OF AUTOGRAPHS.

Price: each series of 30 plates, 7s. 6d.; single plates, with printed text, 3d., or 4d. by post (except a few, now out of print).

FIRST SERIES, 1895. (*Second Edition*, 1898.)

Queen Katherine of Aragon, 1513; Archbishop Cranmer, 1537; Bishop Hugh Latimer (marginal notes by Henry VIII.), about 1538; Edward VI., 1551; Mary, Queen of Scots, 1571; English Commanders against the Spanish Armada, 1588; Queen Elizabeth, 1603; Charles I., 1642; Oliver Cromwell, 1649; Charles II., 1660; James, Duke of Monmouth, 1685; William III., 1689; James Stuart, the Pretender, 1703; John Churchill, Duke of Marlborough, 1706; William Pitt, Earl of Chatham, 1759; George III., 1760; George Washington, 1793; Horatio, Viscount Nelson, and Emma, Lady Hamilton, 1805; Arthur Wellesley, Duke of Wellington, 1815; General Charles George Gordon, 1884; Queen Victoria, 1885.

John Dryden, 1682; Joseph Addison, 1714; S. T. Coleridge, 1815; William Wordsworth, 1834; John Keats, 1820; Charles Dickens, 1870; W. M. Thackeray, 1851; Thomas Carlyle, 1832; Robert Browning, 1868.

SECOND SERIES, 1896.

Henry V., 1419(?); Queen Anne Boleyn, 1528-9; Cardinal Wolsey, 1530; Episcopal Declaration, 1537; William Cecil, Lord Burghley, 1586; Francis Bacon, Lord Verulam, 1595; James I., 1623; Thomas Wentworth, Earl of Strafford, 1633; John Pym, 1643; John Graham of Claverhouse, Viscount of Dundee, 1679; Mary II., 1692; Robert, Lord Clive, 1757; George II., 1757; William Pitt, the younger, 1790; Edmund Burke, 1791.

Frederic II., the Great, of Prussia, 1757; Napoleon Bonaparte, Emperor of the French, 1798 and 1807.

John Milton, 1646-52; Sir Christopher Wren, 1675; Sir Richard Steele, 1720; William Hogarth, after 1751; William Cowper, 1779; Edward Gibbon, 1788; Robert Burns, 1792; George Gordon, Lord Byron, 1810; Percy Bysshe Shelley, 1819; Charles Lamb, 1822; Alfred, Lord Tennyson, 1864.

Martin Luther, 1536; François Marie Arouet de Voltaire, 1760.

THIRD SERIES, 1897.

Edward IV., 1471; Henry VII. and Elizabeth of York; Henry VIII. and Katherine of Aragon; Mary I., 1547; Lady Jane Grey, 1553; Adherents of Queen Mary, 1553; Sir Walter Ralegh, 1586; Archbishop Laud, 1640; the Council of State, 1653; Admiral Robert Blake, 1654; James II., 1680; Robert Harley, Earl of Oxford, 1711; Henry St. John, Viscount Bolingbroke, 1715; "Junius," 1772; Warren Hastings, 1780; Charles James Fox, 1798.

Charles V., Emperor, 1555; Henry IV. of France, 1606.
Ben Jonson, 1609; Sir Isaac Newton, 1682; Alexander Pope, 1714; Jonathan Swift, 1730; Thomas Gray, 1750; Oliver Goldsmith, 1763; Samuel Johnson, 1781; David Hume, 1766; David Garrick, 1776; Sir Walter Scott, 1820; Lord Macaulay, 1839.
Michelagniolo Buonarroti, 1508(?); Desiderius Erasmus, 1525.

FOURTH SERIES, 1898.

Sir Thomas More, 1534; Edward VI., 1547; Sir Philip Sidney, 1586; Sir Francis Drake, 1586; Robert Cecil, Earl of Salisbury, 1598; Sir Walter Ralegh, 1617; George Villiers, Duke of Buckingham, 1623; John Hampden, 1642; Charles I., 1645; Richard Cromwell, Lord Protector, 1660; William Penn, 1681; Queen Anne, 1704; Sir Robert Walpole, 1730; Richard Brinsley Sheridan, 1805; Arthur, Duke of Wellington, 1828; Albert, Prince Consort, 1856.

Philip II. of Spain, 1579; Louis XIV. of France, 1688.
Dr. John Donne, 1602; Henry Purcell, before 1685; John Locke, 1699; Daniel Defoe, 1705; Thomas Ken, Bishop of Bath and Wells, 1709; Laurence Sterne, 1767; Thomas Chatterton, 1769; John Wesley, 1783; "George Eliot," 1859; Alfred, Lord Tennyson, 1872.
Albrecht Dürer, 1523; Jean Jacques Rousseau, 1764.

FIFTH SERIES, 1899.

(In Preparation.)

Henry VIII., 1518; John Knox, 1561; Robert Devereux, Earl of Essex, 1596; James Graham, Marquess of Montrose, 1644; Oliver Cromwell, 1645; Thomas, Lord Fairfax, 1645; John Maitland, Duke of Lauderdale, 1669; Charles II., 1672; William III., 1688; William, Duke of Cumberland, 1746; Benjamin Franklin, 1782; Prince Charles Edward Stuart, 1784; Henry John Temple, Viscount Palmerston, 1832; Benjamin Disraeli, Earl of Beaconsfield, 1833; Richard Cobden, 1848; John Russell, Earl Russell, 1850; William Ewart Gladstone, 1856; John Bright, 1861.
Edmund Spenser, 1588–1598; Jeremy Taylor, 1661; Izaak Walton, 1647–1662; John Milton, 1667; G. F. Handel, 1749–50; Henry Fielding, 1750; Samuel Richardson, 1754; Thomas Gainsborough, about 1760; Sir Joshua Reynolds, 1773; Horace Walpole, 1776; James Boswell, 1795; Elizabeth Barrett Browning, 1859.

www.ingramcontent.com/pod-product-compliance
Lightning Source LLC
Chambersburg PA
CBHW032154160426
43197CB00008B/903